AN INTRODUCTION TO
Richard Wagner's
Der Ring des Nibelungen

Richard Wagner
Drawing by Franz von Lenbach
The original drawing was owned by Cosima Wagner,
whose portrait Lenbach also painted

AN INTRODUCTION TO
Richard Wagner's
Der Ring des Nibelungen

A HANDBOOK BY
WILLIAM O. CORD

Second Edition · Revised and Enlarged

OHIO UNIVERSITY PRESS
ATHENS · OHIO

Ohio University Press, Athens, Ohio 45701

© 1983 and 1995 by William O. Cord.

99 98 97 96   5 4 3

Ohio University Press books are printed on acid-free paper

Library of Congress Cataloging-in-Publication Data
Cord, William O.
An introduction to Richard Wagner's Der Ring des Nibelungen; a handbook / by William O. Cord. — 2nd ed., rev. and enl.
p. cm.
Includes bibliographical references (p.   ) and index.
ISBN 0-8214-1112-8 (pbd.)
1. Wagner, Richard, 1813–1883. Ring des Nibelungen. I. Title.
ML410.W22C67 1995
782.1—dc20
94-40066 CIP MN

DESIGNED BY LAURY A. EGAN

TO

The resolute spirit who thought it so
and the mettled spirits who know it to be true

Contents

Contents

Contents

ix

Illustrations

Tables

The thing shall "sound" in such
fashion that people shall hear
what they cannot see.

Preface to
the Second Edition

Some ten years have passed since the first edition of this work became available. That decade has been witness to an ever-broadening attitude toward Richard Wagner and his music. Larger, more encompassing writings about that art appear now, if not literally each day, at least metaphorically so. Then, too, the number of shorter pieces, on all facets of the man and his work, seem almost to overwhelm reputable journals. Today, the music dramas of the man from Leipzig, their sound and their text, and the concepts and perceptions that they convey, have mesmerized world audiences. There can be little doubt that the man Wagner and the Wagnerism which he generated have become the most studied and discussed artistic bent in human history. This manifest fact, surfacing as it has well over a hundred years after the man's death, may well indicate that the artistic world is presently experiencing the Golden Age of Richard Wagner.

Yet, today, with the world awash in Wagnerian matters, there is that ever-growing company of new arrivals drawn into the fold, where they tend to remain, transfixed. Yet, unfortunately, these newcomers most often stand alone, unaware of what questions to ask, unaware of *who* or *what* or *when* or *why* or *how* are the things Wagnerian in the world of today. They are very much aware that they are present in a new world in which powerful forces are at work. It is the Wagner cosmos which can be summarized if not defined by the two words *music drama*. (Those two words in the English language should rightfully be fused into a single term referring to the musico-dramatic works of Richard Wagner!) Then, stepping one pace beyond the term *music drama*, one discerns that those powers that drive so dynamically and compel so intensely generally are those that ensue when the issue is *Der Ring des Nibelungen*, the *Ring*, the Cycle, the Tetralogy, that massive art work that has so captivated a world, its generations, its epochs, and its cultures.

It is to these newly arrived that this present work attempts to speak, and it is that artwork, the *Ring*, which shall be the single subject. Such was stated in the first Preface, and such still remains paramount: this Handbook is for those who only recently have somehow come upon the *Ring*.

Those readers familiar with the original edition will note that its format has been carefully preserved in the present work. At first glance, one might even believe that this second edition is identical to that first work. However, there is new material here, certain fresh but appropriate matters that have been woven into the text. A few dates have been changed to reflect more accurately the contents of Wagner documents that only recently have been uncovered. Some matters personal to Wagner himself as well as some factors singular to the development of the *Ring*, unclear or perhaps contestable in the past, have been inserted as fitting and proper to the subject at hand. Then, also, on one occasion, what was meant to be a statement of fact (the matter of the composer and *Musikdrama*), was improperly recorded in the first edition, or at best muddled, and the item now has been redone to render Wagner's true personal feelings more understandable. An Appendix C, which contains notes concerning the singers and principals of the command premieres of *Das Rheingold* and *Die Walküre* has been added. The Bibliography has been updated and a second section devoted to Wagner journals has been added.

All in all, the substance of the original work is retained, reworded at times, but such modifications are always intended as an improvement. It is hoped that those new arrivals who are experiencing their first entrance into the world of the *Ring* will find this second edition a fresh and inviting piece of Wagneriana, and that its intent, that is, to introduce to any and all concerned the truly extraordinary artistic masterpiece, *The Ring of the Nibelung*, is realized.

W.O.C.
Rohnert Park
California

Preface to
the First Edition

This handbook is only that, a handbook, a concise work devoted to a single subject, Richard Wagner's *Der Ring des Nibelungen*. I have no desire other than to offer, in an orderly fashion, the pertinent data and information related to the conception, the development into a finished work, and the presentation to the world of one of the landmarks of musico-dramatic history.

This handbook was conceived, designed, and written primarily for those who, for whatever reason, have remained relatively unaware of the fascinating story of this masterpiece and who now, for whatever reasons, wish to know more about the work and to acquire a basic understanding of this celebrated artistic creation. However, it is possible that this handbook can also serve those who have already been introduced to Wagner's work as well as those who have more experience in his works and world.

This handbook is divided into chapters, each of which treats a specific topic of import in the overall picture of *Der Ring des Nibelungen*. Together, in the order of their presentation, these chapters present the composer's artistic intention and the history of his work from its inception through its first performances before world audiences. However, each of the chapters, or indeed each of the numbered paragraphs that speak to individual aspects of the respective chapter titles, may be consulted or read without undue regard for whatever has come before. Every effort has been made to offer each chapter as a unit unto itself and, at the same time, as a complement to all the others in order to reveal the complete story of Wagner's work. A bibliography specific to each chapter is also presented.

I have sought conscientiously to present accurate data. My search took me first to the words of Wagner himself. Lacking certain particulars, I then turned to the works of past and present students and scholars of things Wagnerian, many of whose thoughts and data have been incorporated within the several sections of this handbook.

I consider this volume but an introduction to *Der Ring des*

Nibelungen. Its purpose is to offer a basis for additional, more extensive studies of the multifarious matters associated with the composer and his work. If, then, this presentation arouses in but a single reader a desire to learn more about Wagner, his life, or his creations, I shall consider the several years devoted to its completion worth the time and effort and that one reader's interest will, in itself, be reward enough.

W.O.C.
Rohnert Park
California

The Absolute, that is, the *un*conditioned art work,
which exists only in thought, is not naturally bound
to time or to place, and neither yet to definite
circumstance.

Richard Wagner, 1851

AN INTRODUCTION TO
Richard Wagner's
𝕯𝖊𝖗 𝕽𝖎𝖓𝖌 𝖉𝖊𝖘 𝕹𝖎𝖇𝖊𝖑𝖚𝖓𝖌𝖊𝖓

Chapter One

The Art of Richard Wagner: An Overview

At his death at the age of seventy, Leipzig-born Wilhelm Richard Wagner (1813–1883) was the acknowledged titan of operatic composition, the international monarch of musical innovation, and the most controversial composer ever to have appeared on the musical scene. Despite a life fraught with severe personal anxieties, a life buffeted by political and social upheavals, a life marked by continuous frustration in his artistic endeavors, Wagner fashioned an art form that advanced to the fore and permanently altered the thinking of creative and intellectual minds the world over. The totality of design, content, format, structure, and execution in his musico-dramatic works was highly regarded in his own day and has remained an ever-present archetype and template that, in the modern era, continues to shape and flavor much of the creative work produced in the musico-theatrical world.

If, however, Wagner realized both national and international fame during his lifetime, that success was hard earned. The professional attacks upon him as an artist and the deep bitterness against him as a man were continuous and formidable. As a theorist on matters of drama and music, as a dramatist, and as a composer, he was vigorously vilified. His ideas on art, and later the works that exemplified his thoughts, were made the brunt of much ridicule and scorn by a significant cadre of critics, scholars, and artists. At the same time, his chaotic personal life, his ego-centered character, and his aggressive, often abrasive personality inspired social rejection, even unbridled hatred, in many with whom he came in contact. This multitude of detractors included individuals from the artistic, academic, business, political, social, and religious communities and, within each of these sectors, persons of all measures of knowledge, talent, and skill.

Despite this hectic and tumultuous life, which often brought Wagner to the last stages of mental and physical desperation, his genius could not be denied. No one of his creative order ever before had made his way into public view. It was inevitable that his stamp was to be felt directly and indirectly throughout Western culture by those of all persuasions, even by those constantly in pursuit of his defeat.

The full flowering of Richard Wagner's celebrity came during the second half of his life. If, in his younger years, he had completed two operas of less than meritorious status, *Die Feen (The Fairies)* and *Das Liebesverbot (Love Forbidden)*, he had also created works that confirmed him as a composer of the first rank, *Rienzi, der Letzte der Tribunen (Rienzi, the Last of the Tribunes)*, *Der fliegende Holländer (The Flying Dutchman)*, *Tannhäuser, und der Sängerkrieg auf Wartburg (Tannhäuser and the Song Fest on the Wartburg)*, and *Lohengrin*. However, it was in his later years that he was to establish firmly his artistic kingdom and then to reign over it in a manner unprecedented in musical history (see Appendix A for a chronological summary of Wagner's operatic works).

In the years 1849–1851 Wagner took his first steps along what was to become the artistic pathway down which he would later stride with fixed purpose. During this period, in part because of the necessity of earning a livelihood while a political exile in Switzerland and in part because of his own re-evaluations of the contemporary state of drama and music, he wrote and published several essays and articles. In these writings he proffered then-distinct concepts regarding the objective of drama, the purpose of music, and more importantly, the function of these art forms when wedded as artistic partners in what is generally known as the operatic format.

Among Wagner's essays of these years, three are of paramount importance in revealing his accumulated thoughts about art in general and about opera specifically. Although the substance of each of these works directs itself to the one fundamental aspect of his artistic beliefs, these three studies complement one another, and together they form a mosaic of his ideas, theories, feelings, and reactions. In 1849 Wagner wrote "Die Kunst und die Revolution" ("Art and Revolution"), an essay in which he indicated his belief that his society was culturally manacled, that it was prevented from sharing the profound communal experience possible through the rebirth of the spirit of Greek drama. That same year

Wagner published "Das Kunstwerk der Zukunft" ("The Artwork of the Future") in which he discussed the route of the arts after the decline of Greek dominance. He viewed each medium as having gone its own way, each slowly deteriorating to such a state that there was now widespread among the *Volk* (people) an insistent urge for a renaissance in the quality of these arts and a desire for their union into a single great work of a universal nature.

The third of these tracts was a singular essay that detailed Wagner's concepts of the art form that, in his mind, would reflect that universal character so persistently sought. That art form was *opera*, or as he envisioned it, a special form of opera which became the focal point of this voluminous study (over three hundred pages) published in 1851, entitled *Oper und Drama* (*Opera and Drama*), and subtitled *Die Oper und das Wesen der Kunst* (*Opera and the State of the Art*).

Although written in a language, syntax, and style that thoroughly test and tax the perseverance of the reader (as do most of Wagner's prose works), this volume contains an elaborate discussion of his then-unique, indeed startling, concepts regarding opera and operatic tradition. His concern was directed initially at what he considered to be the underlying artistic poverty of the opera of his time, and he then proceeded to detail a formula to remedy the situation. All of Wagner's interests and concerns, and his subsequent theories, revolved around a single, deep-rooted belief that remained fixed in his mind: In that grandest of art forms, opera, the audiences of the world, both emotionally and intellectually, desired and indeed sought a true and absolute drama, a drama whose power and strength were ever reinforced by a music of expression, authority, and creditability.

Wagner saw the drama of his day as merely a "spoken play" in which diverse characters and their equally diverse actions were presented according to the traditional mechanics of dramatic history. Such drama, he maintained, was designed around a general understanding of a people and their faculties of simple imagination. Wagner envisioned a drama of a greater and more intense fiber, a drama of the more constant stuff of human experience. In a word, he believed that drama should be organic, that it should deeply penetrate the substance of human nature rather than offer the artificial facade that society deems humankind should have.

Wagner was calling for a drama that captured a comprehensive view of humanity. He sought essence, not flavor; he proposed truth, not modality; he preached the infinite, not the temporary and tenuous. Such drama, he continued, should begin at the center of the human organism, develop from within and extend outward, thus concentrating on what he called the *reinmenschlich* (purely human). This "purely human" was emotion, not mere action, and this emotion would be presented without concern for its cause. His drama would examine, probe, and lay bare the essence of the human experience, the heart and the soul. Wagner seemed to gather all his thoughts and ideas into a few words when he wrote in 1851, in his essay "Eine Mitteilung an meine Freunde" ("A Communication to my Friends"):

> The artist addresses himself to the Feeling, and not to the Understanding. If he is answered in terms of the Understanding, then it is as good as said that he has not been understood.

The fruits of Wagner's design plan for drama would be twofold. In the first instance, drama of the type he proposed would meet the public exigency for dramatic power and strength because its appeal would be to human feeling rather than to generic physical senses. It would be a drama that spoke to the entirety of "man's artistic receptivity"; it would communicate with the totality of his "perceptive organism." In the second instance, such drama would rid contemporary cultural thought of the noxious belief that drama was a means of expression, a means to an end, and replace it with the true concept of drama's ultimate purpose, that of being an object of expression, the end itself.

Once Wagner had put forth his concepts of the function and rightful purpose of drama, at least as he viewed matters, he then elaborated upon the material that would serve as the argumentative vehicle of that "true drama." He reasoned that the theater, to date, had not produced drama of the kind he considered so necessary, partly because its contents had dwelled upon themes of a social or historical nature. Wagner argues that such themes prevented the artist from developing a means of total expression in his art because such development was restricted by the capacity of its audience for comprehension. Social themes could be presented only within the context of current social concepts and only by means of the manners exercised by society at that moment. Such limitation distorted or even hid the basic truth that a given social theme might contain. A historical theme, necessarily located in its own time and place, was severely hampered by its being revealed in a physical atmosphere alien to the audience and by means of a representation equally removed, in an emotional sense, from its actual setting. Thus, both social and historical themes were dutifully accommodated to the societal values and priorities of the moment, and such accommodation could result only in a deceptive, fabricated, and therefore unreal present. Both themes could be directed only to understanding in terms of the devised conventions of contemporary manners rather than to feeling, which was innate, recognized, and universal to all ages and to all cultures.

To the question of how to emerge from the textual and thematic bog in which drama had so long been mired and how to achieve the kind of drama that he had concluded was so necessary, Wagner had but one thematic response—myth. For years he had been studying, analyzing, and otherwise absorbing myth and legend, particularly that of Germanic culture, and he was convinced that in myth lay the universal truth, a truth that had been filtered, honed, and shaped by experience throughout history. Myth, he wrote, was truth without end, the truth of forever. Myth was the portrait of humanity, the "purely human" so indispensable to his absolute drama. Further, he maintained, there was to be found in German myth the totality of the essence of German culture and, therefore, the foundation of a real and authentic German drama that, when paired with the music he envisaged, would become a genuine national art form. That Wagner was ever the consistent artist, at least insofar as the matter of *myth* was concerned, is evidenced by his words of later years. In 1860, he wrote in his essay "Zukunftsmusik" ("Music of the Future") that *mythos* was "the poet's ideal stuff." Ten years later, in the second part of a revised *Opera and Drama*, he would add that "mythos is the beginning and the end of history."

Wagner continued his lengthy discourse, next turning his attention to the subject of music, specifically to that of the operatic genre. This was a matter about which he intended to be as resolute as he had been with drama. As a first step, Wagner attacked that operatic music that had become so entrenched as the traditionally accepted model of the day. Such music, he maintained, was essentially a trivial music. He viewed it as a series of separate and unrelated incongruous tunes—arias, duets, choruses, loosely held together by the rhyming words of an irrelevant plot. The aria, he believed, had achieved its popularity through a combination of two equally insignificant factors: The aria served theatrical ego, the artistic vanity of the singer, and at the same time it pleased the shallow, external collective mind of its audiences, a public that desired to be amused rather than be taxed intellectually. Wagner concluded that the aria, if perhaps a pleasant sound, was really a melody of less than meaningful artistic service because, in the final analysis, it could give expression only to the most generic and stereotyped of human emotions. Music, he insisted, should be both a parallel and an extension of the poetry of true drama. As a parallel it would naturally reflect the surface meaning of the words, that meaning acceptable to all society. As an extension, it would penetrate the semantic surface of the poetry and expose the deeper meaning that lay enfolded in the word, a meaning that neither intellectual nor physical powers could transmit, a meaning to which feeling alone could respond. In traditional opera, music had become an end in itself. Wagner would change radically that unfortunate tradition. Music must cease to be the object of expression; his "true drama" now carried that end. Music must serve as a vehicle, a means of expression, and thus be an intimate partner of that drama he had announced in clarion call earlier.

Wagner had a word for this thorough fusion of music and drama: *Gesamtkunstwerk* (total-work-of-art). (Although Wagner used this word on one occasion only, in his essay "The Artwork of the Future," the term was destined to serve as a popular description of Wagner's later musical dramas.) In such a work, the music and the poetic verse of "absolute" drama would serve equally; each would serve to stimulate the other, yet each would also complement the other. Neither would be complete without the other, yet neither would rise above the other. Each of the two art forms would blend and meld into the other, the result being an art form of exceptional unity, an art form whose sway would be greater than that of the separate expressions of its parts.

Such a creation as Wagner envisioned was not "opera" in the tradition of the popular French and Italian schools. It was a new and distinct concept and, in 1851, as he meditated the application of his ideas, Wagner wrote that he would no longer compose "opera." Rather, he would write "drama," a term that later became *Musikdrama* (music drama). In his day, Wagner strongly objected to the use of the word *Musikdrama* as a generic name for his mature musical works. Yet, the term was an apt and appropriate designation for most of his later works, especially so when reference is made to *Der Ring des Nibelungen*. (Wagner expressed his satisfaction with a word that he would create and apply to his work: *Bühnenfestspiel* [stage-festival-drama].) However, throughout the years that followed, the preeminence and predominance of Italian and French operatic styles continued and the word *opera*, if only generically appropriate, is routinely applied to Wagner's works by most audiences throughout the world. Later in life, despite the artistic venom with which he had attacked the term *opera*, even Wagner admitted that perhaps the best generic term for his musical works was simply that term, *opera*.

Such elaborate pronouncements as Wagner had made had wrought confusion and havoc within the artistic world and had perceptibly weakened the solid foundations of accepted beliefs and practices in the worlds of drama and music. His ideas did not represent mere modifications or alterations. Rather, they advocated a completely new or radically different operatic tradition. It was not unnatural, then, that a vast horde of detractors rose in unison. The practiced and the professional, the famous and the near-famous, the scholar and the artist lifted their voices and their pens in denunciation of his ideas. They voiced their disbelief and then branded his theories ridiculous, impertinent, and unwanted.

Accustomed as were these detractors to the operatic fare that had been their lot, their creative minds and their artistic talents could not envision such ideas, let alone accept them as musico-dramatic reality. Wagner's concepts had thrown artistic acid on all that was sacrosanct in the genre, on all that rested so comfortably and so serenely in the minds of the cognoscenti. So frequent and so extensive were these clamors that, in a very short time, a new dimension was added to their reactions. In addition to all else, they said, these ideas of the political exile from Saxony would come to naught because an opera designed and prepared in the Wagner manner was an impossibility!

Wagner paid little heed to the reactions against the substance of his essay. If, in the public eye, his many words merely represented supposition, total conjecture arrived at by casual surmise, Wagner viewed his text in a much different light. In 1851, he, and he alone, knew that his essays, and especially *Oper und Drama*, were not the first step toward music drama, not a theatrical text of abstract ideas that might serve as the basis for some future work. Rather, what he had written was essentially the detailed discussion of a music drama that his creative mind had already fashioned. Well before *Oper und Drama* his fertile talents had conceived a drama that focused on the "purely human" as well as a music that expressed the human experience of his poetry. If the words and the notes of *Der Ring des Nibelungen* had not yet been put on paper as a finished libretto and a full score, they were there, in his mind, developing, emerging, shaping themselves, not as two separate and distinct mediums, but as a seamless strand, a single art form. If, in 1851, a skeptical, rebellious public would have to wait some time before it saw and heard the tangible artistic reality of music drama, for Wagner at least, it existed, it was real, and his essay was simply a way in which he could arrange his thoughts and describe in words what his genius had already effected.

In time, Wagner was to temper somewhat his concepts of the function of music in the "art work of the future." By 1860, nine years after *Oper und Drama*, he had completed more than half of *Der Ring des Nibelungen* as well as *Tristan und Isolde* (*Tristan and Isolde*), the work most exemplary of his initial concepts of music drama. As he completed the latter work, he became aware that music, in its wedding with drama, had become the more forceful, the more dominant element in the partnership. He acknowledged this fact in his essay on the music of the future, and his works that were yet to be would clearly reflect the artistic turn his mind had taken.

Wagner's thoughts on the role of music drama were to undergo still another transformation. His expression of this change came in 1871, by which time he had completed three-fourths of his Nibelung work and had enjoyed the success of *Tristan und Isolde* and *Die Meistersinger von Nürnberg* (*The Master Singers of Nuremberg*). In "Über die Bestimmung der Oper" ("The Destiny of Opera"), a paper delivered before the Berlin Royal Academy of Arts—to which he had been elected as a corresponding member—Wagner admitted that the music of his music drama had ceased to portray in detail the subtleties and nuances of the dramatic argument. He agreed that music drama was essentially opera but added that it was opera on a more extensive, more elaborate and highly colored level. Now, the singer and his presentation had gained a prominence that was not so readily discernible in earlier conceptions. Wagner echoed these sentiments the following year in an essay entitled "Über Schauspieler und Sänger" ("Actors and Singers"). In these two tracts Wagner stated in essence that his earlier concepts had matured and now reflected something of a compromise between music and drama in and of itself and traditional opera as the world knew it. The artistic result of this alteration of musical character was to be heard and seen within a short time in the still-to-be-completed *Götterdämmerung*, the last segment of *Der Ring des Nibelungen*, a section of the total work that is often looked upon today more as opera than as music drama.

Wagner's admirers and detractors remained divided in their reactions to *Der Ring des Nibelungen*. They were equally strong on both sides. Yet despite this great disorder regarding things Wagnerian, the man persisted, recognizing these matters as part of the realities of life. To him, the art was always foremost (after *Der Ring des Nibelungen* he then composed his final music drama, *Parsifal*), and in him there was a dynamism, a magnetism, a uniqueness that made him stand out before all others. He struck his mark forcefully in the artistic ways of his society. He moved on and he would not be dismissed. The magnitude of his genius rose above all else and carried him to greatness in his own day.

The passage of years since Wagner's death has not diminished the interest in the composer and his works. On the contrary, his prominence today remains high. Serious interest in Wagner and in his art has not only grown but has also expanded widely both in scope and in the number of his disciples and followers. His influence upon the musico-dramatic world has been no less than phenomenal, and much of the musical output in this field is considered today in terms of before and after Wagner. His life, his thought, and especially his creations continue to be the center of endless discussions and there has been no dearth of words written about him. His stature is unquestioned. That he was a giant of his age is attested to by the quantity of contemporary studies, analyses, commentaries, monographs, and books that focused on him and his works during his lifetime. While Wagner was yet alive, an ardent admirer, Nikolaus Oesterlein, who would later found a private Richard Wagner museum, had catalogued more than 10,000 publications on and about the composer and his work. That artistic popularity is as great, perhaps greater, in the modern era. A conservative estimate places the number of publications at about 22,500 as of 1983, and scholars predict that this number will rise to 30,000 by the turn of the century. Such has been and remains the world of Richard Wagner.

Chapter Two

Der Ring des Nibelungen: An Overview

Of all the musico-dramatic creations of Richard Wagner, none stands out more as a landmark of artistic and cultural history than *Der Ring des Nibelungen* (*The Ring of the Nibelung*). This protracted piece is the brightest jewel in the ornamented crown that is the work of opera's most innovative and certainly most controversial composer. The *Ring* (or *Ring* Cycle, as it is frequently called), was written and composed as "Ein Bühnenfestspiel für drei Tage und einem Vorabend" ("A Stage-Festival-Play to be produced on Three Days and a Fore-evening"). It premiered 12, 13, 16, and 17 August 1876 in Bayreuth, Bavaria, in a theater designed by the composer and constructed especially for that production. The statistics of the *Ring* offer an exemplary introduction to the magnitude of this musical work. The *Ring* consists of more than 800 pages of dialogue and stage instructions, 3750 pages of music for an orchestra of more than 120 instruments and thirty-six solo voices. These data result in a musico-dramatic work that requires some fifteen hours of playing time. The figures in this lengthy drama includes giants, dwarfs, a pantheon of divine beings, and mortals, each of whom lives in its own mythical world of the universe. The *Ring* also features a giant serpent, flying horses, and a dragon. The dramatic action includes a descent from the surface of the earth into the bowels of the world, as well as a rainbow bridge over which the gods can walk from the earth into the heavens, the flooding of the earth and a cataclysmic fire whose flames reach into the sky to burn the fortress Valhalla.

Prior to its first performance, the *Ring* had already become a much heralded work. Such public notice had come about principally because of Wagner's previous successes, and because of the widespread debates that broke out in reaction to his writings on opera and its status or non-status as art. At this first presentation, the *Ring* immediately became a topic of popular and critical study, and today, more than a century later, it remains one of the most-discussed artistic creations in history. Designed by Wagner to be performed on four successive evenings (an intention seldom realized because of the excessive theatrical and physical demands on both performers and technicians), the *Ring* is therefore the longest stage piece with a continuous theme ever created. Its nearest competitor in these terms is the *Passion Play* (a miracle drama of the sufferings of Christ between the night of the Last Supper and the Crucifixion) that is performed once every decade in the German city of Oberammergau.

Comparable to the length of the *Ring* drama is the amount of time Wagner devoted to its composition. From 1848, the date of the composer's initial sketch of what eventually became the *Ring* as it is known today, until the premiere, some twenty-eight years were to pass. Indeed, for some five years prior to 1848 Wagner read, studied, and in all ways immersed himself in Germanic myth, legend and history. In 1845, some six years before he thought of the *Ring* as a definite project, Wagner had decided to prepare a work on Germany's legendary hero, Siegfried, and from that date, if at first only nonspecifically, he continuously sorted out his players and properties and thought deeply about what particular new musical concepts would serve the dramatic ends he pondered. Wagner was thirty-three years old when his interest in what were to be *Ring* matters began to manifest itself. He was sixty-one when he wrote the last musical note of his *Ring*, and sixty-three at the time of its first complete performance.

The argument of *Der Ring des Nibelungen* reveals the fusion into a complex dramatic form of Wagner's version of two separate and unrelated themes from the societal, cultural, and literary history of the German people. The first is a story line in which the ancient gods of the Teutonic world, by their actions, create a moral dilemma which ultimately results in their downfall and the destruction of their world by fire and flood. The second theme focuses on the adventures of the celebrated German hero, Siegfried, who was known as a *Nibelung* in German legend, but whom Wagner converts into a Volsung (Wälsung), as he was known in Nordic tales.

Wagner shaped and fashioned his poetic drama from the numerous myths of the vast Germanic world and the popular legends of his native soil. From this extensive oral and recorded literature, he extracted figures, incidents, symbols, and other related matters as they had been interpreted through the ages. Incorporating his own thematic modifications, he poeticized the whole into an extensive drama for which he then composed the music.

In its final form *Der Ring des Nibelungen* is an allegory. The poem relates the actions and events that lead to and conclude with the destruction of the ancient gods, the doom of the corrupt world they had shaped, and the rebirth of the universe, cleansed and newly undefiled, through the thoughts and deeds of a valorous, virtuous champion. This total cataclysm and moral rebirth included other participants whose roles in that event had been designed by Wagner: the dark dwellers beneath the earth, the inhabitants of the waters of the earth, those—both mortal and supernatural—of the earth itself, and a gallery of ancient, pre-Christian Germanic gods.

For his drama of mortals, assorted supernatural and divine beings, and demigods, Wagner created an overwhelmingly persuasive music, a symphonic music that served not so much as a vehicle to facilitate dramatic expression, but rather as music that was an expression of the drama itself. Wagner conceived this music as a manifestation of the revelations of the drama, and as an exposition of the emotional and intellectual nuances of his poem—as a communion, so to speak, with the very words that gave it form.

Wagner's music inundated the world with a new and distinct sound. (That sound had been anticipated by an earlier Wagner work, *Tristan und Islode,* which had premiered in 1865.) To many listeners, this new music was strange, incongruous, and unacceptable because it so flagrantly violated the traditional, accepted forms and structures of operatic form which had gained dominance through the widespread popularity of French and Italian compositions. To others, this innovative music moved beyond what they considered innocuous melodies that served as diversions for inactive minds. To the latter, Wagner's new sound was indeed "the music of the future," as the composer had termed it. In the final analysis, however, Wagner's music possessed formidable power to stimulate deep emotion and to effect strong reaction.

Wagner's music slowly gained a vast audience. In time, it was acknowledged an impressive, sometimes overpowering, force that penetrated the core of human thought and emotion as had no other sound ever created, a sweeping expression of the "purely human." Fused as it was with poetry, Wagner's music and his drama together became the

Gesamtkunstwerk he had sought, the "total-work-of-art" about which he had thought and written so prodigiously.

Prior to the *Ring*, nothing of this musico-dramatic stamp had ever been conceived or even imagined, and it is most unlikely that any work of similar character will ever again be created. Today, as in 1876, the *Ring* reflects an artistic imagination of unbridled scope. It is a work whose every limit stretches well beyond the accepted patterns of art pieces. Regardless of the temper or the posture of subjective interpretation—and the *Ring* invites those of all hues and molds—Wagner's masterpiece stands as a singular creation. It is one of the most majestic artistic achievements in history, one that permanently transformed the course of the world's concepts of drama and music. In the modern day, *Der Ring des Nibelungen* remains an unparalleled endeavor, a legacy and a treasure in the field of creative arts.

Perhaps the late Carl Dahlhaus, an eminent Wagnerian scholar, depicted more lucidly and more succinctly than others the matter of the mature works of Richard Wagner, which, of course, are dominated by the *Ring*. Dahlhaus wrote:

> A Wagnerian music drama, like a Beethoven symphony, is a work of art, an inviolable text to be taken at its word and conveyed to the understanding of an audience capable of aesthetic contemplation by means of a staged interpretation that serves the work. By contrast, an Italian opera, for example by Rossini or even the early middle Verdi, was nothing more than a blueprint for an evening at the theater, and the production succeeded or failed on those grounds alone.[1]

---

[1] "Wagner's Place in the History of Music." *Wagner Handbook*, 101.

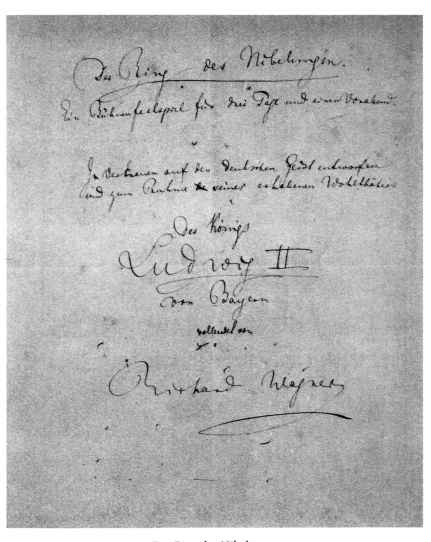

Der Ring des Nibelungen
Title page with dedication to King Ludwig II, 1873
(after a photocopy)

16

Chapter Three

The Format of the *Ring*

3.1 DIVISIONS

Der Ring des Nibelungen is a music drama consisting of four parts. Each of the parts has its own dramatic argument and, therefore, can be performed as a single work, independent of the others. However, the four dramas together form a greater stage piece whose theme is continuous and whose total argument is developed according to the requirements of dramatic literature. The music of the *Ring*, similarly, is at once individual to each of the four parts, yet that music is also repetitive and overlapping in accordance with both the dictates of the argument and the composer's artistic intent.

Wagner entitled each of the four music dramas in a manner most descriptive of the central theme or figure of each part. The main title, *The Ring of the Nibelung*, reflects the major theme that runs throughout the four dramas. The dramas of the *Ring*, listed in the order of the intended presentation—with internal divisions and approximate playing time—are provided in Table 1.

3.2 ORIGINAL TITLES

The titles of the four dramas of the *Ring* as well as that of the complete work—as we know them today—are not those that Wagner originally assigned. The changes of the titles, in the main, are significant because they reflect a modification in dramatic emphasis as the composer made numerous revisions in the poems, revisions that became necessary because of the turns in his dramatic thoughts.

17

Der Ring des Nibelungen

In 1852, after the text of the four dramas had been completed, Wagner brought the quartet of poems together under the title *Der Gold des Nibelungen* (*The Nibelung's Gold*). This title was later changed to *Der Reif des Nibelungen* (*The Nibelung's Circlet*) (*Reif* means "Ring" in the sense of "circle" or "hoop"). Wagner sensed that neither of these titles conveyed the importance of the Ring as part of the great Nibelung treasure, and thus settled on the title by which the tetralogy is known today.

Das Rheingold

Wagner's original title for the first drama of the *Ring* Cycle was *Der Raub des Rheingoldes* (*Rape of the Rhine Gold*). Aware that the single act of theft of the Gold was of less dramatic significance in the total work than the Gold itself, Wagner then changed the original to the new title.

Table 1
The Dramas of the *Ring*

Title	Acts/Scenes	Playing Time	Total
Das Rheingold (*The Rhine Gold*)	1/4	2'30"	2'30"
Die Walküre (*The Valkyrie*)	3/11		
ACT I	3 scenes	1'10"	
ACT II	5 scenes	1'30"	
ACT III	3 scenes	1'10"	3'50"
Siegfried (Siegfried)	3/9		
ACT I	3 scenes	1'20"	
ACT II	3 scenes	1'15"	
ACT III	3 scenes	1'25"	4'00"
Götterdämmerüng (*Twilight of the Gods*)	3/13		
Prelude	2 scenes		
ACT I	2 scenes	2'00"	
ACT II	5 scenes	1'10"	
ACT III	3 scenes	1'20"	4'30"
Totals	10/37	14'50"	14'50"

Die Walküre

The original title of the second drama was *Siegmund und Sieglinde: Der Bestrafung der Walküre* (*Siegmund and Sieglinde: The Punishment of the Valkyrie*). Wagner's dramatic acumen told him that a shorter title was necessary. Realizing that the focus of the argument was on the principal Valkyrie, he then renamed his drama.

Siegfried

Der junge Siegfried (*The Young Siegfried*) was the first title that Wagner gave to this third drama of the Ring. In time he determined that the word young was superfluous and that the text of his poem would reveal the youthful character of the Volsung hero. The title was then reduced to its present form.

Götterdämmerung

The fourth drama of the tetralogy, the first in the order of composition, was written as *Siegfrieds Tod* (*Siegfried's Death*). The retitling of the drama reflects a significant shift of emphasis in a radically revised final scene.

The term 'Twilight [dusk] of the Gods' is a literal translation of the Old Norse term *ragnarökkr*. This word refers to the end of the gods in a metaphoric sense, that is, 'shadow,' 'dusk,' or 'twilight.' Early on, this term, *ragnarökkr*, became semantically enmeshed with *ragnarök*, which depicts the "fate" or "destiny" of the gods, that is, their downfall at the hands of their enemies and then the destruction of the universe by a cataclysmic fire and flood. From these terms Wagner fashioned his title which, in light of the mythical past and the final events of his drama, was most appropriate.

3.3 THE PLAYERS—TYPES

The players in *Der Ring des Nibelungen* are many and varied, an amalgamation that existed and, in certain ways, continues to exist in the societal mind of the Germanic peoples. In the *Ring*, these figures are of two groups:

1. Personified deities, demigods, and supernaturals who satisfied the Germanic spiritual and cultural needs of the pre-Christian races.
2. Legendary mortals whose deeds and adventures represented the actions of romanticized champions.

The figures of both groups transcend the limits of material existence but are bound to the reality of mankind by their human forms, their attributes, and their overall conduct which pattern, in one manner or another, that of earthly life.

The *dramatis personae* of the *Ring* number thirty-six solo vocal roles. Of this total, two of the representations are enacted by players who each appear in two distinct physical forms, transformations brought about by magical or divine powers. The roles of the *Ring*, grouped according to nature types, and their number, are as follows:

1. *Deities* (6)

   Donner — God of Thunder and Lightning
   Erda — Earth Mother, Goddess of Wisdom
   Freia — Goddess of Eternal Youth
   Fricka — Goddess of Wedlock and Fidelity
   Froh — God of Light, God of the Fields
   Wotan — King of the Gods, the Allfather

(Of this group of gods and goddesses, Wotan transforms himself, through divine powers, into mortal form and wanders the earth.)

2. *Demigods* (1)

   Loge — Guardian of Fire

3. *Divine Beings* (12)

   a) Valkyries (9)
   Brünnhilde
   Gerhilde
   Grimgerde
   Helmwige
   Ortlinde
   Rossweisse
   Schwertleite
   Siegrune
   Waltraute

(The principal warrior-maiden, Brünnhilde, is banished from the World of the Gods and her divinity is replaced with mortal life and being.)

b) The Fates (3)
   First Norn
   Second Norn
   Third Norn

4. *Supernaturals* (7)

   a) Dwarfs (Black Elves) (2)
      Alberich
      Mime

   b) Earth Giants (2)
      Fafner
      Fasolt

(Fafner, by means of magical powers, transforms himself into the Dragon.)

   c) Nymphs (Nixies) (3)
      Flosshilde
      Wellgunde
      Woglinde

5. *Mortals* (8)

   a) Wanderer — transformed King of the Gods

   b) Siegmund and Sieglinde — mortal twin children of the transformed King of the Gods and mortal woman

   c) Siegfried — child of Siegmund and Sieglinde

   d) Hunding — mortal husband of Sieglinde

   e) Hagen — son of Alberich and the mortal Grimhild who is also the wife of Gibich and the mother of Gunther and Gutrune

   f) Gunther — ruler of the Gibichung kingdom on the Rhine

   g) Gutrune — sister of Gunther

6. *Animals* (2)

   a) Forest bird

   b) Dragon (This figure is the Giant Fafner, transformed by the powers of a magic helmet.)

The complement of solo players is enlarged by a group of nonsinging dwarfs and a chorus of mortal vassals which, depending on production means and facilities, may number between forty and one hundred. (Wagner specified twenty-eight men and nine women for his original chorus.)

3.4 THE PLAYERS—DESCRIPTIONS

The following list presents, in alphabetical order, the names of each of the solo players of the *Ring* with a brief description of the part each plays as the drama develops. Immediately after each name, in parenthesis, the type of voice for which Wagner wrote his music is indicated, and the drama(s) in which each figure appears (**R**-*Das Rheingold*; **W**-*Die Walküre*; **S**-*Siegfried*; **G**-*Götterdämmerung*).

Alberich (Bass-baritone; **R, S, G**)

A scurrilous Black Dwarf; father of Hagen and brother to Mime; a Nibelung, the race of metalsmiths who inhabit Nibelheim, a cavern in the bowels of the earth. Teased, taunted, and then spurned by the Rhine Daughters,[1] Alberich forswears love and steals the Rhine Gold, from which he forges the Ring with which the possessor may rule the Universe. With the Ring he enslaves the Nibelungs, whom he forces to mine a huge treasure of gold, makes himself Lord of Nibelheim, and forces his brother Mime to make the Tarnhelm, a helmet of gold which permits the wearer to assume any form desired, including invisibility. When the gold treasures are taken from him, he places a death curse on any possessor of the Ring, and then schemes continuously to regain the Ring and the power that it affords.

Brünnhilde (Soprano; **W, S, G**)

Eldest and mightiest of the nine Valkyries, Wish-Maidens, and daughters of Wotan and Erda.[2] Brünnhilde is the favorite daughter of Wotan,

---

[1] Wagner's primary and principal reference to these three nixies is as *Rhinetöchter*, literally *Rhine Daughters*. In turn, the trio refers to the Rhine with the word *Vater* (Father). It is only rarely that the composer uses the term *Rheinmädchen* (*Rhine Maidens*). However, for whatever reason, English-speaking Wagnerians overwhelmingly seem to prefer the term *Maiden(s)* when referring to any or all of this trio of water spirits.

[2] Some scholars maintain that only Brünnhilde is the daughter of Wotan and Erda, while making no claim as to the parentage of the other eight Valkyries.

King of the Gods; she serves as the god's *Will*. Because she attempted to protect the mortal Siegmund, against her father's command, the latter banishes her from the World of the Gods. Her divinity is taken from her and replaced with mortal life, and she is condemned to a prolonged sleep on a fire-girded rock from which she can be rescued only by a fearless hero. Siegfried penetrates the fire and awakens her, and the two pledge their love. She then gives Siegfried her strength and her wisdom. When she believes that she has been deceived by Siegfried, she is tricked into revealing where his vulnerability lies, which disclosure results in his murder. Realizing that she has been duped into causing the hero's death, she puts a firebrand to his pyre, the flames of which reach Valhalla and the gods. As destruction comes to the world, she returns the Ring to the Rhine and then immolates herself on Siegfried's pyre.

Donner (Baritone; **R**)

God of Thunder and Lightning, which he calls forth by means of his magical hammer; brother of Freia, Fricka, and Froh. With the other gods, he urges Wotan to gain possession of the Gold in order to use it as a substitute payment to the Giants for their construction of Valhalla. The original promise of reward for this work had been the goddess Freia.

Dragon (Bass; **S**)

The giant Fafner, who—after killing his brother in an argument over possession of the Gold given to them as payment for their work on Valhalla—flees to Neidhöhle (Hate Cavern) where, by means of the Tarnhelm, he transforms himself into a dragon and stands guard over the Treasure. He is killed by Siegfried, who then takes the Ring and the Tarnhelm for himself. It is the taste of the Dragon's blood that gives Siegfried the power to understand the language of birds and to understand the thoughts of the scheming Mime.

Erda (Contralto; **R, S**)

Earth Mother, Goddess of Wisdom, mother of the Norns. Seduced by Wotan, she gave birth to the Valkyries.[3] Erda resides in the vaults of the Earth from which, as eternal woman of wisdom (*Vala* or *Ur Vala*), she rises to warn Wotan of the impending doom if he does not return the Gold that he has taken from Alberich.

[3] See note 2.

Fafner (Bass; **R**, **S**)

Last of the Earth Giants whose home is Riesenheim (Land of the Giants). After killing his brother, Fasolt, in a dispute over possession of the Gold that Wotan had paid the pair—in lieu of Freia—for their building of Valhalla, he flees with the Treasure to Neidhöhle (Hate Cavern) where he transforms himself into the Dragon by the magic of the Tarnhelm. He is slain by Siegfried, who then becomes possessor of the Hoard.

Fasolt (Bass; **R**)

An Earth Giant who is killed by his brother, Fafner, in an argument over possession of the Gold that Wotan had paid them, in lieu of Freia, for their work on Valhalla.

Flosshilde (Mezzo-Soprano; **R**, **G**)

[*See* Rhine Daughters]

Forest Bird (Soprano; **S**)

A bird whose language Siegfried understands because he has tasted of the Dragon's blood. Through her song, she reveals to the hero that Fafner's lair is the hiding place of the Gold, and counsels the hero on its power. She then warns him of the crafty Mime, and later she guides the hero to the banished Brünnhilde, who sleeps on the fire-ringed rock.

Freia (Soprano; **R**)

Goddess of Eternal Youth; Guardian of the Golden Apples, the source of eternal youth for the gods; sister of Donner, Fricka, and Froh. She is promised by Wotan to the Giants Fafner and Fasolt as reward for their building of Valhalla, but later is rescued from their hands when the Giants decide to accept the Gold as their payment.

Fricka (Mezzo-Soprano; **R**, **W**)

Goddess of Wedlock and Fidelity; Queen of the Gods; spouse to Wotan; sister to Donner, Freia, and Froh. She is the censurer, and correctly so, of almost every action of Wotan although she urges him to take the Gold from Alberich in order to use it as payment to the Giants Fafner and Fasolt, in lieu of Freia, for their labors on Valhalla.

Froh (Tenor; **R**)

God of the Fields; Guardian of Light; brother of Donner, Freia and Fricka; Guardian of the Rainbow Bridge that serves the gods as the entrance to Valhalla.

Gerhilde (Soprano; **W**)

[*See* Valkyries]

Giants

Fafner and Fasolt, the last of the Earth Giants. Fafner kills his brother in order to possess all the gold treasure that Wotan has given them. Fafner then uses the Tarnhelm that is part of the hoard to transform himself into a dragon, to lie guard over the Gold. Fafner is later slain by Siegfried who seeks out this dragon in order to learn the meaning of fear.

Grimgerde (Mezzo-Soprano; **W**)

[*See* Valkyries]

Gunther (Baritone; **G**)

A Gibichung mortal, son of King Gibich and Grimhild; King of the Gibichungs in his Kingdom on the Rhine; brother to Gutrune and half-brother to Hagen through their mother. Gunther is concerned about his personal fame. When Hagen tells him that he should have a noble wife, but that he cannot win the most illustrious maid, Brünnhilde, for himself, he plots with him to drug Siegfried to cause the hero, by means of the Tarnhelm, to assume his disguise and to win Brünnhilde for him as his bride. Later, after Hagen has killed Siegfried—with whom Gunther had taken an oath of blood brotherhood—Gunther attempts to gain the Ring for himself, and he is also slain by Hagen.

Gutrune (Soprano; **G**)

A Gibichung mortal; sister to Gunther and half-sister to Hagen through their mother, Grimhild. Gutrune takes the eager but drugged Siegfried as her husband in payment for her role in the scheme to have the hero win Brünnhilde for her brother.

Hagen (Bass; **G**)

Son of mortal Grimhild and the Black Dwarf Alberich; half-brother to Gunther and Gutrune through their mother, Grimhild. With Gunther and Gutrune, Hagen plots to have Siegfried win Brünnhilde as bride for Gunther. He continues to plot to win the Gold for himself by causing Brünnhilde to reveal the secret of Siegfried's vulnerability. After he kills Siegfried, he then murders Gunther and attempts to claim the Ring. As he rushes to retrieve it when it is returned to the Rhine, the Rhine Daughters take him to his death in the waters.

Helmwige (Soprano; **W**)

[*See* Valkyries]

Hunding (Bass; **W**)

A mortal of the Neiding race; lawful husband of Sieglinde whom he took against her will. He is suspicious of the resemblance between Sieglinde and Siegmund. When he becomes aware that it was Siegmund who killed his kin, he challenges him and later kills him in battle. He is then struck dead by the vengeful Wotan.

Loge (Tenor; **R**)

Guardian of Fire. Loge is a wily, cunning demigod who has searched the world to find a suitable substitute payment with which Wotan can pay the Giants for their construction of Valhalla. He informs Wotan, the King of the Gods, of Alberich's Gold and its powers, encourages the god to steal it, then leads him to Nibelheim where the fire god tricks the Black Dwarf so that he may be captured and the Gold taken from him. Later, when Wotan banishes Brünnhilde from the World of the Gods, he calls upon Loge to surround the Valkyrie in her forced sleep; in the final destruction of the gods, Brünnhilde calls upon him to leap from Siegfried's pyre into Valhalla to consume the Home of the gods and all who reside there.

Mime (Tenor; **R, S**)

A treacherous Nibelung Black Dwarf; brother to Alberich, who enslaves him through the powers of the Ring and who forces him to make the Tarnhelm. Lusting for power and the lordship of Nibelheim, Mime raises Siegfried from infancy in order that the hero one day will confront the Dragon that guards the Gold, hoping that the two will kill each other, thereby permitting him to gain the Gold for himself. He is slain by Siegfried when the latter learns of his evil plans.

Norns

First Norn (Contralto; **G**)
Second Norn (Mezzo-Soprano; **G**)
Third Norn (Soprano; **G**)
The three daughters of Erda, who conveys to them her wisdom and knowledge. They are the spinners of the Cord of Destiny that determines the fate of all things.

Ortlinde (Soprano; **W**)

[*See* Valkyries]

Rhine Daughters (Nixies)

Flosshilde, Wellgunde, Woglinde. Three nymphs, daughters of the Rhine King, and Guardians of the Gold that rests in the Rhine. The Treasure is stolen from them by Alberich and passes through the hands of several possessors, ultimately to be returned to them at the time of the destruction of the gods.

Rossweisse (Mezzo-Soprano; **W**)

[*See* Valkyries]

Schwertleite (Mezzo-Soprano; **W**)

[*See* Valkyries]

Siegfried (Tenor; **S, G**)

Mortal son of Siegmund and Sieglinde and mightiest of the Volsungs. Sieglinde dies in childbirth, and the hero is raised by Mime, who schemes to have the youth one day kill the Dragon and, in turn, be killed. In this way, Mime will gain the Gold and its magic powers. Siegfried is the fearless hero who reforges the pieces of his father's shattered sword, Notung, and with it kills the Dragon and then retrieves the Ring and the Tarnhelm, which he considers to be curios. Having tasted the Dragon's blood, he is able to understand the language of birds; and through Forest Bird he learns of Mime's evil plotting. He kills the Dwarf and is then led to Brünnhilde's Rock by Forest Bird. At the foot of the rock he encounters Wotan, who tries to bar his way. Siegfried does not know the King of the Gods, whom he defies and whose Spear of Authority he breaks. Siegfried then climbs the rock on which Brünnhilde sleeps, penetrates the fire, and awakens the banished Valkyrie. Their feelings of love are aroused, and they pledge themselves to each other. Brünnhilde, now a mortal, gives Siegfried her strength and her wisdom. He then travels to the Gibichungs on the Rhine where he swears blood brotherhood with Gunther. Siegfried then becomes the pawn in Hagen's scheme to get the Gold; drugged by a potion, he assumes Gunther's form and wins Brünnhilde as bride for the King of the Gibichungs. As reward, Siegfried is given Gutrune as his bride. Brünnhilde becomes aware of the deception, vows Siegfried's destruction, and reveals to Hagen the hero's vulnerability. On a hunt, Hagen kills Siegfried by plunging a spear into the vulnerable spot on his back. Brünnhilde, now aware of all that has happened, declares the purity and nobility of Siegfried, and then sets a torch to his pyre. After removing the Ring from Siegfried's hand, she returns it to the Rhine Daughters and then immolates herself as the flames reach into the sky to destroy Valhalla and the gods.

Sieglinde (Soprano; **W**)

Mortal daughter of Wotan and mortal woman; twin sister to Siegmund; lawful but unwilling wife of Hunding. Sieglinde receives the lost stranger Siegmund into her dwelling. In time, as the two recognize each other as brother and sister, and as their love unfolds, she tells him the story of the sword that a mysterious stranger long ago buried in the tree. The two then vow their love. Siegmund takes the sword from the tree, and they flee together. Siegmund is killed by Hunding in a battle in which the sword is broken into two pieces. Sieglinde, now with child, is aided by Brünnhilde, who directs her to escape into the forest. Carrying the pieces of Siegmund's broken sword, Sieglinde takes refuge in the woods where she dies giving birth to Siegfried.

Siegmund (Tenor; **W**)

A Volsung, and mortal son of Wotan and mortal woman; twin brother of Sieglinde. As a stranger in Sieglinde's dwelling, he tells of his sad life and his lost father's promise of a sword in the time of his greatest need. Sieglinde tells him of a sword embedded in the tree by a mysterious stranger. In time, the two recognize each other, are attracted, and pledge their love as Siegmund claims the sword as that promised by his father. He names it Notung. He and Sieglinde flee. Siegmund is later slain by Hunding, Sieglinde's husband, to avenge his kin who were slain by Siegmund. During the dispute, Siegmund's sword is broken into two pieces that are retrieved by Brünnhilde who, against Wotan's command, had attempted to aid the Volsung.

Siegrune (Mezzo-Soprano; **W**)

[*See* Valkyries]

Valkyries

Brünnhilde, Gerhilde, Grimgerde, Helmwige, Ortlinde, Rossweisse, Schwertleite, Siegrune, Waltraute; the nine daughters of Wotan and Erda.[4] They are the Wish-Maidens of Wotan who serve him and the raised mortal heroes of Valhalla, chosen by Wotan because of their valor during battle and brought by the Valkyries to the Home of the Gods. The Valkyries, on their way to Valhalla, gather at Brünnhildenstein (Brünnhilde's Rock) to await Brünnhilde's arrival. The latter arrives, with Sieglinde, and implores her sisters' aid for Sieglinde, who is carrying Siegmund's child.

Waltraute (Mezzo-Soprano; **W**, **G**)

A Valkyrie. In defiance of the dejected Wotan, she travels on her steed from Valhalla to Brünnhilde's Rock to ask her sister to save the forlorn gods from impending doom by causing the accursed Ring to be returned to the Rhine.

Wellgunde (Mezzo-Soprano; **R**, **G**)

[*See* Rhine Daughters]

Wood Bird

[*See* Forest Bird]

---

[4] See note 2.

Woglinde (Soprano; **R**, **G**)

[*See* Rhine Daughters]

Wanderer (Baritone; **S**)

Wotan, transformed into a mortal by his divine powers. In this guise, he travels about the world.

Wotan (Baritone; **R**, **W** and *Wanderer* in **S**)

King of the Gods; Allfather; Guardian of Pacts and Pledges; ruler of the world through his Spear, a branch from the World Ash Tree on which are carved the runes of his power; husband of Fricka; father of the Valkyries.[5] To rescue Freia, whom he had promised to the Giants Fafner and Fasolt as payment for their construction of Valhalla, he and Loge trick Alberich out of the Gold and then offer it to the Giants as their reward. Cautioned by Erda to return the cursed Ring to the Rhine Daughters, Wotan understands that, as Guardian of Pacts and Pledges, he has already broken his word to the Giants and therefore cannot use force to retrieve the Ring. To have this deed accomplished for him, Wotan fathers—with a mortal woman—the Wälsung (Volsung) twins, Siegmund and Sieglinde, anticipating that the mortal hero will, of his own accord, bring about such action. Berated by his wife for fostering the incestuous love of the brother and sister, and causing an act of infidelity within the lawful wedlock of Sieglinde and Hunding, Wotan commands that Siegmund must die at Hunding's hand. Brünnhilde, moved by the love the twins have for each other, understands Wotan's true wishes, that is, that Siegmund not die, and disobeys his command by attempting to protect Siegmund. Because of her actions, Wotan punishes Brünnhilde by removing her divinity and condemning her to a fire-girded rock where he kisses her into a sleep from which she can be awakened only by a hero who knows no fear. In time, Siegfried, led by Forest Bird, approaches Brünnhilde's Rock and the sleeping Valkyrie. Wotan attempts to prevent the son of Siegmund and Sieglinde from reaching his daughter, but the fearless Siegfried breaks Wotan's Spear of authority with his sword Notung. Defeated, the King of the Gods withdraws and retires to Valhalla to await the fulfillment of the curse that he has brought upon the gods by his actions in the theft of the Ring.

[5] See note 2.

Table 2
The Players—A Chart of Relationships

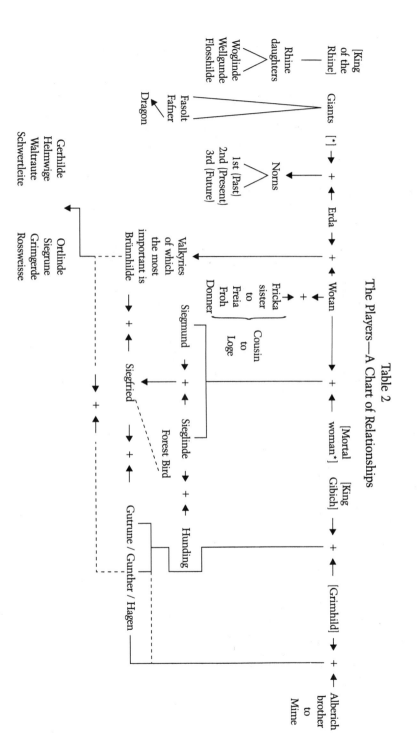

* Is not named in the drama

[ ] Does not appear in the drama although reference is made to the figure

Table 3
The Players—A Chart of Appearances

Legend: ■ Singing role □ Non-singing role

Column key (opera / act / scene):
Rg = Das Rheingold (scenes 1–4);
WI, WII, WIII = Die Walküre Acts I (1–3), II (1–5), III (1–3);
SI, SII, SIII = Siegfried Acts I, II, III (each 1–3);
GdI, GdII, GdIII = Götterdämmerung Act I (P,1,2,3), Act II (1–5), Act III (1–3).

Dramatis Personae (in the order of first appearance)	Rg1	Rg2	Rg3	Rg4	WI-1	WI-2	WI-3	WII-1	WII-2	WII-3	WII-4	WII-5	WIII-1	WIII-2	WIII-3	SI-1	SI-2	SI-3	SII-1	SII-2	SII-3	SIII-1	SIII-2	SIII-3	GdI-P	GdI-1	GdI-2	GdI-3	GdII-1	GdII-2	GdII-3	GdII-4	GdII-5	GdIII-1	GdIII-2	GdIII-3
Das Rheingold																																				
The Rhine Daughters																																				
Woglinde	■			■																														■		□
Wellgunde	■			■																														■		□
Floshilde	■			■																														■		□
Alberich	■		■	■															■	■									■							
Fricka		■		■				■																												
Wotan		■	■	■				■	■			■		■	■		■		■			■	■													
Freia		■		■																																
Fasolt		■		■																																
Fafner		■		■															■	■																
Froh		■		■																																
Donner		■		■																																
Loge		■	■	■																																
Mime			■													■	■	■		■	■															
Nibelung Dwarfs			□	□																																
Erda				■																		■														
Die Walküre																																				
Siegmund					■	■	■			■	■	■																								
Sieglinde					■	■	■			■	■		■																							
Hunding						■						■																								
Brünnhilde								■		■	■	■	■	■	■									■	■			■				■	■			■
The Valkyries																																				
Gerhilde													■	■																						
Waltraute													■	■														■								
Schwertleite													■	■																						
Ortlinde													■	■																						
Helmwige													■	■																						
Siegrune													■	■																						
Grimgerde													■	■																						
Rossweisse													■	■																						
Siegfried																																				
Siegfried																■		■		■	■		■	■	■		■				■	■		■	■	
Forest Bird																				■	■															
Götterdämmerung																																				
The Norns																																				
1st Norn																									■											
2nd Norn																									■											
3rd Norn																									■											
Gunther																										■	■					■	■		■	
Hagen																										■	■		■	■	■	■	■		■	■
Gutrune																										■	■					■	■			■
Gibichung Vassals																															■	■			■	□

■ Singing role □ Non-singing role

Note: Design adapted from Albert Lavignac, *The Music Dramas of Richard Wagner and his Festival Theater*, translated by Ester Singleton. 1904; reprinted, New York: AMS Press, 1970, 154ff.

For a graphic depiction of the complex interrelationships among these players, see Table 2.

See Table 3 for the *dramatis personae* and the order and distribution of their appearances throughout the Cycle.

3.5 MAJOR PROPERTIES

Apples

[*See* Golden Apples]

Bridge

[*See* Rainbow Bridge]

Donner's Hammer

[*See* Hammer]

Gold

In a very real sense, the Gold is the protagonist of the *Ring* drama. Sometimes referred to as "Hoard" or "Treasure," it is the stimulus for the chain of major actions and mental attitudes that dominate the argument. If the Gold reflects the dual symbolism of wealth and power that has been attached to it throughout cultural history, that concept is heightened in the *Ring* by the addition of magical powers. In this capacity, the presence of the Gold is keenly sensed throughout the drama. To know the path of the Gold is to know not only the dramatic framework of the *Ring*, but also the lust, the greed, the hatred, the havoc, the malevolence, indeed the tragedy, of the tetralogy.

The Gold appears in the first moments of the opening drama. It rests serenely in the depths of the Rhine where it is guarded by the three daughters of the Rhine King. The Gold possesses special powers in that whoever renounces love can then fashion from it a ring with which the possessor may rule the universe. Alberich, the Nibelung Dwarf, vengeful at the rejection of his advances by the Rhine Daughters, steals the Gold, forswears love, and creates the Ring. The Dwarf then enslaves the Nibelungs and forces his brother Mime to make the Tarnhelm.

The Hoard, of which the Ring and the Tarnhelm are a part, then continues its fateful journey. Wotan, using trickery, forces Alberich to

33

give up the Treasure; the Dwarf then places a death curse on the Ring. From Wotan, the treasure passes in turn to Fasolt and Fafner, to Fafner alone, then to Siegfried, to Brünnhilde, who, at the downfall of the gods, returns it to its home in the Rhine. In the course of its travels, the Ring is coveted by Mime, Gunther, and Hagen, upon whom, as with all the possessors, the death curse is realized.

Golden Apples

Cultivated only by Freia, Goddess of Eternal Youth, the Golden Apples are the source of everlasting youth for the gods, a means of life without sorrow. When Freia is accepted by the Giants as payment for their work on Valhalla, the gods are deprived of their Golden Apples, and they begin to age and grow weak as life slowly fades away. Once the goddess is returned and the Apples are again cultivated, the gods regain their vigor and spirit.

Hammer

Possessed of magical powers, the Hammer belongs to Donner, God of Thunder. The god uses the Hammer to threaten the Giants, and with it he also brings a great storm of thunder and lightning to clear away the mists as the gods prepare to enter Valhalla for the first time.

Hoard

[*See* Gold]

Notung

[*See* Sword]

Rainbow Bridge

The Bridge—whose guardian is Froh, God of Light—serves as the pathway over which the gods cross as they leave the mountain top to enter the celestial Valhalla.

Ring

The magic Ring is fashioned by Alberich from the Gold that he has stolen from the Rhine Daughters; because he has forsworn love, he can use it to become ruler of the universe. Using the powers of the Ring, the Dwarf enslaves the Nibelung race, forces them to mine a gold treasure for him, and then forces his brother Mime to use the Gold to make the Tarnhelm, a magic helmet that permits its wearer to assume any form desired, even absence of form, invisibility. When the Ring is taken from Alberich, he places a death curse on it. The Ring is coveted by Mime, Hagen, and Gunther, and in turn, after Alberich, it is possessed by the gods through Wotan, the Giants, the Dragon, Siegfried, and Brünnhilde, upon each of whom the death curse is ultimately invoked. In an act of salvation and redemption, Brünnhilde returns the Ring to its home in the Rhine where the waters of the river cleanse, purify, and return it, as Gold, to its original noble state.

Spear

The Spear carried by Wotan is at once the authority by which the King of the Gods rules the World and the symbol of that divine authority. The spear originally was a branch of the World Ash Tree, torn away by Wotan, who then carved upon its shaft the runes of his godhead and his powers, including the rune of Truth in Pacts and Pledges. At such times in the drama when Wotan lays aside the spear, he is abandoning, symbolically at least, the attributes of a god and donning those of a lesser being. The Spear has no name although Wotan refers to it as "Heerschaft Haft" (The Haft of Lordship") and later the Second Norn calls it "Haft der Welt" (The Haft of the World). The powers of the Spear are superseded by those of the Ring, and later by those of the sword Notung, which, in Siegfried's hand, splinters the spear, thus ending Wotan's divine rule and removing the final barrier to the fated doom and destruction of the gods and the world over which they had divine supremacy.

Sword

In the distant past a stranger embedded a sword in the trunk of the ash tree that rises in the center of Hunding's dwelling. Many have tried to remove it, but all have failed. As Sieglinde and Siegmund, the mortal Volsung children of Wotan, recognize each other as brother and sister and become lovers, she tells him of the stranger and the sword. The pair then realizes that the stranger was Wälse (Volsa)—Wotan transformed—their father, and Siegmund knows that the sword is the weapon his lost father had promised him in the hour of his greatest need. Withdrawing the sword from the tree, he names it Notung (Needful). The sword was placed in the tree by Wotan to serve in the rescue of the Gold and its return to its home in the Rhine, an act of force which the King of the Gods, as Guardian of Pacts and Pledges, is not free to do himself, and for which he fathered the Wälsung (Volsung) race. In battle with Hunding, lawful husband of Sieglinde, Siegmund is killed, and the sword is broken into two pieces. Brünnhilde rescues the pieces and gives them to Sieglinde, whom she helps to escape. After Sieglinde's death while giving birth to Siegfried, the pieces pass to Mime whose scheme is to raise the youth to kill the dragon and at the same time be killed, thus allowing the Nibelung Dwarf to become possessor of the Gold. Mime is unable to reforge the pieces, and years later this feat is accomplished by the grown Siegfried. With Notung, Siegfried slays the Dragon and then kills the scheming Mime. Led by Forest Bird, Siegfried then proceeds to Brünnhilde's Rock where he encounters Wotan, who attempts to stop the youth from rescuing the banished Valkyrie. The fearless Siegfried uses Notung to shatter Wotan's Spear of Authority and, as the powerless King of the Gods turns away, Siegfried continues to the rock where he uses the sword to sever the bonds of Brünnhilde's breastplate. Brünnhilde is awakened, and in time the two discover each other, declare their love, and take their vows. The hero then sets out on new adventures. Siegfried travels to the land of the Gibichungs where he pledges the might of Notung to the service of King Gunther and then uses it to draw blood for the ritual of the oath of blood brotherhood. Notung then becomes the witness to chastity and fidelity as the drugged Siegfried places it between himself and Brünnhilde, whom he has vowed to win for Gunther. Later, in an encounter with the Rhine Daughters, Siegfried proclaims that if the Norns have woven into the Cord of Destiny a strand for his death, Notung will sever that cord. In its final adventure, the sword is sheathed at Siegfried's side, along with the Tarnhelm, as the hero is run through by Hagen's spear. In a last effort, Siegfried draws the sword, but he dies without being able to put it to use.

Tarnhelm

The Tarnhelm is a magic helmet made from the Gold by Mime at Alberich's order and instruction. The powers of the Tarnhelm permit the wearer to become invisible or to assume any form desired. Alberich becomes invisible, to watch over the Nibelungs, whom he has enslaved, and later, to impress Wotan and Loge, he uses the Tarnhelm to turn himself into a serpent and then into a toad. In the latter form he is made prisoner by Wotan, who then becomes possessor of the Tarnhelm as part of the Treasure, all of which he turns over to the Giants as ransom for the return of Freia. Once the Gold is in the possession of the Giants, the brothers argue over their respective shares. Fafner then kills Fasolt, and by means of the Tarnhelm transforms himself into a Dragon and flees to a cave with the Gold where he will guard the treasure as his own. Siegfried kills the Dragon and takes the Tarnhelm (and the Ring), which he later uses to assume the form of Gunther as a means to win Brünnhilde as the Gibichung's bride. The Tarnhelm hangs at Siegfried's side (along with Notung) when the hero is killed and placed atop a funeral pyre. Siegfried and the Tarnhelm and the sword are then consumed in the flames of the pyre, which reach to Valhalla and the gods.

Treasure

[*See* Gold]

Valhalla

This great fortress is the Home of the Gods and the Hall of the Chosen. It was built for Wotan by the Giants Fafner and Fasolt. To this lordly abode the Valkyries bring the bodies of valiant warriors who have died in battle. In Valhalla the fallen heroes are returned to life, to serve as the army of the King of the Gods. Valhalla is located in the celestial heights and is entered by crossing the Rainbow Bridge. In the final destruction, Wotan orders that the World Ash Tree be felled and its wood be placed around Valhalla. There, the gods await the doom of Loge's flames, which will rise from Siegfried's pyre to consume them and the universe.

World Ash Tree

The guardian tree of the universe, whose limbs spread over the World and in times past bore lush foliage. At its base flowed the Spring of Wisdom from which waters Wotan once drank, giving one of his eyes as payment. From the tree, Wotan took a branch that became the Spear on which are carved the runes of his powers and those of his godhead. When the branch was snapped from the tree, the latter began to wither and the Spring of Wisdom ceased to flow. The blight grew worse. When the hero Siegfried splintered Wotan's Spear, the tree could no longer house the Cord of Destiny woven by the Norns. Wotan, aware of the inevitable doom of the World, then ordered the tree felled and its branches placed around Valhalla, all to be consumed by the flames that rose from Siegfried's pyre.

Chapter Four

The Composition of the *Ring*

4.1 THE DRAMAS

Wagner devoted four years, from 1848 to 1852, to the composition of the four dramatic poems that constitute the *Ring*. In preparation, he had spent some five years prior to 1848 reading and studying the many myths and legends of the Germanic peoples. By 1848 he had decided to write one single drama, but in time that drama spawned another to precede it in the plot; the latter then occasioned two additional dramas, each argumentatively preceding the others. Wagner thus composed his four dramas of the *Ring* in the reverse order of its plot development, a procedure that later was to give rise to many problems of revision and modification.

The first manuscript that became the basis for what would become the *Ring* was completed in October 1848. It was a relatively short sketch of some eleven pages in which Wagner, for his own benefit, attempted to sort out and to give some order to his version of the many events, figures, and properties—and their relationships—which he had encountered in his extensive studies. Wagner entitled this sketch "Der Nibelungen Mythus, als Entwurf zu einem Drama" ("The Nibelung Myth as Sketch for a Drama," hereafter, the *Sketch*), the first lines of which read:

> From the womb of night and death there came into being a race that lives in Nibelheim (Nebelheim), that is, in gloomy subterranean caverns and crevices. They are called *Nibelungs*, and they burrow through the bowels of the earth with erratic, restless agility,

like worms in a dead body. They smelt, they refine, and they forge hard metals. *Alberich* seized the pure and noble gold of the Rhine, took it from the waters' depths, and with cunning magic fashioned from it a ring that gave him supreme domination over all his race, the Nibelungs.

At the time of the writing of the *Sketch*, Wagner was living in Dresden where he was serving as Hofkapellmeister at the Royal Opera and, at the same time, involving himself in the political rumblings that were growing against the monarch of his native Saxony.

Immediately after completing the *Sketch*, the manuscript of which is housed in Wagner's home in Bayreuth, Wagner completed a prose scenario which he then developed into a three-act poem-drama. He completed this dramatic work during the final week of November 1848. Wagner titled his poem *Siegfrieds Tod* (*Siegfried's Death*), and beneath the title he wrote: "A Grand Heroic Opera in Three Acts."

One of Wagner's colleagues read the text of the poem and suggested change. The friend felt that the audience would not understand the intense amorous relationship which, according to Wagner, had existed between Siegfried and Brünnhilde before the drama begins. This was a thematic element that Wagner had not developed in the drama, and the audience would witness only the acrimonious confrontation of the pair, an explosive action that Wagner had brought into the second act. Further, it is the heated quarrel between Siegfried and Brünnhilde that resulted, ultimately, in the hero's death. Wagner concurred with his friend, and he immediately set about to remedy the situation. He made no alterations in the three acts that he had written, but rather prepared a *Vorspiel* ("Prelude") to the drama itself. The new scene that was to be in the "Prelude" brought Siegfried and Brünnhilde together and depicted the genuine dedication and devotion that the pair had for each other, as well as the intense love that their vows had sealed. Without doubt, this scene allowed for a stronger and more firmly woven dramatic framework for the entire work.

At the same time, Wagner attempted to make the drama's story line even more explicit by means of yet another scene that he would now include in this "Prelude." This scene, which would open the drama, would focus on the three Norns, the 'fates' of early Teutonic thought. The dramatic task of this significant trio of Germanic mythical figures was that of unveiling much of the past actions of the god Wotan.

The Norn scene would be Wagner's first significant step into ancient Teutonic myth. The thematic material of this scene, geared to promote a fuller comprehension of all that was to follow, seriously influenced the composer's thoughts about yet another Siegfried drama that would soon enter the dramatic scene. It was also the addition of the Norn scene that rightly prompted Wagner to remove his words that heralded the drama as "A Grand Heroic Opera in Three Acts."

The story of *Siegfrieds Tod* was the dramatist's version of the death of the German hero of legend and folk story, Siegfried the Nibelung. Siegfried, having won the much-coveted Gold of the Rhine as his own and having taken Brünnhilde as his wife, becomes involved with the Gibichungs and the treacherous Hagen who plots to take the Gold for himself. Siegfried is murdered by Hagen, and the devoted Brünnhilde then immolates herself on the hero's pyre as she returns the Gold to its home in the depths of the Rhine. This final act saves the gods from the impending doom that was to be theirs because of a prior act of theft involving the Gold. This final scene was later radically revised. Instead of the restoration of authority and power to the gods, the divine ones are brought to total destruction by the force and power of their own wills. It was because of this changed ending and the resultant shift of philosophic intent and dramatic emphasis that Wagner retitled his poem *Götterdämmerung*. (In 1872, Wagner considered changing the title once more, this time from *Götterdämmerung* to *Göttergericht*, a term which can be translated to *Judgment of the Gods*. This possibility occurred to him when he questioned if people truly understood what *Götterdämmerung* (*Twilight of the Gods*) really meant. He stated that the Nordic term that included the catastrophic fate of the deities, that is, *ragnarökkr*, essentially denoted 'judgment of the gods,' and since the principal female character of his drama, Brünnhilde, was, in effect, passing judgment on the divine ones, the title would be most appropriate. Wagner never acted on his thoughts.)

Wagner intended to compose the music for his Siegfried drama immediately. As was his usual manner, much of that music had been conceived in his mind as he wrote the poem. He had even made several musical notations in the margins of his manuscript. However, Wagner was not to realize his intent. Some two and one-half years were to pass before he could apply himself directly to his work, and by that time his dramatic ideas had undergone significant revisionary considerations.

During the weeks that Wagner had been concerned with *Siegfrieds Tod*, his involvement in the unsuccessful movement of the people against the monarchy had become most intense, so much so that on 16 May 1849, a warrant for his arrest was issued. The warrant was published three days later in Dresden's daily newspaper, and for all intents, Wagner was a wanted man. He was accused of being a political revolutionary. Informed of the warrant, Wagner made what preparations he could and on May 24 he fled Dresden, going first to Weimar (where he sought help from his friend Franz Liszt), and then on to Zürich, Switzerland. Wagner's flight would become the beginning of an exile of some twelve years from Germany.

Wagner was essentially without funds or assistance in his new home in Zürich. He was to receive some financial help from friends, but such assistance was meager at best, and he soon set about earning much needed funds. He attempted to earn a livelihood by writing essays on music and drama, and by conducting in and around the city. In time, Wagner established himself as a reputable conductor. During the years 1851–1855 he conducted no fewer than twenty-two concerts for one of the several musical groups of Zürich. Such activity naturally prevented Wagner from working on the music of *Siegfrieds Tod*, but the drama was never out of his mind. As he gave thought to the poem, he began to sense that it contained an excessive amount of dialogue whose only reason for inclusion was to cite, and perhaps to elaborate upon, those matters that had been the dramatic basis for the poem at hand. Wagner was convinced that such text was vital for an understanding of the substance of *Siegfrieds Tod*. At the same time, however, he was aware that this dialogue lengthened the drama inordinately, and also detracted somewhat from his main argument. Yet, Wagner also sensed that more of his tale should be told in order to give a complete thematic order to his story. Slowly there began to evolve in Wagner's mind a new dramatic plan: extract from *Siegfrieds Tod* those thematic elements that were not directly a part of that plot and with them prepare another drama. Such a move, he concluded, would realize two significant ends: *Siegfrieds Tod* would, in itself, become a more compact work dramatically, and the second drama would not only be complete within itself, but would also present the dramatic basis necessary for a comprehension of *Siegfrieds Tod*. Each drama would contain its own separate argument, yet the two would become essentially a single work because of the common theme that runs through them.

In May 1851, Wagner found himself in the appropriate mental and economic states to resume work on his drama. He had considered carefully the idea of this second drama and, laying aside the matter of the music for *Siegfrieds Tod*, he prepared a sketch for his new drama which he entitled *Der junge Siegfried* (*The Young Siegfried*), later to be revised and retitled simply *Siegfried*. The dramatic substance of this drama would be the hero's early life, his slaying of the Dragon and his rescue of the Gold, and his awakening of Brünnhilde. After the initial sketch of *Der junge Siegfried*, Wagner developed a full prose sketch and then put these ideas into verse, completing the entire process within a period of six weeks, the final lines of the poem being written in June of that year.

As Wagner developed his story of the life of the young Siegfried, he was again overcome with hesitation. His dramatic intuition suggested a serious doubt, one not unlike that which he had known during the writing of *Siegfrieds Tod*. He felt that his drama of Siegfried was quite lengthy, yet he was certain that he could not reduce this account if an audience was to comprehend the drama's plot. Somehow, he must tell the story, but vital to the tale were certain events which predated the life of the Volsung, matters that he had included in *Der junge Siegfried*. Wagner's concern was great. It was a period of indecision.

Within four months after completing *Der junge Siegfried*, Wagner conceived yet another plan. Now, he developed an artistic concept that was without precedent in the history of the creative mind, a plan so imposing, so grandiose, that it would be considered by even the most liberal of minds to be impossible of realization. Wagner determined that he would write two additional dramas to give his two completed poems the dramatic fullness and thematic thoroughness that he sensed they needed. The first of these works would recount events prior to Siegfried's birth, specifically the union of his parents, Siegmund and Sieglinde, the death of his father, the flight of his mother, and the wrath of Wotan and his banishment of his Valkyrie daughter Brünnhilde for disobeying his command that she not give aid to Siegfried's father. The second of the proposed works, which would be populated only with Teutonic gods and other supernaturals, would serve as a prologue to the Siegfried story and would present the tale of the original theft of the Rhine Gold and that of Wotan's dilemma, which arises essentially because he has reneged on a pledge that he had made to the giants Fasolt and Fafner. (The god had promised the Giants that he would give them the goddess Freia as payment if they would build the fortress Valhalla for him. The Giants carried out their part of the agreement, but Wotan, pressed by the other gods, broke his word and caused the brothers to accept the Nibelung Gold in lieu of the goddess. When the Giants agree to the substitution, Wotan and Loge descend into Nibelheim and by means of trickery take the Gold from Alberich.)

Wagner lost no time in his new endeavor. He was enthusiastic and he worked diligently. He studied carefully the *Sketch* he had made three years before; it had served him well for his first two poems. Now that *Sketch* would become his guide for two more works. Wagner prepared an initial sketch for each of the two dramas, work that he finished before the end of the year; and by spring 1852 he had written a full prose sketch of his prologue drama. Laying aside this piece, he turned to the sketch of what was to become the second poem in the plot development. By

May he had turned his first ideas into a complete prose sketch, and then, within a month, he completed his poems. He entitled the drama *Siegmund und Sieglinde: Die Bestrafung der Walküre* (*Siegmund and Sieglinde: The Punishment of the Valkyrie*), a title that he later reduced to *Die Walküre* (*The Valkyrie*).

Wagner rested only briefly. He turned almost immediately to the sketch of his prologue drama. Instead of following through with his original idea of a drama in three acts, he revised his plan and prepared a drama whose action was restricted to a single act, completing the poem during the first week of November 1852. His first title for this poem was *Der Raub des Rheingoldes* (*Rape of the Rhine Gold*), which later was shortened to *Das Rheingold* (*The Rhine Gold*).

Wagner was hesitant about the title for this yet-to-be-written tetralogy. His first choice was *Der Gold des Nibelungen* (*The Nibelung's Gold*). He then changed that title to *Der Reif des Nibelungen* (*The Nibelung's Circlet*). In the end, he settled on *Der Ring des Nibelungen*, which he then described as "A Stage-Festival-Play to be produced on Three Days and a Fore-evening."

The four versified dramas of the *Ring* were completed by mid-1852. However, the composition of the complex multipart argument, in the reverse order of plot progression, and the circumstances that occasioned such a procedure, were to give Wagner much to worry about. It was only natural that each drama would require some internal changes—language, minor incidents, dialogue, scenic matters, and other related items. Such matters could be remedied with little difficulty. Of more concern, however, was the total argument, which presented several compositional problems, such as the need for an acceptable dramatic flow in thematic order, the need for the proper development of character and events and for appropriate carry-over of these and other details from one drama to the next, and the necessity of dramatic transition from one part to another. After *Siegfrieds Tod*, as Wagner completed each of the other dramas, he found it necessary to return to his previous work to make revisions, to add, to delete, or otherwise to change a multitude of argumentative details. An alteration of any one factor in a given scene could necessitate a series of changes throughout the poem. Such revisions were not only numerous but often extensive because Wagner's intent was twofold. He desired to prepare a single dramatic piece in which the four parts meshed into a continuous, comprehensive argument, a poem that satisfied all the requirements of effective drama. At the same time he wanted a work in which each of the four parts individually boasted those same attributes in order that each could stand alone as a separate and distinct drama. Wagner devoted a great deal of thought and labor to this task. The seriousness of his concern and the scope of his efforts to realize his dramatic goals are evidenced by the hundreds of pages he needed to write his notes, sketches, scenarios, revisions, and the final poem itself.

(An extreme example of the concerns that plagued the composer was the final scene of *Götterdämmerung*, the climactic ending to the lengthy *Ring*. Wagner initially wrote several versions of the words that Brünnhilde was to sing as the gods were forgiven for their wrongdoing. Then, he changed radically the plot-line and the gods would now be destroyed because of that same wrongdoing. Over the years, he continued to alter and to rearrange Brünnhilde's final words, preparing several versions and then modifying those texts in some way. Wagner was considering changes in this text as late as 1872! It would seem that most of these several textual versions are known today, if uncollected. One version of these words did not surface until 1893, ten years after Wagner's death and some sixteen years after the *Ring's* premiere.)

In the main, these revisions were accomplished with artful dramatic skill. Many were effected during the active period of composition. However, some four additional years were to pass before the poem of the *Ring* was essentially in finished thematic form. Time has confirmed Wagner's success in his work. Yet there are some scholars of the *Ring* who claim that there are what may be called "contradictions" in the plot, despite the dramatist's care and concern. If these so-called "contradictions" have no significant effect on the total drama, they remain as curiosities because Wagner could not have been unaware of their existence. Wagner never offered an explanation for these matters.

Immediately after he had completed the last of his four poems, Wagner expressed the desire to have them published. Within three months he had prepared and published at his own expense a limited, deluxe edition of the *Ring*. He then began to search out commercial publishers, but he was unsuccessful in this venture. Commercial publishers were hesitant to accept the work because the music had not been completed and because of the real possibility that numerous textual changes would be made later. Three years later, in 1856, Wagner negotiated with a Leipzig firm for publication of a now substantially revised poem. The efforts proved fruitless as the parties could not agree on terms. Again, in late 1858, Wagner reopened negotiations with the publisher in Leipzig, but this second round of talks had the same result as the first dealings. It was not until 1863 that the first public edition of the *Ring* was published. This edition included the title changes and the extensive dramatic revisions he had made during the years 1852–1856, and the poem was prefaced with a lengthy introduction in which, almost prophetically, Wagner wrote of things to come. He spoke of his intent to produce his music drama as a festival performance in a new theater—one constructed from his design, especially for the *Ring*—one that would accommodate the drama's unprecedented theatrical demands, a theater that would incorporate his then-radical concepts of orchestra placement, audience view line, and related innovations. Wagner was aware of how ambitious were his plans, and in his Preface he asked if there was not somewhere a sympathetic prince who understood what he wished to accomplish, a prince who would open to him the royal purse.

[The temporal relationships among the *Sketch*, the prose scenarios, and the poem of each drama are seen in Table 4, which includes some notes of interest about the several manuscripts.]

Table 4
The Dramas—A Chart of Dates

Der Nibelungen Mythus als Entwurf zu einem Drama[1] Endated: 4 October 1848			
	Initial sketch or Scenario	Full Prose Sketch	Poem
Das Rheingold[2]	3–10 November 1851[3]	23–31 March 1852[4]	15 September –3 November 1852
Die Walküre	November 1851	17–26 May 1852[5]	1 June–1 July 1852
Siegfried	3–10 May 1851[6]	24 May– 1 June 1851	3–24 June 1851
Götterdämmerung	Completed: 20 October 1848 ----- 11–28 November 1848[7]		12–28 November 1848[8]

[1]This manuscript is housed today in Wahnfried, Wagner's residence in Bayreuth, which was converted into the Richard Wagner Museum in 1973.

[2]The original titles of the four dramas will be found in Chapter Three.

[3]The sketch indicates that the work is to be a drama in three acts.

[4]The format of the manuscript is now that of a drama in one act with four scenes.

[5]Wagner utilized his initial prose sketch for this prose design and supplemented it with numerous notes that he had made while preparing the full prose text of *Das Rheingold*.

[6]This is a short sketch, written in pencil, to which Wagner later added several marginal notes.

[7]This is a supplementary sketch that became the *Vorspiel* ("Prelude") of the finished poem.

[8]Over the years this manuscript was revised frequently and in significant ways. In the early years, the Royal Court at Weimar offered Wagner 500 thalers for *Siegfrieds Tod* provided the composer could complete the work, with full score, by 1 July 1852.

4.2 THE MUSIC

The composition of the music of *Der Ring des Nibelungen* occupied a period of twenty-two years. Even though work on the *Ring* was always a major concern to Wagner, during these years a number of factors forced him to give way to other artistic urges. At the same time, these were years of much turbulence in his daily life. Wagner knew professional as well as personal rejection, obvious frustration with the cultural scene of the day, and numerous personal reverses of several kinds. (In 1840, he had been jailed in Clichy, France, for non-payment of debts.) He remained a political exile from Germany until 1860 and from his native Saxony until 1862. During the last years of this period he was also inordinately consumed by his desire to realize a special theater in which to produce the *Ring*. However, throughout this time of political, economic, and artistic turmoil, the genius of the man prevailed.

Time, however, was of little import to Richard Wagner's creative mind. His art was always primary and, in the composition of the *Ring*, the span of twenty-two years became much more a stimulus than a hindrance. Wagner did not "compose" music in the manner of stereotyped definitions; he did not "set words to music." His dramas and his music emerged and evolved almost as a single creation; they complemented each other; he wanted them to flow as one art form. Neither were his words created for his music nor his music for his words. Each was intended as an expression of the other. Thus, as Wagner conceived his prose scenarios and sketches and later, as he converted those ideas into poetic dramas, he was at the same time developing in his mind the music that was to be an artistic partner in his art form. What he conceived as music was not a finished score. At times his initial music was only fragmentary, a theme perhaps, or a rhythm, or even a harmonic movement. Yet, as he wrote his poems, the total music somehow was there within him; his mind saw it if his pen had not yet set it to paper. Early in his career he wrote a friend that once he had prepared his text and put the scenes and acts together as a finished piece, the "entire musical aura" and the "complete sound" were well in place in his mind, and in a figurative sense the opera had been written. (Some years later, Wagner would make statements that somewhat contradicted his earlier remarks.) Time, then, was needed to elaborate, to expand those musical ideas; time was needed to build and to shape them into the orchestral scores we know today. Given the final results of the *Ring*, history has proved that time was Wagner's greatest ally.

Once Wagner had determined his musical routes, the labor of putting the ideas into written form was one to which he devoted relatively little time. It was essentially a mechanical process, one to which he gave several hours each day, but also one in which he was totally absorbed and to which he was always completely dedicated. The unique thematic, dramatic, and theatrical nature of the *Ring* required a distinct musical layout. In his autobiography Wagner noted that he did not follow the usual procedure of writing the vocal line accompanied by the compressed orchestral material. Rather, he found it necessary to prepare a miniature orchestral score as a first step. The meshing and intertwining of musical ideas and their expanded and often altered expressions forced him to designate specific instrumentation, frequent changes of key, and often unusual musical relations of one key or one chord to another. As he prepared these scores, new ideas frequently suggested themselves, both in the work at hand and in other parts of the drama. Once this first semi-orchestral composition had been completed, its expansion into a full orchestral score, if complex, actually involved only the physical task of putting into a finished form the work he had already completed.

Unlike the reverse order in which he had written the four poems, Wagner began the music of the *Ring* with the opening scene of *Das Rheingold*. He spent some ten weeks preparing this draft, which he finished in January 1854. On the last page, under his initials, he wrote, "Und weiter nichts?? Weiter nichts??" ("And nothing more?? Nothing more??"). The full orchestral score was completed in May of that year and then copied into finished manuscript form. Wagner autographed this *reinschrift* (fair copy) in September.

While the manuscript of *Das Rheingold* was being copied, Wagner began the compositional sketch of *Die Walküre*. This draft of the three acts was begun in June and completed in December 1854. He then set to work immediately on the full orchestral score. More than a year was to pass before the final note was written. It was not that Wagner had difficulty with the score; rather, unrelated circumstances prevented him from giving full attention to his creation. Between February and June 1855 he fulfilled a contract to conduct eight concerts in London. Both the city and the concerts proved to be exhausting ordeals, and upon his departure from England he was in great need of rest. His mental and physical weariness were complicated by his usual bad health, and his only recourse was a six-week "cure." By March of the following year, 1856, however, he had completed the full score of the second drama of the *Ring*, and on the twenty-third of the month he began a fair copy of his work.

If the music of *Das Rheingold* and *Die Walküre* came into existence in a relatively routine fashion, that of *Siegfried* had a different history.

After completing *Die Walküre*, Wagner again took a "cure," during which time he doubtlessly acknowledged to himself that the stimulus to continue work on the *Ring* was waning. His interests were taking other directions, and in that summer of 1856 he wrote a prose sketch for a proposed music drama with a Buddhist theme, *Die Sieger* (*The Victors*), a work that never developed beyond the draft-prose stage. In September he returned to the *Ring*. He began the draft of Act I of *Siegfried* and, curiously, within a month he also started work on the orchestral score of that act. This latter action was initiated despite the fact that the compositional sketch, which in the past had served as a musical plan for the score, was also incomplete. For some three months Wagner worked simultaneously on both the sketch and the score of this first act. He persisted, however, and the draft of this act was completed in January 1857. The full score was finished in late March of that year. Two months later he began the draft of Act II.

By this time *Siegfried* was giving him no little trouble. Two significant distractions that had been personal concerns now broke into the open. For some time the state of his private affairs had been such that stirring within him was a growing urge to create a music drama in which a sublime love between man and woman was developed to the fullest, the kind of love that he had never known in his own life, the kind of love for which he had longed and perhaps could experience, if only vicariously, by means of the tragic tale of *Tristan and Isolde*. At that same time he was stirred and stimulated by an attraction to Mathilde Wesendonck, the charming and sympathetic wife of Otto Wesendonck, his benefactor of the day. Here was an amorous eagerness which, during the first months of 1857, resulted in an intimate involvement and an association that Wagner no doubt related to his creative bent of the moment. The relationship between Wagner and Frau Wesendonck became known to the composer's wife, Minna, whom he had married in 1836, and immediately caused another serious upset in their already insecure marriage. By midyear the Wesendonck affair and his interest in the legendary lovers had reduced his creative interest in *Siegfried* and had given rise to the need for a crucial decision. In late June, with only about half of the second act of *Siegfried* drafted, Wagner wrote to his friend Franz Liszt to inform him that he was laying the work aside. However, he forced himself to complete the draft of Act II before turning to other interests in late July. More than eight years would elapse before this second act would be fully scored, and nearly six more years would be required to complete the music drama.

Wagner returned to *Siegfried* in late 1864. The several years of separation from the *Ring*, however, had not been a period of creative idleness. During the two-year period from 1857 to 1859, he had concentrated on the book and the music of the lovers' tale that had so fascinated him, and the result was one of the truly great operatic masterpieces of all time, *Tristan und Isolde*. This was a work that perhaps more than all others exemplified the tenets of music drama as they had been set down by Wagner some years earlier and as they would filter through the artistic conscience of the time. After *Tristan und Isolde*, Wagner turned to a theme that had interested him since 1845 when he had prepared a prose sketch for an opera. In the years 1861–1867 he developed the poem and the music for this project, which became *Die Meistersinger von Nürnberg*, a work that would be acclaimed by critics as his single greatest artistic triumph. It was also during this same period, in 1864, that there appeared on the scene that royal prince and purse that Wagner had sought so eagerly in his Preface to the 1863 public edition of the *Ring* poem. In May of 1864, the new king of Bavaria, the eighteen-year-old Ludwig II, stepped forward to answer Wagner's call for financial aid. Ludwig, who had been king for less than two months and who would later be known as the *Dream King*, was to become Wagner's most important admirer and patron, and his appearance on the Wagner scene provided the financial basis of much that was Wagnerian, including, ultimately, the reality of a festival theater in which the composer could produce his *Ring*.

Wagner's return to the *Ring* and to his work on *Siegfried* was of relatively short duration and produced nothing of musical substance. He reviewed some of his prior work, but only in a passive manner, and he could only dabble with his musical intent. Wagner soon set aside his work once again. This cessation was not the result of his desire to compose other pieces, as had been the situation years before. Rather, the composer now found himself much embroiled in a personal matter not entirely conducive to creative work, one that was to cause him and others a great deal of uneasiness, uncertainty, and public embarrassment. In April 1865, Cosima Liszt, daughter of his close friend Franz Liszt and wife of Hans von Bülow, a devoted friend and admirer, gave birth to Wagner's child. The matter of the relationship between Richard Wagner and Cosima would generate much deceit and misrepresentation and would become a topic widely discussed in social and political circles. Cosima would give birth to two more of Wagner's children before a divorce from her husband and her marriage to Wagner in 1870. (Cosima Wagner was twenty-four years her husband's junior and she lived on for forty-seven years after his death.)

By 1869 Wagner felt himself ready to resume work on *Siegfried*. In February of that year he made some minor revisions in Act II and then devoted four months to the musical sketch of Act III, after which he began work on the orchestral score. As this scoring progressed, he turned to the last of the four dramas, *Götterdämmerung*, for which he began the draft of the Prelude and Act I. Intermingling work on these music dramas, the two poems he had envisioned first as his version of the Siegfried legend, Wagner also involved himself in the realities of planning for a festival theater largely of his own concept in which he would premiere his *Ring*. By early February 1871 the full orchestral score of *Siegfried* was completed.

As 1871 passed, the visions of Bayreuth, the city in which he had decided to build his theater, were taking shape in Wagner's mind. If only vaguely, he saw this theater, and in it the performances of the *Ring*, as he deemed they should be. Yet the music of the fourth drama remained unfinished. Thus, he prepared the draft of Act II of *Götterdämmerung* and proceeded immediately to Act III, whose compositional sketch he completed in April 1872.

Demands on Wagner's time increased. Bayreuth was to become fact, but to make it so required large sums of money. These funds did not come easily, and Wagner found it necessary to participate actively in the several promotional efforts that had been planned. Much of his time was taken up with travel and concerts that he conducted in behalf of the Bayreuth idea. Finally, in mid-1873, he began the orchestral score of *Götterdämmerung*, work that was to be interrupted almost daily by the need for his presence to supervise the construction of the theater that was slowly rising on the outskirts of the Bavarian city. Finally, after a year and a half, the full score of his fourth drama of the *Ring* was finished.

On 21 November 1874, some twenty-six years after he had drawn up a sketch from which he could prepare a single Nibelung drama, Richard Wagner wrote the last note of the gigantic *Ring*. (For a chart depicting all the relevant compositional dates, see Table 5.) Despite the many frustrations that had plagued him through the years, despite the obstacles that had confronted him so often, despite the great fatigue that had come with his gargantuan endeavor, *The Ring of the Nibelung* was finished. If nothing more, it would be a monument to dedication and to discipline.

As he finished the great score, Wagner turned to the last page and, in the simplest of terms, penned an epilogue that bespoke his thoughts. He wrote:

Vollendet am Wahnfried am 21 November 1874. Ich sage nichts mehr!

(Completed at Wahnfried on 21 November, 1874. I say no more!)

Table 5
The Music—A Chart of Dates

	Compositional Sketch	Orchestral Score
Das Rheingold	1 November 1853–14 January 1854	1 February–28 May 1854
Die Walküre	ACT I 28 June–1 September 1854 ACT II 4 September–18 November 1854 ACT III 20 November–27 December 1854	January 1855–23 March 1856
Siegfried	ACT I 20 September 1856–20 January 1857 ACT II 22 May–9 August 1857 ACT III 1 March–4 August 1869	ACT I 11 October 1856–31 March 1857 ACT II (First draft) 22 December 1864–2 December 1865 (Second draft) Completed 23 February 1869 ACT III 25 August 1869–2 February 1871
Götterdämmerung	PRELUDE/ACT I 2 October 1869–5 June 1870 ACT II 24 June–25 October 1871 ACT III 4 January–10 April 1872	3 May 1873–21 November 1874

Chapter Five

The Origins and the Sources of the *Ring*

5.1 Origins

In his 1848 *Sketch* Richard Wagner set down the sum and substance of what was to become, years later, the drama of *Der Ring des Nibelungen*. This short prose piece presented Wagner's arrangement and elaboration of the story of the birth and then the death of the German legendary figure Siegfried, and an unrelated tale—if only thinly suggested—that included assorted supernaturals of ancient Teutonic thought, including the supreme god, Wotan. The former had long existed in oral tradition and had been recorded in numerous versions in many medieval lays and songs. The gods and their activities had dominated Germanic culture since early times and had endured in prose and poetry in both the southern (German) and the northern (Scandinavian) regions of the Teutonic peoples.

Wagner's *Sketch*, as an artistic idea for a dramatic poem, was the result of thematic concepts that had begun to evolve in his mind during the first years of the 1840s. Into these ideas he blended those that came to him during his lengthy study of the vast literature of German myth, legend, culture, and history.

The artistic route that let Wagner to his *Sketch* and from there to the *Ring* was an anomalous one. He did not resort to a single literary piece but rather followed a pathway of extensive study of many works, a study that shaped his theatrical vision and, as time passed, prepared the road that led to his monumental libretto-drama. However, there can be no doubt that Wagner's specific direction originated in certain thematic sensibilities that had existed in German society for centuries.

The Nibelung legend has been one of the most enduring stories in German history. Originating in the early centuries after Christ, the story, in oral form, passed from generation to generation. During the period of the great migration, it made its way into Scandinavia to appear later, at least in part, in written form, in *The Poetic Edda*. Its spread into the German world was equally wide and its popularity continues. In the first years of the thirteenth century it was preserved in a manuscript known as *Nibelungenlied* (*Song of the Nibelung*). In 1472 a manuscript that carried the title *Lied von hürnen Seyfrid* (*Song of the Horned-Skinned Siegfried*) was a version of the Siegfried tale. Yet another version of the earlier poems appeared in printed form in 1527; and in 1557 Hans Sachs (1494–1576), one of the most prolific writers of the sixteenth century and a principal figure in Wagner's *Die Meistersinger von Nürnberg*, used several previous works as a source for his seven-act tragedy entitled *Der hürnen Seufrid* (*The Horned-Skin Siegfried.*)

Interest in the tale of the Nibelung Siegfried continued unabated in Germany. In 1726 a prose narrative version of the story, based on Sach's play, appeared in a *Volksbuch* (chapbook), a term applied to those popular collections of German prose romances which concentrated on themes of a literary nature. In 1803, Friedrich Heinrich Karl Fouqué, Baron de la Motte (1777–1843), perhaps the most widely read of the romantic authors of his day, wrote the first of his Siegfried sketches which he entitles *Der gehörnte Siegfried in der Schmied* (*The Horn-Skin Siegfried in the Smithy*). Seven years later, Fouqué de la Motte converted his sketches into a trilogy of plays under the title *Der Held des Nordens* (*The Hero of the North*). The first drama was titled *Sigurd der Schlangentöter* (*Siegfried, the Dragon Killer*); the second of the three dramas bore the title *Sigurds Rache* (*Siegfried's Revenge*); the final drama was entitled *Aslauga* (*Aslaug*), who was the daughter born to Brünnhilde and Siegfried.

As the recorded accounts continued to appear, the story of Siegfried also persisted as oral literature in the form of untold numbers of songs and poems, each elaborated according to the talents of the tellers.

The eminence of the fascinating Nibelung tale and its place in German cultural and literary history could not have escaped Wagner's receptive mind. The interest of past ages in Siegfried continued, and the young composer witnessed first hand the magnetic draw that the hero and his adventures held for those of his own era.

In 1828 *Der Nibelungenhort* (*The Hoard of the Nibelungs*), a five-act spoken drama by Ernst Raupach (1784–1852), premiered. With this work, Raupach, a voluminous writer of some 117 now-forgotten plays, brought the story of the Nibelungs to the nineteenth-century stage. Wagner later worked with Raupach and obviously knew of his drama, although the piece had no direct impact on the composer's thoughts— even if, in its own way, it did bring the theme closer to his mind and, along with other works, helped to prepare the way for his own eventual dramatic adventures.

The Siegfried theme was again in the public eye a few years later. In a remarkable essay on German opera, Floretin von Zuccalmaglio, an immigrant from Italy, argued persuasively for the adaptability of such drama to musical interpretation in operatic format. In his essay "Der deutsche Oper" ("German Opera") of 1837, Zuccalmaglio continued the discussion by selecting the Siegfried tale as a most appropriate legend for this artistic treatment.

Although there seems to be no record of Wagner's acknowledgment of the work, there is the probability that he was familiar with a comedy-drama based on the Siegfried theme that appeared in 1842. The work was written by Anastasius Grün, who gave his work the title *Nibelungen in Frac* (*The Nibelung in Evening Dress*). Grün, whose real name was Anton Alexander Graf von Auersperg, gave his Siegfried a quixotic-like role, and set the piece in the eighteenth century.

The Siegfried story continued to be a popular theme in German letters, even as Wagner worked with his tale of the legendary hero. At least two major works that focused on the Siegfried matter appeared after Wagner had composed his text and some or all of the *Ring's* music. In 1862, Friedrich Hebel, an avid student of *The Song of the Nibelung*, completed a trilogy of dramas that depicted the life and death of the hero and his widow's search for revenge on her husband's killers. In 1867, Wilhelm Jordan completed his two-part poem *Die Nibelunge* (*The Nibelung*). In 1872, Cosima Wagner wrote in her *Diaries* that she and Wagner were *re-reading* the works of Hebel and Jordan. She stated that she and her husband were convinced that the manner in which these two men expressed themselves could easily turn people away from the Siegfried theme!

The concept of myth and legend as opera, at the time in its initial stage before the German public, was also emerging in Wagner's creative mind. In 1840, while living in Paris, Wagner read several of the German romances found in the *Volksbucher*, and at the same time he was drawn to a legendary theme that was to be the source of a poem and then an opera. The work was *Der fliegende Holländer* (*The Flying Dutchman*), and its theme was radically unlike those in his previous works. Wagner had finished his first complete opera, *Die Feen* (*The Fairies*), in 1833–1834. He based his text on the comedy *La donna serpente* (which Wagner translated as *Die Frau als Schlange*) written in 1762 by Carlo Gozzi (1720–1806), and whose music was patterned after that of German romantic opera. His second opera, *Das Liebesverbot* (*Love Forbidden*), completed in 1836, had as textual source Shakespeare's *Measure for Measure*, and a music that hinted at a Bellini influence. Wagner's third opera, *Rienze, der Letzte der Tribunen* (*Rienze, The Last of the Tribunes*), was historical in theme and had been inspired by Lord Edward Bulwer-Lytton's 1835 novel *Rienzi*. As Wagner completed the score of *Rienzi*, the haunting tale of the Dutch sailor who was condemned to roam the seas until Judgment Day hovered persistently in his mind. In early spring, Wagner prepared a sketch of the story, which he sent to the influential French librettist, Eugène Scribe. Wagner had hoped that this work would help establish him as a librettist and composer in France. Scribe totally ignored both Wagner and the libretto. Ultimately, because of lack of funds, Wagner was forced to sell his sketch to the Director of the Paris Opera, who, in turn, ordered the libretto completely rewritten and then set to music by another Frenchman, Pierre-Louis Dietsch. The work endured eleven performances! Wagner, who never lost interest in the Dutchman, then began his own poem and the music, all of which he completed in late 1841.

If *Rienzi*, by its success, was to launch Wagner's career as a ranked composer of opera, it was *Der fliegende Holländer* that was to give him the thematic direction along which that career ultimately would rise until it reached unprecedented heights. In the preparation of his first three operas, Wagner had felt limited by the arguments that had served as his sources. Their words, their players, and their themes reflected specific social, political, or historical concepts that had denied him the freedom of his own expression, and such restrictions further frustrated him in the development of the musical ideas forming within him. The story of the Dutchman, on the other hand, was essentially *legend*; and if not wholly so, it was at least legendary in character. As such, it invited elaboration and allowed him a kind of artistic license, both thematic and musical, with which he was more at ease. If he did not realize it at the time, *Der fliegende Holländer*, or more specifically legend, had given Wagner the mold that was to shape all of his successive works.

After *Der fliegende Holländer*, Wagner again sought out legend as source material for a dramatic poem. He turned this time to the many tales of his own land, to those of wholly German origin. Within six months of the completion of *Holländer*, Wagner had begun the prose sketch of the poem in which he would join two popular but unrelated tales into a single story: the medieval legend of Dannheuser (Tann-häuser), the minnesinger who sojourns with Venus in her grotto in the Hörselberg, and the account of the great song tournaments that were held in the thirteenth century, in the castle of the Landgraves of Thuringia that had been built on the Wartburg, a hill that overlooked the city of Eisenach. Wagner first entitled his poem, which he completed in April 1843, *Der Venusberg*, but after some reflection on that title (literally, Mount Venus or *mons veneris, mons pubis*) Wagner changed it to that by which the work is known today, *Tannhäuser und der Sängerkrieg auf Wartburg* (*Tannhäuser and the Song Contest on the Wartburg*). This "grand romantic opera," whose score was completed in April 1845, concerned Tannhäuser's life with Venus, his participation in one of the song contests at the Wartburg Castle, and subsequently, his repudiation of his worldly existence, his forgiveness, and his death.

As Wagner worked on *Tannhäuser*, he became even more aware that legend greatly appealed to his artistic and creative instincts. The dramatic and musical liberty he had sensed during the preparation of *Der fliegende Holländer* and the greater awareness of that independence that came with *Tannhäuser* aroused in him something more than simple artistic curiosity. His theatrical mind, combined with a natural inclination toward matters of a national flavor, spurred him to learn more of the popular foundations of his culture. His attention turned to *Geschichte der poetischen Nationalliteratur der Deutschen* (*History of German National Poetry*) (1835–1842) by Georg Gottfried Gervinus (1805–1871), a work that was to lay before him a necessary literary perspective. At the same time, he began a study of Jakob Grimm's monumental work on German mythology, *Deutsche Mythologie* (1835), a work that was to influence him greatly in the choice of subject matter for his subsequent dramas.

At the same time as Wagner began to focus increasingly on such themes, a literary work of such proportions that the composer could not have been unaware of its existence appeared, a work that Ernest Newman, Wagner's eminent biographer, suggests was important in encouraging the composer to take a serious interest in the Siegfried matter. The publication, which appeared in 1844, was the second volume of *Kritische Gange* (*The Pathway of Criticism*) by Friedrich Theodor Vischer (1807–1887), a respected professor, philosopher and aesthetician. This volume contained a lengthy essay in which Vischer offered ample argument to justify his belief that German society and culture had developed to such an intellectual and artistic level that the time was now appropriate for the production of an art work of truly German foundation, a work that was thoroughly the product of the German mind. As a means to that end, Vischer suggested that the thematic source for such an art work lay in the medieval epic the *Nibelungenlied*. Vischer maintained not only that this national poem contained the dramatic ingredients for a distinct form of operatic composition but also that it was wholly of German origin and depicted the totality of the multifaceted German character. (Curiously, Vischer later became one of those numerous Germans who found delight in writing essays and/or fictional material that ridiculed, belittled, or even scorned Wagner's musical works, or even his person. These writers took great pleasure in indulging in strong satire, mockery, or any other form of negative expression. Vischer's contribution to this deluge of invectives was *Yet Another*, a forceful parody of *Das Rheingold*, which he published in 1879.)

Vischer's essay could have been to Wagner no less than an open invitation. In essence Vischer's message lay bare a belief long held and deeply seated in the composer's mind. Early in his life Wagner had become convinced that the German personality accepted unchallenged a persistent notion that its Teutonic heritage was much inferior to that of the Latin world, that the German culture was founded on insignificance and strewn with trivia. Wagner viewed this conviction as a serious flaw in a national character that merited a high position in the world of cultures. In time, by means of the *Ring*, Vischer's suggestion would be answered and Wagner's concerns addressed. However, as 1844 closed, that art form, that national expression, and that national theme were but an embryonic glimmer in the composer's creative thoughts, faintly present, but as yet unrecognized.

Within three months after the completion of *Tannhäuser*, Wagner was well into another drama whose subject he had drawn from German legend. The story was that of Lohengrin, the swan-knight and son of Parsifal, who leaves the Holy Grail on Monsalvat, in Spain, to champion the distressed and innocent Elsa, but who must return when he is asked his name and his origin. The themes of his two previous works, plus that of *Lohengrin*, indicate that legend was evidently becoming a fixed and foremost source of material for Wagner. These themes afforded such creative leeway that he then began to implement in fuller form the musical ideas that were in his mind. If *Dutchman* and *Tannhäuser* had allowed Wagner a dramatic and musical liberty that he had not known before, and which had constituted a step away from the traditional operatic form of the day, *Lohengrin* provided a definite and indeed permanent aesthetic separation from the pathway that traditional French and Italian opera had taken. Now, Wagner was well on an artistic journey that would lead to what is known regularly today as *music drama*.

Although Wagner was busy composing, his continuous study of German myths and epics never slackened. As he roamed through Grimm's mythological-legendary world, always aware of the profound impact through the ages of the Nibelung theme on the German people—and faced with the ceaseless flow of writing that dealt with the theme—Wagner found himself attracted more and more to the deeds of Siegfried and the actions of the other figures.

For a while he turned from myth and legend to concentrate on German history. In 1846 he prepared a prose sketch on Friedrich Barbarossa, the most renowned of the Hohenstaufens, the German family of Holy Roman emperors between 1138 and 1254. The idea for a drama on this historic figure never went beyond the preliminary-sketch stage; his intuition and his past experience told him that its limitations were such that the drama could not be in harmony with the artistic concepts straining within him for expression. The sketch for *Friedrich I* really amounted to nothing more than a response to an urge to create. As if led by a more powerful force, he soon abandoned *Friedrich I* and returned to the world of myth—and particularly to the figure of Siegfried.

Wagner continued to probe deeply into the foundations of his culture. He read and studied carefully the many sagas and poems. He steeped himself in the numerous accounts and versions of the Siegfried theme. He versed himself in the movements of Wotan, Fricka, and the other Teutonic gods. He came to know of redes and runes, of dwarfs and giants, of Valkyries and nymphs. As he contemplated the universe of the gods, and as he watched Siegfried pass from adventure to adventure, his mind was sorting out incidents, events, ideas, and figures; and he was unconsciously embroidering his own unique pattern of the relationships of these two worlds of the ancient past.

When 1848 arrived, Wagner's mind was a tangled mass of German myth, legend, history, and tradition. This information, as yet unordered and unassembled, brought him to the crux of his creative dilemma. He realized the need to clarify his thoughts, to put into a recognizable shape the encyclopedic materials he had absorbed over the years. The result was a long essay "Die Wibelungen: Weltgeschichte aus der Saga" ("The Wibelungs: World-history as Revealed in Saga"). Written in a language that is at times as incomprehensible as are some of the ideas, the essay presents an incredible, often fantastic, arrangement and disposition of medieval German history. The substance of the initial pages of this essay returned to the Friedrich theme. Wagner attempted to demonstrate that the royal dynasty of the historic Hohenstaufens was really that of the Nibelungs of sagas. Soon, however, a new figure appears in the composer's creative mind. This figure is the heroic Siegfried who—

at least in this early Wagnerian thought—reflected a radiance that was so bright and so beneficial that it was the grantor of all of mankind's happiness and joy. Wagner saw this Siegfried, first as the God of Light, and then as the God of the Sun. It is this Siegfried who slays the monster and takes possession of the great Nibelung Hoard which contained arms and weapons as well as gold and jewels, and was, therefore, the source of the world's power and force. The Hoard and all that it represented, Wagner continues, was also the cause of all the stress and struggle of the human race. Wagner concludes his essay by stating that Siegfried, in reality, is the son of God, the figure known to the world as Jesus Christ!

In its own way, the Wibelung essay allowed Wagner a means for putting in order his personal philosophical foundations for art. Somehow, in a manner clear only to himself, this work gave him an understanding of his own dramatic goal and a recognition of the means by which to achieve that end. He learned that what he sought was an expression of the human condition, the experience that transcends the historicity of time and place and person. He learned why myth and legend so attracted him—that what he had found in myth and legend had brought him closer to the elusive artistic pinnacle toward which he had been striving and toward which *Rienzi*, *Der fliegende Holländer*, *Tannhäuser*, and *Lohengrin* had each been steps, one higher than the other, but none the ultimate one. The Wibelung essay itself does not rank among Wagner's prose as superior writing, yet its importance in the formation of the dramatist-composer's artistic and creative thought must never be disregarded; this essay must be considered a most significant factor in Wagner's journey to the *Ring*.

With the Wibelung essay and its artistic thesis fresh in his mind, Wagner then prepared a prose sketch for a three-act drama entitled *Jesus von Nazareth* (*Jesus of Nazareth*). This sketch concerned a god, created by a divine father, who willed his own downfall and destruction. If the idea and the sketch proved to be more an exercise in compositional fantasy than a serious project, the theme definitely foreshadowed things soon to come.

Within three months of completing the Wibelung essay, Wagner abandoned the sketch for *Jesus of Nazareth* and embarked on a new idea that would fulfill the germinal thought with which he had been concerned for so long. Braced by time and history, encouraged by the roots of his own culture, and goaded by his studies, in October 1848 Wagner completed his *Sketch* from which he would write a drama on the death of Siegfried. *Der Ring des Nibelungen* was underway. (For a chronological summary of Wagner's operatic works, see Appendix A.)

5.2 SOURCES

5.2.1 THE GERMANIC WORLD

The thematic warp and woof that became the dramatic fabric of *Der Ring des Nibelungen* are to be found in the pre-Christian myths and legends of the Teutonic peoples as recorded in their medieval literature.

These peoples were a branch of the Indo-Europeans who spoke one or another of several Germanic dialects and who were otherwise related by what might be termed a common culture. These people lived in the northern and western regions of Europe. Specific boundaries varied through the ages because of wars, invasions, and explorations; however, in the main, the territory was bounded on the north by Iceland, southern Norway and Sweden, Denmark, and the islands of the Baltic Sea. The Teutonic region then extended southward into continental Europe and included northern and central Germany, the Netherlands, and part of Poland. It was bounded on the west by the Rhine, and on the south by the Danube. In the east, the boundary was the Vistula, also known as the Wisða, which flows slightly west of twentieth-century Warsaw. Those lands that are on the continent proper are frequently referred to as the southern section of the Germanic world, and the rest is known as the northern region. (In the modern day, the peoples who originally inhabited this expanse of territory are generally divided into no less than eleven nationalities: Afrikaners, Danish, Dutch, English, Faroese, Fleming, Frisian, German, Icelander, Norwegian, and Swedish.)

5.2.2 WAGNER'S STATEMENT ON HIS SOURCES

For the preparation of his *Ring* drama, Wagner did not restrict himself to a single source. Rather, he conceived, shaped, and molded his story around the many figures, events, incidents, themes, and symbols he had encountered in the poems, lays, sagas, songs, tales, and related writings that he read during the years 1841–1848, the period during which he devoted so much of his time to a study of Germanic culture.

Despite Wagner's voluminous outpouring of correspondence and prose writings, the composer wrote little about the source materials that served him in the development of the argument of the *Ring* poem. (More than ten thousand Wagner letters have been preserved and the composer's collected prose writings have been published in ten volumes. There is an eight-volume set of translations of the prose works into English.) Ernest Newman, in his detailed account of Wagner's life, writes that there is only one letter extant in which Wagner addressed himself directly to this matter. The letter is dated 1856 and was written to Franz Müller, then Court Councilor at Weimar, who was an ardent admirer of Wagner's works and who had inquired about the sources the composer had used. Wagner indicated that the following works figured in the thematic preparation of this drama:

a. *Edda Saemundar*
b. *Völsungasaga*
c. *Nibelungen Nôt und die Klage*
d. *Deutsche Mythologie*
e. *Die deutsche Heldensage*
f. *Deutsches Heldenbuch*
g. *Heimskringla*
h. *Wilkinasaga*
i. Studies of Franz Joseph Mone
j. Studies of Karl Lachman.

The first three works cited furnished Wagner with the principal elements of what may be termed his "story line," and hence should be considered primary sources. The remaining works and studies contained related data and information and were more referential than thematic. These latter items must be accepted as secondary sources.

5.3 Primary Sources

5.3.1 *Edda Saemundar*

The *Edda Saemundar*, more frequently known as *The Poetic Edda* or *The Elder Edda*, is a collection of thirty-five to thirty-nine poems; the number is determined by the procedure by which a specific editor joins the stanzas to form a given tale. The verses were recorded in Old Norse in Iceland, and the original manuscript of this work was prepared sometime during the second half of the twelfth century.

The poems of *The Poetic Edda* are of two distinct types, and the work is divided accordingly into two sections. The first section consists of fourteen poems (again a number that varies according to the decisions of specific editors) that are mythological in subject matter. The poems are called "Lays of the Gods." These are the poems that present the entire pantheon of the Teutonic gods of the North, along with an even larger gallery of secondary divinities, their activities, their personal relationships, as well as their relative positions in the divine hierarchy. These poems draw a vivid picture of the stark, humorless world of the

Nordic peoples, a world Wagner so skillfully captured in the *Ring*. Even a casual look at these poems will immediately reveal how basic is their substance to Wagner's drama. A more careful study of the poems will uncover a myriad of mythological details that Wagner incorporated into his drama.

The second section of *The Poetic Edda* is entitled "Lays of the Heroes." These twenty-one to twenty-five poems represent the heroic treasure of the kindred Germanic races, the legendary substance accepted and respected throughout the Teutonic world. The poems can be separated thematically into four groupings, each with its own figures and story line. There is, however, a kind of thematic unity evidenced throughout these lays, a unity achieved mostly by means of marriage or assumed blood-lines. The ballads of one of these groupings focus on Sigurð (Siegfried) or the Volsungr (Volsung) of Rhineland and the Niflungas (Nibelungs).

The poems of *The Poetic Edda* are the written versions of the oral poetry that came into existence in several regions of the Teutonic world. The poems about the gods and their activities, most of which probably originated in Iceland and Norway, were carried south into Europe, many during the period of the migration of A.D. 300–600. Those stanzas that deal with Siegfried and the Nibelung tragedy originated in the Valley of the Rhine and, as they circulated among the people and were handed down through the generations, they eventually made their way into Scandinavia. There are several theories regarding the time and place of the origin of the poems, especially those that deal with the gods, but it is generally agreed that all of them reached the height of their popularity and cultural influence during the explosive period of the Vikings (A.D. 800–1100).

Throughout their existence as oral poetry, the essence of these stanzas remained intact. In the main, major figures were retained, and they usually continued in their original roles. Likewise, incidents, events, properties, and important concepts were preserved. However, as the poems passed from one region to another and from one people to another, changes of some kind naturally occurred. Such changes are evident specifically in the Siegfried legend, which was of particular interest to Wagner. In the nineteenth century, literary scholars uncovered early German manuscripts in which the story of the Volsung was distinct from that found in the poetry of *The Poetic Edda*. Although the principal characters appeared in both versions, on occasion the relationships were different; many of the deeds and adventures of the hero were the same in these separate stories, but some were accomplished in alternative ways. At times, circumstances of a given situation varied, and frequently there were shifts of emphasis and even alterations of chronology. To distinguish these related but distinct interpretations of the same tale, scholars have designated the poetry that originated in the area of the Rhine as the "southern" version of the Siegfried tale and that which is a part of *The Poetic Edda* as the "northern" version. It is possible that the poems about the gods, which reflect the basic religious concepts of the people, underwent changes of a similar nature as they circulated in the Teutonic world. However, to date, no southern manuscript that pertains to this mythical matter is known to exist, and it is therefore the Nordic interpretation, as found in *The Poetic Edda*, that has come to be looked upon as the authentic mythology of the numerous Germanic clans.

The importance of *The Poetic Edda* to Wagner's development of the *Ring* is without question. When the *Edda* and the *Ring* are viewed side by side, it becomes obvious immediately that Wagner drew extensively from this medieval masterpiece for his dramatic argument. The "Lays of the Gods" and those poems of the "Lays of the Heroes" which focus on Siegfried serve as the principal font for much of his version of the Nibelung story. If at times Wagner developed his own dramatic chronology, intermeshed certain themes and events, utilized German names, and otherwise extracted certain matters to serve his own thematic purposes, he was nevertheless still faithful to the mythological body of the verses and respectful of their place in German culture.

5.3.2 *Völsungasaga*

Völsungasaga (*Saga of the Volsungs*), the second of Wagner's primary sources for his argument of the *Ring*, is the most important, and one of the most interesting, of Iceland's sagas. This work dates from the midthirteenth century and, like other writings of its kind, recounts the deeds of heroes, one of those many tales that was developed in the oral tradition and which was retold countless times as a form of entertainment. The story in *Völsungasaga* is the tragic saga of Sigurð (Siegfried) the Volsung and is a preservation of an earlier version of the Nibelung tragedy. The work had as its foundation Old Norse poems, a few unknown elsewhere, but mostly those heroic poems found in *The Poetic Edda*, of which it is essentially a prose paraphrase. The pervasive cultural ambiance in *Völsungasaga* is, however, more that of the southern Teutonic people than that of the people of the Nordic region.

Völsungasaga was invaluable to Wagner and his *Ring*. Much of the work found its way into his story, including the lineage of his Siegfried, that is, as a descendent of the god Wotan. Although thematic properties were really those of *The Poetic Edda, Völsungasaga* possessed a secondary feature that was a great aid to Wagner: the work was written in prose. Unrestricted by the requirements and limitations of poetics, the unknown author was free to let his literary imagination and his thematic fantasy roam at large. Thus, in telling the Siegfried story, the tale was permeated with Germanic medieval romanticism richly blended with the colorful southern heroic tradition.

5.3.3 *Nibelungen Nôt und die Klage*

Nibelungen Nôt (Fall of the Nibelungs) is the title of a Middle High German poem that, in time, became known by the more popular title *Nibelungenlied (Song of the Nibelungs)*. This early thirteenth-century poem by an anonymous author is preserved in thirty-four manuscripts, only three of which contain the complete poem. This work is an excellent example of the *Heldenepos* ("heroic epic"), a verse form frequently used in early German heroic poetry. The poem was quite popular until the sixteenth century, after which it lay dormant for some two hundred years. The work was revived in the middle of the eighteenth century and went on to become a true national piece of German literature. Today, the poem is looked upon as the national epic of Germany, although its hero is quite distinct from the Cid of Spain and Roland of France. The *Nibelungenlied* is the only German work—written in German and wholly of German origin and development—that Wagner used as a primary source for his *Ring*. Wagner's library in his home in Bayreuth contained four editions of the epic; two had been written in Middle High German and two were written in modern German. In 1874, Wagner's wife wrote in her *Diaries* that *Nibelungenlied* still held, after all the years, its attraction for her husband and that both she and Wagner appreciated the pictures illustrating elements of the poem that hung on the walls of their home.

The story that unfolds in *Nibelungenlied* is the southern and the original version of the Nibelung tale as handed down through oral tradition. Its story is really two separate tales. The first, presented in the first nineteen chapters (âventiuren) of the poem, is the tale of Kriemhild, Brünhild, and Siegfried. It is this tale that figures prominently as a primary source for the Siegfried theme in the *Ring*. The remaining twenty chapters of *Nibelungenlied* are devoted to an account of the life and actions of Kriemhild as she persists in the desire to avenge the murder of her husband, Siegfried. Wagner entirely passed over this second theme when he devised his version of the Nibelung story.

Each of the two tales of this epic is of Frankish origin, the creation of those people who, in the third century, established themselves along the Rhine River. Each story has its setting in the region of the Rhine and each was separately incorporated into songs, poems, and lays, probably during the fifth century. The popularity of the poems of the two tales was such that they were in continuous circulation, gathering linguistic and thematic variations as they passed from group to group. At some unknown time the two themes began to merge, and several hundred years later they appeared together as a single poem. The themes traveled north during the period of the great migration and, substantially altered, are found in the poems of *The Poetic Edda* and in many sagas of Scandinavia.

It is only natural that *Nibelungenlied* became part and parcel of Wagner's dramatic thought. The thematic aspects of the poem were such that he was provided with a most appropriate source out of which he felt he could realize a dramatization of what later he would call the *purely human (reinmenschlich)*. The work was one of the vehicles that he proposed for such an undertaking. Given also Wagner's desire to strike a chord for German nationalism in art, the epic was a logical choice. It was entirely of German origin and imbued throughout with the essence of German thought. In the poem Wagner saw a reflection of the German people, a cultural mosaic of honor, pride, moral and physical strength, virtue, loyalty, and valor, those traits which he insisted were typical of German society, the attributes that he wished so much to bring before the public in order that the nation could come to know its true self. If in the preparation of the *Ring* Wagner drew heavily from *The Poetic Edda* for his argument, it was in *Nibelungenlied* that he found the tone, the timbre, and the cultural posture for his drama.

Die Klage (The Mourning) is, at best, but an addendum to *Nibelungenlied*. It was created to satisfy the listeners' yearning for a continuation of the epic's story, and it is essentially a lament for the heroes who were victims of the Nibelung tragedy. The substance of this work was provided by the epic itself. *Die Klage* is seldom included in editions of *Nibelungenlied*, and although Wagner was well aware of its existence, the poem served no significant role in the preparation of the *Ring*.

5.4 Secondary Sources

5.4.1 *Deutsche Mythologie*

The most valuable source of information for Wagner in his development of the *Ring* drama was, without doubt, *Deutsche Mythologie*. This multivolume study by Jakob Grimm (1785–1863), which was published in 1835, continues to be both the authoritative work on German antiquity and a primary source for the study of any aspect of German mythology. (Wagner's library contained the second edition published in Göttingen in 1844.) This monumental work was one of thirty volumes of research Grimm published. In collaboration with his equally renowned brother, Wilhelm, he published another thirty-four.

In a manner and with a scope that has seldom been rivaled, Grimm prepared an incomparable work. He researched, studied, sorted out, compiled, and discussed what is probably every known facet of the mythological world of the German people. This immense storehouse of knowledge encompasses the most significant as well as the least significant features of the culture, the entire gamut of matters that formed the thoughts, beliefs, and creeds of the Teutonic races. Grimm's attention ranged from the origins and histories of the deities and the rites associated with them to the influence of these matters on contemporary life, from the heroes of the age to the language, from superstitions of the culture to the herbs used in daily life.

The *Deutsche Mythologie* was indispensable to Wagner as a work of reference. Other sources provided the basis for his argument of the *Ring*; Grimm's study allowed for a more thorough and more comprehensive awareness of the culture he was dramatizing. The work was significant in that it permitted him an understanding of the relevancy of the minor but essential cultural details that were to become a part of his drama. It was by means of Grimm's work, combined with his own devotion and dedication to his project and his natural cultural acquisitions, that Wagner succeeded in dramatizing quite authentically the Teutonic ambiance and was able to embody within the *Ring* vital foundations of the Germanic culture.

5.4.2 *Die deutsche Heldensage*

Die deutsche Heldensage, published in Göttingen in 1829, is generally considered to be the greatest achievement of Wilhelm Grimm (1786–1859), a respected and prolific writer (eighteen volumes) in his own right as well as in his collaboration with his equally famous brother, Jakob. (Perhaps their most widely known joint effort was *Kinder- und Hausmärchen* [*Children's and Household Tales*], more popularly known in English as the Grimm Brothers' *Fairy Tales*.)

Die deutsche Heldensage was essentially a retelling of the story lines of epic tales. Unlike previous publications in which he had arranged heroic legends, folk tales, and fairy tales according to content, Grimm carefully researched the period A.D. 600–1600 to determine the origins of the epic tales and then made his presentations in chronological order. He included excerpts from the original poems and enhanced the usefulness of his study with a selection of other relevant poetry and prose of that thousand-year period. This unique work concluded with Grimm's essay on the origin and development of the German epic tale.

Much of the content of *Die deutsche Heldensage* derives from Grimm's continuous investigation, study, and collection of things Germanic. He had long held in high regard the epic poetry of Germany; and his work, which attracted popular as well as scholarly audiences, was instrumental in establishing the epic as a subject for serious study, thereby stimulating others to investigate Germany's epic past. Grimm's study was an invaluable aid to Wagner in his preparation of the *Ring* drama. By this means the dramatist familiarized himself with the numerous heroic stories, and, in turn, these tales allowed him a greater knowledge of German antiquity, culture, structure, and ambiance. The scope of the tales gave Wagner greater insight into a national concept, a concept that he sought to achieve in his drama.

5.4.3 *Deutsches Heldenbuch*

Deutsches Heldenbuch (*The German Book of Heroes*) is a series of six volumes published in the years from 1843 to 1849 by Karl Simrock (1802–1876). These works are essentially Simrock's translation into contemporary German of much medieval poetry, including his earlier translation of *Nibelungenlied* (1827).

Simrock, a student and later a professor at Bonn University, pursued studies in literature and philology. He became widely known for both his original poetry and his translations of medieval poetry, which included his version of *The Poetic Edda* (1851), a copy of which was in Wagner's library.

As with other secondary sources, Wagner acquired vast amounts of information from Simrock's works. In addition to the rich treasure trove of data and details that contributed to his comprehension of the mainsprings of Germanic culture, Wagner had at hand, through Simrock, translations of two of the three primary sources that he utilized for his thematic development of the *Ring*.

5.4.4 *Heimskringla*

Heimskringla (*Circle of the World*) is the second of two significant works by the Icelander Snorri Sturluson (1179–1241). Subtitled *A Chron-*

icle of the Norwegian Kings, this fascinating study, which was completed sometime between the years 1220 and 1230, is an attempt by the author to present a broad and balanced history of the chiefs of that country. Utilizing the records and the accounts of the more prominent sagas, the poetry of the royal courts, and the oral material heard during his extensive travels, Snorri assembled a remarkably accurate account of the kings of Norway from ancient times through the year 1177.

However much it is a masterpiece in its own right, *Heimskringla* was only of indirect value to Wagner and the *Ring*. Although the work clearly reflects the stamp of Christianity, which had recently reached the North, it is nevertheless sprinkled throughout with indirect references as well as certain details of a mythological nature. At times there are vivid descriptions of non-Christian customs and traditions of earlier times. *Heimskringla* obviously made no contribution to the thematic aspects of the *Ring*. However, its ancient Teutonic ambiance certainly had an impact on Wagner as he accumulated his extensive knowledge of the Germanic world. As late as 1871 the composer was still reading Sturluson's work.

5.4.5 *Wilkinasaga*

Wilkinasaga (Vilkina Saga), more correctly entitled *Thidrekssaga (Dietrich's Saga)*, is the account of the exploits and adventures of Theodoric the Great (A.D. 454–526), ruler of the Ostrogoths (an eastern group of the Germanic peoples) from the year 475, and king of the Romans from 493. (The term *Wilkina* as a title for this work was applied to the tale by the first editor, who took the word from within the story itself.) Scholars are divided as to the country of origin of this saga, Iceland or Norway. The work was written, however, in Old Norse, late in the thirteenth century. A Swedish version was completed some two hundred years later. In German, Theodoric the Great is Dietrich von Bern (Dietrich of Verona, that city being one of Theodoric's two capitals). This is the same Dietrich who appears in *Nibelungenlied* as the avenger of the Amelungs and, in the final chapter of that work, as the conqueror of Siegfried's murderer, Hagen, whom he then delivers to the hero's vengeful wife, Queen Kriemhild.

Although there is a vast difference between the life of Theodoric and the legendary history of Dietrich, their appearances as one and the same person provided a popular theme throughout German medieval literature. History relates that Theodoric, as a young man, was driven from his kingdom in northern Italy by his uncle, and that many years later, with a large army, he returned to conquer the country. Legend states that Theodoric, as Dietrich, spent his long exile in the court of King Etzel (Attila), where he gained the great respect of the people as a thoughtful, fearless leader and as an honorable man and an exemplary knight. In short, Dietrich was the perfect reflection of the heroic ideal. It was this supposed association with Etzel's court which became the tie that joined Dietrich to the Nibelung story. (Such a relationship could not actually have been possible because the reign of Attila ended in A.D. 453, one year before the birth of Theodoric.)

Such was the figure of Dietrich in Attila's court and such was his popularity among the people that he became the central character in numerous poems and songs of German medieval literature. One of these poems, "Biterolf und Dietleib" ("Biterolf and Dietleib"), recounts how Dietleib goes into the world to seek his father, and another, "Eckenlied" ("Song of Ecke"), tells of Dietleib's adventures with the giant Ecke and his brother Fasolt.

Although Dietrich is obviously the protagonist of the saga that bears his name, the hero Siegfried also plays a somewhat prominent, if detached, role in the work. As here presented, Siegfried is the son of Siegmund and the daughter of the king of Spain! Quite by accident, the newborn child floats down a river in a wooden box that eventually is banked on the shore, near a forest. The infant is nourished first by a deer, and then, in time, is discovered by a smith, Mimir, who takes the child as his stepson. Siegfried grows to manhood and marries Grimhild, the daughter of King Aldrian of Nibelungenland and Queen Oda. Wagner found little use for these thematic matters that developed the Siegfried story in the saga. However, he may have been struck by a rather detailed physical description of the youth, a description that is not to be found in any of the major works that deal with the hero.

If these popular poems presented specific incidents in Dietrich's life, it remained for *Thidrekssaga* to draw the strands of that legendary life into a single story, one in which Dietrich's lengthy stay in the land of Attila caused much of the Nibelung legend to appear. If *Thidrekssaga* is less an artistic accomplishment than *Nibelungenlied*, it is, nevertheless, a work that is imbued with the essence of the southern heroic tradition. Scholars are divided in their opinions regarding the sources that gave rise to the saga: some believe the author drew directly from the earlier *Nibelungenlied*, while others maintain that each of the writers had access to similar, if not the same, sources. Although Wagner disregarded the figure of Dietrich and the tales of his heroics as well as those thematic elements that are here concerned with Siegfried, the dramatist-composer did find in *Thidrekssaga* much that helped him in the development of the *Ring* drama, much that reflected the German sentiment that he wished to incorporate into his poem.

5.4.6 THE STUDIES OF FRANZ JOSEF MONE

Franz Josef Mone (1796–1871), the son of a Dutchman (Moonen), was a much-respected Germanist and literary scholar. His studies at Heidelberg, though varied, focused principally on law, philology, and history. His professional career included work as a librarian, as a professor, and as general director of the Ducal Archives in Karlsruhe.

Mone published his first study in 1816. This work was followed by numerous other publications on language, poetry, literature, and religion. Wagner's wife writes in her *Diaries* that in 1869 her husband was rereading Mone's study on German heroic sagas *Untersuchungen zur Geschichte der deutschen Heldensage* (*Investigations into the History of the German Heroic Sagas*) which had been published in Quedlinburg in 1836 and which intrigued Wagner very much. Years later, in 1872, she writes that she and Wagner were reading again the author's collection of medieval plays, *Altdeutsche Schauspiele* (1841). Wagner was never specific regarding which of Mone's other studies he had consulted, although there are several that may have been useful to the dramatist in his research into German antiquity. The following is a selected list of Mone's publications which, in one manner or another, may have been helpful to Wagner during the long incubation period of his *Ring* project:

a. *Einleitung in das* Nibelungenlied (*Introduction to the* Nibelungenlied). Heidelberg, 1818.

b. *Quellen und Forschungen zur Geschichte der deutsche Literatur und Sprach* (*Sources and Research Relating to the History of German Literature and Language*). Leipzig, 1830.

c. *Geschichte des Heidenthums im nördlichen Europa* (*The History of Paganism in Northern Europe*). Darmstadt, 1822–1833.

d. *Übersicht der niederländischen Volksliteratur älterer zeit* (*Summary of Dutch Folk Literature of Earlier Times*). Tübingen, 1838.

5.4.7 THE STUDIES OF KARL LACHMANN

Karl Lachmann (1793–1851) was one of the first eminent scholars of German philosophy. He gained renown because of his original, occasionally provocative, writings that included a number of tracts on writers relatively unknown in his day, a translation into German of *Macbeth*, the first German translation of Shakespeare's sonnets, and undisputedly important studies of the national epic poem *Nibelungenlied*.

Lachmann's work on *Nibelungenlied* was substantial and extensive. His *Liedertheorie* ("song theory") garnered immediate national attention. In this study Lachmann proposed that *Nibelungenlied* was not a single poem composed by one author, but rather a collection of twenty separate songs or lays that had been arranged in proper sequential order and then united into one single work by means of appropriate connective material. Lachmann's theory was not discounted until after his death. He followed his *Liedertheorie* with a volume of those twenty songs that he had concluded were the foundation of *Nibelungenlied*.

Other pertinent studies by Lachmann to which Wagner had access include his editions of two of the three principal manuscripts of *Nibelungenlied* and several tracts on specific aspects of the Nibelung poem. These studies were published in the years 1816–1841. Although Wagner acknowledged his study of Lachmann's investigations, he never specified to what extent he was familiar with that scholar's work.

Chapter Six

Bayreuth

Bayreuth (spelled *Baireuth* in earlier times) is both a city and a symbol. Geographically, Bayreuth is a relatively unpretentious town located in central Germany, in the state (*Land*) of Bavaria, a short distance from Nuremberg and some 125 miles north of Munich. However, with the premiere in Bayreuth of Wagner's *Der Ring des Nibelungen*, that city ceased to be merely a nondescript German town and became the international symbol for all that is Wagner as an artist and all that is Wagnerian in art. Since 1876 Bayreuth has been no less than an aesthetic phenomenon, and as such it stands by itself among the cities of the world.

Wagner took up residence in Bayreuth in 1872 and remained there until his death. In 1874 he and his second wife, Cosima, and their family of three children moved into Wahnfried, the home Wagner had designed and built for himself and near which both he and Cosima are buried. Through the years, members of the family have lived in Wahnfried, which today serves as a Wagner museum.

The indissoluble association of Bayreuth with Wagner began in 1876 with the first performance in the *Ring* in the Festspielhaus ("Festival Theater"), the theater that Wagner conceived, designed, and built especially for the staging of his music drama. The Festspielhaus, originally called by Wagner "Bühnenfestspielhaus" (Stage Festival Theater), still stands today; and through the years since 1876 it has been the mecca of Wagnerites who visit the Bavarian city annually for the summer festival of Wagner operas. This Festival Theater, which itself has been the subject of many volumes, is the only theater in the world dedicated solely to performances of the work of one person. Officially, no work other than that of Richard Wagner has been performed in the Festival Theater in its more than one-hundred-year history. (During World War II, when the forces of the United States occupied Bayreuth, servicemen were stationed throughout the town, and at times, they were in the bombed theater and made use of the musical instruments and other items that had been stored there.) It is appropriate to note here that three of Wagner's thirteen completed operas have never been performed in the Festspielhaus in Bayreuth. These early works, *Die Feen*, *Das Liebesverbot*, and *Rienzi*, reflect a definite influence of the Italian and the French styles of opera, styles which Wagner, in his later years, considered to be artistically corrupt and debased.

Wagner got his first view of Bayreuth in 1835. At the time he was serving as conductor of the orchestra of Magdeburg, in Saxony, some eighty miles west of Berlin. Certain of Wagner's duties required travel to other cities and on one of the journeys, the then young composer passed through this quiet village, which dates from the twelfth century. Although some thirty-five years would pass before Bayreuth would become prominent in Wagner's life and, in turn, be catapulted into the international public eye, the name of the town for some unknown reason became fixed in his mind. In 1866, as he worked on *Die Meistersinger*, whose setting was in Nuremberg, Wagner suggested to the king of Bavaria that the royal government be located in that city, then neighboring Bayreuth could become the composer's residence.

In 1850, a time when Bayreuth was still quite separate in association from Richard Wagner, several artistic concepts were germinating in the dramatist-composer's fertile brain. He had completed the poem *Siegfrieds Tod*, and the idea of a second drama was stirring within him. Even then he knew that *Siegfrieds Tod*, in its final form, would be a work distinct from the traditional operatic fare of the day, and thus a work whose demanding combination of theatrical-dramatic-musical requirements could not be met by any of the theaters then in existence. In that year, from his exile in Switzerland, he wrote his musician-friend Theodor Uhlig that a new and different theater was necessary if an appropriate production of his drama was to be given. (Wagner's ideas regarding a properly designed theatrical atmosphere were not concepts that he was devising only now. In May 1848, he had written an unsolicited plan for a theater and its necessary equipment. His essay, "Entwurf zur Organisation eines deutschen Nationaltheaters für das Königreich Sachsen" ["Plan for the Organization of a German National Theater for the Kingdom of Saxony"], was rejected out of hand by the royal authorities.) Wagner now called only for a temporary structure, one to be made of wood and to be erected in some field near Zürich. Wagner's letter represents the first tangible evidence of what would become, twenty-six years later, a festival theater and a summer program of opera. At the time only Wagner understood what ideas and concepts he was developing; the full meaning of his words was lost on others, even on his close friend.

Wagner's idea of a special theater not only persisted, but grew. As *Siegfrieds Tod* expanded into two dramas and those two into four, Wagner began to nourish an added element regarding the unfinished tetralogy. Although some work on the poem still remained and all of the music was still to be composed, Wagner conceived the idea of a "cycle-festival," a production of his Nibelung music drama as a four-day program in a special theater to be built somewhere on the Rhine. Within a year he had added another detail to his grandiose scheme. In a letter to his friend and future father-in-law, Franz Liszt, Wagner described the kind of city in which he wished to see his theater rise. It was to be a small city, one remote from the commotion of an industrialized area, one in which the cultural attitude and tastes of the inhabitants had not been overly developed and which had not been sullied by foreign (French and Italian) musical works. As he worked on the *Ring*, his active mind continued to envision that future first performance in that yet unnamed town in that yet unbuilt theater.

As he contemplated these matters, Wagner was also giving much thought to the music that he would compose and to the talents that his singers would have to possess in order to perform his work as he would write it. By 1853 his artistic intuition had convinced him that even the finest performers of the day were ill-equipped, vocally and dramatically, to undertake the severe and stringent interpretations he was incorporating into the many roles of his drama. These singers, he concluded, had succumbed so thoroughly to the operatic traditions of the day that without intense training they would never be able to adjust or to adapt to his drama and its music. In his mind the performers of the *Ring* would require individual instruction and disciplined rehearsal if they were to carry out successfully their dramatic and vocal assignments.

During the ensuing years Wagner's ideas on the performance of his music drama grew both in scope and detail. By 1863 he was secure enough in his own mind to bring his ideas together and to present the plan that now had become whole. In the Preface to the first public edition of *Der Ring des Nibelungen*, Wagner explained his desires and intentions. He would mount the *Ring* in a theater of his own design. It would be a sparse structure, possibly only a provisional theater that at a later date could be taken over and upgraded by some government. (Until the establishment of the German empire in 1871, Germany was really a number of individual kingdoms, each governed separately.) He hinted at innovation when he wrote that there would be nothing in or on the structure that did not contribute directly to the dramatic production. He would build his theater in some unimportant town in Germany, a town small enough to be without a theater but large enough to receive what he called "unusual" guests. Regarding the performers, Wagner wrote that they would be selected from the staffs of German opera houses. They would be brought together in the spring of the year for continuous, intensive training and rehearsals, during which time they must be free of any outside commitments, artistic or otherwise. After this strenuous ordeal, there would be a period for rest and unpressured study of their roles; then, during the summer, a performance of the *Ring* would be given.

Wagner's concept of a "festival" production of his *Ring* apparently had reached maturity. However, if his artistic ideas seemed to have had no bounds, the economic realities of such a project had not escaped him. He realized that such an undertaking would be costly, far greater than the personal means of an individual. At the same time, convinced as he was that his art was really a national art, he deemed that its proper execution merited governmental assistance. He concluded his Preface by asking if there was somewhere a prince who would come forward to make this grand adventure a reality for the German people.

Wagner did not have to wait long for an answer to his question. There was such a prince as he had sought! And that prince came forward! In May 1864, Wagner was summoned to appear in Munich for a meeting with Bavaria's young new king, Ludwig II.

As history would record, the reign of Ludwig II was an incredible, quixotic dream world ruled over by a much misunderstood king. Ludwig II gave realization to the fantasy of his own cultural dreams and became known as the romantic idealist of Germany's monarchs, and in the end Ludwig II, more than anyone else, would give Richard Wagner the means by which the composer's much maligned ideas would become reality.

Ludwig, son of Maximilian II and grandson of Ludwig I, was born on 25 August 1845 in the Nymphenburg Palace, the royal summer home near Munich. As a boy he was attracted to the arts, and by his early teens he was already intensely interested in Wagner's works. By the time he was thirteen, he had read Wagner's *Oper und Drama*. He read and reread *Tannhäuser* and *Lohengrin*, whose texts he memorized. In February 1861, at the age of fifteen, Ludwig saw his first performance of a Wagner work, *Lohengrin*. So taken was he by the drama and its music that at his request a command performance of the work was given four months later. In February 1862, Ludwig first heard *Tann-häuser*. The prince's interest in the arts, the special hold that Wagner's dramas had upon him, and the intense rapture that he had known during his attendance at the two performances of Wagner's works drew him deeper into the world of the German master. In early 1864 Ludwig heard another *Lohengrin*, a production mounted at his own insistence, and now he was so emotionally bound to Wagner's works and so overcome by Wagner's art that his obsession and his admiration were to cast him in the role of Wagner's most devoted benefactor. And Ludwig had read Wagner's Preface to the 1863 edition of the *Ring* poems. The prince had studied the composer's ideas for a cycle-festival; he had pondered Wagner's stated need for a theater whose facilities were adequate for a production of the *Ring*; he had considered the master's arguments that a reschooling of singers was necessary. He also read Wagner's plea for financial aid for such a plan, for some royal house to assist in the realization of this great work of national art. Wagner's closing words resounded in his mind: "Will such a Prince be found?"

On 14 March 1864, Prince Ludwig—not yet nineteen—became King Ludwig II of Bavaria. His father had died on the tenth of March, and during the four days of official mourning Ludwig contemplated his role as king. On 16 April 1864, less than five weeks after he had assumed the crown, Ludwig issued an order that Richard Wagner be brought to his court. The Secretary to the King of Bavaria had difficulty in finding the composer, but on the fourth of May, Wagner appeared before the king. From the first moment of that historic meeting, all things Wagnerian were destined to be rerouted along paths that have no parallel in cultural history. Wagner had found his prince!

The first meeting of the monarch and the master was the moment when the unreal became real and reality and fantasy overlapped. For Ludwig the session represented a union with the one whose works had forged a love that transcended the limits of mankind's understanding— those works that had laid bare the beauty of the human soul, those works that had brought some consolation to a young and restive spirit. For Ludwig the purpose of the audience was to inform Wagner that he, as king, would now do all possible to allow his Saxon subject the means by which he could dedicate himself to the continuation of his art, free of the plaguing concerns of day-to-day life. For Wagner the meeting represented the resolution of his artistic ambitions, a pathway out of his dramatic dilemma, and perhaps more significant to him at the time, freedom from his severe economic problems. If in his fifty-one years he had suffered political persecution, long exile, rejection of his dramatic and musical concepts, theories, and ideas, and if he had known personal economic deprivation, even to the point of near-starvation, and if once he had been jailed for failure to pay certain debts, and if, more than once, he had thought of suicide, he now had found Ludwig, the rescuer who would change radically all aspects of his life.

The conditions of Ludwig's proposal were uncomplicated. Wagner was to continue his work, to create, to carry out his self-proclaimed mission on behalf of German culture. In return for such service, Ludwig would free Wagner forever from any monetary concerns. Ludwig promised the composer a generous pension; he promised a production of the *Ring* as Wagner wished it; he promised Wagner a school in which singers could be trained and instructed for performance in the music drama; he promised Wagner his theater. Ludwig was a man of his word, and within a month of that fateful meeting he had given Wagner two large sums with which the composer could satisfy his long list of creditors. Ludwig then followed these gifts with one of a large home in Munich in which Wagner could live and work undisturbed. Wagner's prince indeed had come forward! There can be no equal to that meeting in 1864 between the Dream King of Bavaria and the controversial artist from Saxony. If it is true that the genius of Wagner, in time, would have surfaced before the world, there can be no doubt that the generosity of Ludwig, spurred by his sincere admiration and unquestioned love of the man and his art—and in turn his desire to facilitate that art—hastened that time and made history see and know the richness that is Richard Wagner.

In October of that year (1864) a contract containing ten clauses was drawn up between Ludwig and Wagner. As the king had promised, he would furnish Wagner the means and the facilities for the realization of his artistic intentions. In return, the royal house was to receive the property rights to the *Ring* and to the composer's yet-to-be-written works, as well as performance rights. Wagner, in his turn, was not ungrateful for Ludwig's actions. Yet it was a gratitude that was less deeply felt than that of other men, for Wagner was guided by a deep-rooted conviction that as an artist, and one of national calling, such aid was his natural due. Such assistance, he maintained, would allow him to work; it would be a prepayment for his art that would then be available forever to the German people.

The ensuing years were to see the contract between Ludwig and Wagner become a document of mere formality, more a symbol of the long relationship between the two men. Frequently the terms were modified, always to Wagner's advantage. If, through the years, each party violated the pact, the violations were uniquely indicative of the respective attitudes of each of the men. For his part, Ludwig exceeded his obligations. So intense was his feeling for Wagner's art that he never

Ludwig II at the age of twenty; painting by F. Piloty.

Ludwig II, in his early forties; posthumous portrait
completed in 1887 by G. Schachinger.

failed to give way to the aggressive tactics that Wagner used so well. Wagner never deviated from his belief that all he received was his "right," and as a consequence he was not above deception if such action benefited him. It is a fact that Wagner resorted to lies and stooped to artistic sabotage to get what he wanted. Wagner looked upon the king as an endless source of funds, and Ludwig, in return, never abandoned his artistic hero. Often embarrassed, hurt, many times humiliated by Wagner's words and actions, Ludwig always remained devoted to Wagner. At Ludwig's death in 1886, apparently by suicide, it could be said that no man before him had done so much for art in general and at the same time endured so much from the one person who had benefited most from that aid.

The six years following Ludwig's appearance were rewarding if tempestuous times for Wagner. His personal abrasiveness continued to encourage detractors, and now their numbers included persons high in the Bavarian government. Yet, through it all, his talent was victorious as he sat alone in the royal chair of German composers and the musical world began to re-evaluate itself in terms of his art. In 1865 his *Tristan und Isolde* premiered in Munich. Three years later, again in Munich, he enjoyed another success at the first performance of *Die Meistersinger von Nürnberg*. The following year, despite Wagner's bold and certainly questionable efforts to thwart him, Ludwig commanded the first performance of the first *Ring* drama, *Das Rheingold* (September 22, 1869). The young king was so taken with what he heard and saw that he ordered a premiere production of the second drama, *Die Walküre*, a performance that took place on 26 June 1870. (For names and notes on principals, see Appendix C.)

In 1870 Wagner was fifty-seven years old. (At this time he was living with Cosima von Bülow, then wife to the talented German conductor and musician, Hans von Bülow, and the daughter of Franz Liszt.) His position in the world of music was secure despite the efforts of those who argued violently against him. Had he never written another note, his name would still be found today high on the list of the greatest composers of all time. However, his most significant work, the *Ring*, was still to come. And the desire for a special theater for this unfinished work and for a school in which to train its singers was still strong. Ludwig, true to his word, had ordered plans drawn up for the theater and had decreed the establishment of a musical school in the Bavarian capital. Yet within eighteen months of that fateful meeting between Ludwig and the composer, the combination of Wagner's overbearing, often insolent behavior, his costly style of living, and his rather scandalous personal life had incited much of the public of Munich against him. (During these months, Cosima von Bülow, the wife of the noted conductor, had begun her life with Wagner, and, as previously noted, gave birth in April 1865, to Wagner's daughter, Isolde. At the time, Wagner was still married to Minna. It was this open relationship that weighed heavily in the public vigilance against Wagner.) So strong became the outcry against Wagner that eventually even the king could find no way to allow the composer to remain in the city. In December 1865, Ludwig felt compelled to remove Wagner from Munich, an action that made forever impossible the realization of the theater and the music school in that city.

Despite the notoriety that attached to Wagner the man, as of 1870 his stature as a dramatist and as a composer was such that he could have had his theater in any one of several cities in Germany. Officials in a number of cities (Berlin, Baden-Baden, Darmstadt) seriously considered such a project. Interested parties in Chicago, London, and Strasbourg, France, were also discussing the feasibility of this Wagnerian adventure. As of the moment, however, Wagner had not found anywhere the conditions and facilities that years before he had determined were necessary.

In March 1870, Cosima[1] encouraged him to read again an article on the city of Bayreuth. During the months that followed, Wagner directed certain of his closest friends to gather more information for him about this minor city in central Germany, a course of action known only to the composer and those he had entrusted with the assignment. From his sources he learned that Bayreuth was a relatively small city with some twenty thousand inhabitants, and that it had not been spoiled by industrialization. In Bayreuth there was a theater that reputedly had the largest stage of any in the country, yet it was not in any sense a public theater because the town lacked any true public entertainment and it could not boast any cultural resources. (The theater was the Markgräfliches Opernhaus, the Court Theater which the sister of Frederick the Great, Margravine Wilhelmine, had commissioned. The theater was completed in 1748.) Wagner was taken by what he had learned about Bayreuth, and always the shrewd and practical realist, he recognized the importance of the facts that the city was in Bavaria and that Ludwig II was the king of Bavaria.

In April of the following year, Wagner traveled to Bayreuth, a town he had first visited many years earlier. Although he soon discovered

---

[1] Cosima was granted a divorce from her husband on 18 July, 1870, and on the twenty-fifth of the following month, the birthdate of Ludwig II, she and Wagner were married in Lucerne, in a Protestant ceremony.

that the theater, whose huge stage had drawn his attention, could in no way serve the purposes he had in mind for a production of the *Ring*, he was interested. He observed, inspected, and made inquiries. His interest grew as he measured the town's qualifications in light of his own ambitions. Wagner liked Bayreuth, and his decision was not long in coming. He approached the authorities of the town to explain his plan. He proposed that a theater be constructed, his theater, in which he would present a festival performance of the *Ring*. In addition, he would build for himself and his family a residence, a house that would be his permanent home and from which he would supervise all aspects of the undertaking that would result in the presentation of a great national work of art to the German people. Bayreuth was receptive, both the town officials and the citizenry. A special committee was formed, the most prominent members being the mayor of Bayreuth, Theodor Muncker, and the director of the local bank, Friedrich Feustel. The latter, who was to become a close friend of the Wagner family, was especially eager to bring the Wagnerian world to his city, and it was by means of his persuasiveness that the committee agreed that the land for the Wagner theater should be a contribution of the people of Bayreuth. (The site that the city eventually donated for the Wagner theater was known as Bürgerreuth Hill, more popularly known as Green Hill.) Negotiations followed; then specific details of a plan were discussed; the next month (5 May 1871), in Leipzig, Wagner announced that in Bayreuth, in the summer of 1873, there would be a festival production of *Der Ring des Nibelungen*, in a new theater constructed especially for the occasion.

Wagner's announcement set off a flurry of activity among the Wagnerites of the day. It was no secret, however, that the project obviously would be a costly venture. Emil Heckel, a piano maker in Mannheim and a follower of the Wagner art, believed that an interested public would be most willing to assist financially, and to that end he suggested that a Wagner Society be established in several cities throughout Germany. Heckel anticipated that many persons would become members of such societies and then contribute to the Wagner cause according to their means. Wagner approved the idea and the first Richard Wagner Society was founded by Heckel in his native Mannheim. Soon, other Wagner Societies came into being. Berlin inaugurated a Society in 1871 and, in time, Wagner Societies were established outside the country, specifically in London and New York. In February 1872, a *Patronatverein* (Society of Patrons) was organized in Bayreuth. Baron Loën, the intendant at the Weimar Theater, chaired the group whose intent was to demonstrate an acknowledgement of private subscription to the Bayreuth project by selling one thousand share-certificates at three hundred thalers per share. The certificates were also to serve as entrance to the *Ring* production at such time as it premiered. If, however, there was general enthusiasm in Wagnerian circles, the overall public reaction to the project at Bayreuth was less than favorable. The press vividly remembered Wagner's actions over the years and especially those of recent times, and it was, in the main, much opposed to the Wagner-Bayreuth plans. In addition, there was a small but vehement segment of the German public which, for any number of reasons, was hostile to the venture because Wagner had in the past so often behaved disreputably in both public and private. Politics, too, played its role in the negative reaction to Bayreuth: Several German cities had requested the premiere of the *Ring*, and in their disappointment at not being selected, they responded to the Bayreuth plan with a silence filled with meaning.

Ludwig had never been consulted regarding the Bayreuth idea. In March 1871, Wagner had written the king to explain his concepts and ideas for a festival theater. However, at that time he did not mention Bayreuth and made reference only to "a place in Bavaria." Wagner's announcement came as a surprise. Ludwig was disappointed, but even if he had wished that Wagner, his theater, and his music school could have been near him, he also understood that the negative tone and temper of the court and the feelings of the inhabitants of the capital ruled out those possibilities. Moreover, he could have exercised his royal prerogative and brought the Bayreuth plan to a halt, but he chose to stand aside, not to interfere. Despite the painful relationship he had endured with Wagner, he remained faithful to the man he most admired in all the world. Ludwig understood Wagner, and thus, rather than impede the project, he decided to assist. He offered no objection to Wagner's use of the theater design plans that had been drawn up in 1865 at his expense for the proposed theater in Munich. (Gottfried Semper, a famed German architect who had designed the Dresden Opera House and who would later be involved in the plans for the South Kensington Museum in London, had worked with Wagner and had drawn the plans for the theater in Munich. However, if Semper's plans were used as the basis for the theater in Bayreuth, Wagner would employ Otto Brückwald as the construction supervisor. Semper later brought a legal suit against Wagner.) As a further gesture of his sympathetic nature, Ludwig then subscribed a sizable amount toward the purchase of the patron's certificates, a sum that later, in his devotion to Wagner, he directed to the composer's personal use for the construction of the planned residence.

Despite the noticeable lack of success of the fund-raising plans, the foundation stone of Wagner's festival theater was laid on 22 May 1872, the composer's fifty-ninth birthday. Wagner officiated at the ceremony

Richard Wagner's Festival Theater in Bayreuth

during which he placed a telegram from Ludwig and a verse of his own in a small box that was then placed under the stone. Wagner had written:

> Here I enclose a secret,
> and here it may rest
> many a hundred years:
> So long as the stone preserves it,
> so long will it manifest itself
> to the world.

Wagner made a short speech and then, as he tapped the stone into place, said, "Be blessed, my stone; stand long and hold fast." Early that evening, in the theater whose stage he once rejected, he conducted the Ninth Symphony of Ludwig von Beethoven, his favorite composer. Wagner's theater was at last underway, more than twenty years after the Zürich days in which he first mentioned it to a friend.

The economic state of the Wagner fund left much to be desired. As early as the Fall of 1872 it was obvious that unless much more money was soon forthcoming, work on the theater would have to cease. The situation did not improve, and it was necessary to admit that a festival program the following summer was impossible. By the end of the year, as Wagner and his wife undertook a tour of opera houses throughout Germany to seek out singers for the *Ring*, it was determined that less than five percent of the needed funds was in hand, and outside enthusiasm for the project continued weak, almost nonexistent. Wagner, however, was not dissuaded from his goal, although the need for additional money necessitated added effort on his part. During January and February of 1873 he undertook a series of concerts in several German cities to arouse public interest in the Bayreuth plans. The travel and the conducting were especially tiring to him because the task came soon after a five-week trip to sixteen cities, during which he had searched for singers to participate in the yet uncertain first performance of the *Ring*. The concert tour and the search for performers were an added burden on top of his already extensive obligations as overseer of every detail of the Bayreuth project, as well as those relative to the construction of his personal residence. Furthermore, there was still much work to be done to complete the fourth of the *Ring* music dramas.

As of mid-1873 less than one-fourth of the necessary funds was on hand. The money available was sufficient only to complete the shell of the theater. As August arrived and the frame was finished and the theater topped (2 August 1873), work all but halted. A few days later Wagner, with a fervent plea, turned to his friend and benefactor, Ludwig. The king was receptive to Wagner's request for funds, but he felt that the entire matter had been the composer's doing and that since he had taken no part in the decision, he had no obligation, either contractual or moral, to come to the composer's aid. Although Ludwig desired very much to assist, he was forced to refuse, forced perhaps by a citizenry that was truly concerned about the large sums with which he had favored the composer.

By October the economic situation was such that desperate action of some kind was necessary. Only one-third of the patrons' certificates had been sold, and most of these to Ludwig; the concert tours had done little to help financially; the funds in the project treasury had been depleted; the opposition of the press continued its ever-mounting clamor; the public remained indifferent; Ludwig, on whom Wagner had depended so much in the past, remained on the sidelines, his royal coffers closed. A meeting of some of the leaders of the Wagner Society was called in Bayreuth at which time the composer broached the subject of the possible necessity of boarding up the theater and calling an end to the entire matter. Those present at the meeting studied the situation with care and with grave concern. They did not wish to admit defeat and, after much discussion, agreed that a personal appeal should be made to those most sympathetic to the arts, to those whose livelihood was derived directly from the sale of artistic materials. This appeal for funds was to go to the book, art, and music publishers and vendors throughout Germany. To give the plea the nobility and dignity it merited, Wagner requested that his close friend at the time, Friedrich Nietzsche, write the letter of request. The brilliant young professor eagerly complied. However, when the delegates read the draft that Nietzsche had prepared which he called "Admonition to the Germans," they immediately rejected it because, in their consideration, its wording was too strong an assertion of the weakness of public taste. A second letter of request was written by a less distinguished professor, and it was then forwarded to some four thousand addresses throughout the country. The project was notable only for its failure to raise anything more than a minuscule sum.

Wagner's disappointment was deeply felt. Almost as a last desperate move, he then turned again to the one person into whose purse he had so often before dipped his hand. On 6 November 1873, Wagner addressed a personal plea to Ludwig, an appeal in which the composer, more than any other time, opened himself fully to the monarch. The ever-gentle victim carefully read the master's words. Some six weeks passed without a response. On 6 January 1874, Ludwig forwarded his response to Wagner: The request for additional financial assistance was denied.

As 1874 began, a cessation of work on the Bayreuth project seemed imminent. The theater was but a frame; no work had been done on the all-important interior. Still remaining to be acquired were such things as stage equipment, theatrical machinery, scenery, costumes, and the myriad of miscellaneous but necessary items that are a part of every theatrical house. And there were no funds! With Ludwig's answer vividly etched in his mind, Wagner then attempted to contact several of the royal families of Germany. Convinced as he was that his *Ring* would give the country a true national art, he was equally certain that the nation should lend its support. In mid-January Wagner wrote a most proper but sincere plea to the emperor in a letter in which he proposed that the *Ring* be performed as a celebration of the 1871 unification of all the German kingdoms into one nation. Such a celebration, of course, required financial assistance!

If Wagner's suggestion and request were to receive only passing notice from the royal deputies, his financial woes were soon to be relieved. On January 25 Ludwig wrote again to Wagner. The king had reconsidered the situation, and in yet another gesture of his strong faith in the man he had determined that the festival plan should not fail. Within a month a contract was drawn up which stipulated that Wagner was to receive a large sum (300,000 marks) as a loan to be secured by the equipment it purchased and to be repaid with funds acquired from the sale of certificates, and the receipts from an 1875 premiere of the *Ring*, which Wagner now promised. Although Ludwig's generosity again had rescued Wagner and his plan, he gave firm notice that this latest aid would be his last financial action in behalf of Bayreuth.

Ludwig's loan holds a special significance in the Wagner chronicles. Although every contribution to the Bayreuth project, regardless of amount, was important in and of itself, and it was obvious that additional funds would be needed, the king's benevolence in this instance would take a distinctive place in the Wagner records. The sizable sum that Ludwig bestowed on the composer, and the later rearrangement of the terms of the loan, permitted Wagner to continue his venture and in a very real sense allowed him to advance it sufficiently to envision its successful completion. It is most probable that had Ludwig not come forward at this time with his offer, the *Ring* and the festival theater would not have been realized.

During the turmoil associated with festival matters, Wagner's new home rose as planned, financed in the main through Ludwig's earlier gift. On 28 April 1874, Wagner moved from the villa in which he had been living into *Wahnfriedheim*. He was accompanied by his wife Cosima and their family. A few days later Wagner reduced the name of the home to *Wahnfried*, and he related to Cosima the lines that he had composed to explain why he had chosen this name: "Hier wo mein Wahnen Frieden fand, 'Wahnfried,' sei dieses Haus von mir bennant!" ("Here where my torment found 'Peace from Torment,' so let this house be named by me!") (Some scholars believe that the term *Wahnfried* is a derivation of *Wanfried*, the name of a town in the German state of Hessen.)

Although Wagner had given his new residence a specific name, it was not always as *Wahnfried* that he referred to this house, at least in private. Plagued as he had been during the construction of the building, bothered by the many delays, shortages, errors both of design and of construction, lack of skilled workmen and knowledgeable supervisors, and numerous other problems, the composer frequently called his home *Ärgersheim* (House of Vexation).

Wahnfried had been constructed in accordance with Wagner's design ideas. A marble tablet was placed over the front entrance, and on it was inscribed the name Wagner had chosen. At Cosima's suggestion, a large Nibelung sgraffito of Wagner's design was executed by the Dresden artist Robert Krausse and placed over the front entrance. The central figure of this work was Wotan dressed as the Wanderer, the large brim of his hat covering his right eye. The face of Wotan was a likeness of Ludwig Schnorr (1836–1865), who so successfully performed the role of Tristan at that opera's premiere performance in 1865. Above Wotan's shoulders, one on either side, two ravens descend to bring the news of the world to the King of the Gods. (The Wotan of Teutonic mythology had given an eye to drink at the Spring of Wisdom. When the god roamed the earth as Wanderer, he wore a large-brimmed hat that covered the bad eye and a large, blue cape. The god also carried with him his spear, Gungnir, which guaranteed him victory against any foe at whom he hurled the weapon. The god also had two ravens, Hugin [Thought] and Munin [Memory]. Wotan sent the ravens out into the world each day in order that they could gather the news of the universe for him.) Standing at Wotan's right is a female figure, Tragedy, with the face of Wilhelmine Schröder-Devrient (1804–1860), a singer whom Wagner had first seen perform in 1829 and whose dramatic talents had influenced him greatly in the formation of this ideas regarding acting in musico-dramatic performances. To Wotan's left stands a second female figure, Music, whose resemblance is to Cosima. Between Wotan and Music stands a small boy whose face is that of Wagner's son Siegfried. The boy wears a helmet and carries a sword as he looks up to his mother, Music. (Obviously, the sword and the helmet represent the sword Notung and the Tarnhelm, two dramatic properties that play significant roles in the final text of the *Ring*.) In either upper corner are single dragonlike figures. The entire scene is enclosed in a filigreed framelike border. In front of the house a large, circular grass area was prepared, and there in 1875 a twice-life-size bronze bust of Ludwig was placed on a pedestal.

The remainder of 1874 was a frantic period for Wagner. The orchestration of *Götterdämmerung* was of great concern to him. The supervision of the many details of the construction of the Festival Theater lay on his shoulders. He was continuously in search of singers for the three cycles of the *Ring*, which now was rescheduled for the summer of 1876. There were matters of scenery, costume, and study of the score with some of the musicians who had already agreed to be part of the orchestra. And, of course, he was ever busy, searching for much-needed funds to ensure continuation of the entire project.

The spring of 1875 found Wagner again on concert tours to Vienna, Budapest, Leipzig, Berlin, and other cities. As usual, he was doing all possible to secure financial support. In midyear, during the months of July and August, as specific schedules began to emerge, he worked daily with the singers and musicians whom he had recruited and who had come to Bayreuth for first rehearsals. Yet, over all hung the storm cloud of fiscal disaster that threatened to ruin all he planned. As time passed and conditions worsened, the treasury became so depleted that many people entertained serious doubts that the program could be carried out. King Ludwig, who continued to hold himself outside all these activities, had nevertheless kept himself abreast of the situation. He knew of the financial straits that had again descended on the project, and he was also aware that many people had been working with great intensity to bring the festival idea to successful realization. At the same time, he had never lost his love and admiration of Wagner and his art. Finally, Ludwig tucked his hurt and his disappointments well away from his romantic heart, and despite his statement issued after the loan arranged some nineteen months before, he once again came to Wagner's aid. In September 1875, the king agreed to new terms for the 1874 loan contract: Instead of the payments consisting of all funds received from the sale of certificates, he now would accept a portion of those receipts, the remainder to be available for immediate festival matters. If Ludwig's action essentially guaranteed the continuation of activity, it would not be his last modification of the contract. In late June of the following year, some six weeks before the scheduled performance of the *Ring*, he stipulated that payments on the loan could be deferred until eight hundred certificates had been purchased.

The Festival Theater that Wagner planned was unlike any other theater in the world. It rose on a slight hill, a short distance from the

Haus Wahnfried

Sgraffito at Wahnfried

center of Bayreuth; this site was the third chosen. The first proved to be impractical for construction, and the second was unavailable because of the objection of a local businessman. The theater faced south, its greatest exterior extension being approximately 237 feet (73m) both wide and deep. (In 1925, large storage areas were added to the rear of the stage, lengthening the measurement to 325 feet [100m].) The rafters that supported the roof over the auditorium were 85 feet (26m) above the floor, while those over the stage were 120 feet (37m) above the performance area. Although patterned after the theater that had been planned for Munich a few years earlier, the Festival Theater was constructed as a provisional or temporary building; wood was the primary material, with the outer walls covered with lath and plaster. (Wagner's original idea to allow the government to replace it later with a permanent structure never came to fruition.) That exterior reflected simplicity with minimal decoration and ornamentation.

The interior of the theater was to serve one purpose—the performance. Any element or item that did not contribute directly to that end was excluded. The stage was large: 89 feet (27m) wide, including wings, with a total depth of 115 feet (35m), the front stage 72 feet (22m) and the rear stage 43 feet (13m). The stage of the Festspielhaus sloped toward the auditorium, slightly less than one inch (2.5cm) per foot. Beneath the stage was a work area some 36 feet (11m) in depth. Such was the size of the stage and adjacent areas that scenery could be moved to and from either side of the performance area and raised and lowered as necessary. Wagner had planned carefully for this section of the theater. Because of the numerous scene transitions that he had written into the *Ring* and which he directed should be accomplished without interruption of the performance, he considered such a stage an absolute necessity.

The auditorium also received Wagner's careful attention. He shaped it as an amphitheater, patterned after the Greek theaters, the design of which had always appealed to him. The total seating capacity could accommodate some 1800 persons. (Since Wagner's day construction on the theater has allowed additional seating, totalling today 1925, but there are no tiers, balconies, or boxes.) The seats were arranged in semicircular rows. Each of the thirty-one rows rose in steps from the first to the last, and each row contained more seats than the row before it. The first row contained thirty-two seats and the last, sixty-four. In addition to these seats, intended for patrons, there were places for some three hundred journalists and artists and their families. It is understandable that he included special seating for royalty. This auditorium measured 112 feet (34m) wide and 105 feet (32m) deep. The peaked roof, with an interior covering of sailcloth, was 52 feet (16m) above the seats. Along either side, from the rear to the stage, stood hollow columns that had been constructed for their acoustic qualities. They were placed so as to serve as directional guides for the audience sight line, which was unimpaired from every seat.

The design, the construction, and the materials of the interior of the theater created unparalleled acoustics, which allowed every vocal and instrumental sound to reach and surround every seat holder. It is no doubt true that one of the reasons that no significant alterations have been made to the theater since its construction has been the fear of disturbing the superb acoustics that Wagner achieved. (Air-conditioning was installed during the 1930s, but at that time, the technology was not advanced enough to prevent its operation from interfering with the acoustics. The equipment was soon dismantled and removed. In the late 1980s a less-than-effective cooling system was installed.)

Wagner's intent was to develop a physical arrangement that, as much as possible, would create an ambiance that encouraged total audience interest in the performance. He was eager for complete attention to be focused on the stage. Like the sight line and the absence of distracting decorations, he gave consideration to other details that he believed would help achieve his end. He removed the prompter's box from its traditional location center-stage front and placed it off stage in the right wing, behind the curtain. And, probably to the surprise of the generally talkative and eagerly see-and-be-seen audiences of the day, he directed that the auditorium be totally darkened during the performances, an innovation that has since been adopted by theaters throughout the world.

The most innovative concept that Wagner built into the theater was his plan for the orchestra and its placement. Since his days as Hofkapell-meister in Dresden (1843–1849), he had given much careful consideration to this matter. Two essential factors had always been uppermost in his mind. In the traditional theater the orchestra separated the singers from the audience, and such an arrangement placed the performers and musicians in a competitive situation. Wagner recognized a dramatic futility in such an arrangement, especially in regard to his *Ring*. Only he understood how his large orchestra and the intense symphonic score he was creating for it could cause great artistic harm to even the finest of performances by the most accomplished of singers. His second concern was directly related to the first. The usual placement of the orchestra not only affected the performance itself but also distracted the audience. The movement of the musicians as they played and the motions of the conductor as he led provided constant physical as well as psychological competition with the dramatic action. To resolve the two problems created by the traditional orchestral placement, Wagner wished to create an "invisible orchestra." The conventional orchestral pit thereupon became just that, a *pit* that began in front of the first row of seats and sloped downward toward the stage to a depth of 16 feet (5m). He then extended the stage outward to cover many of the musicians and erected a curved wooden partition, which he called a *Schalldeckel* (also *Schalldekke*), a "sound reflector," between the audience and the orchestra; this partition extended from the floor to well above the conductor's head. This "mystical abyss," as it came to be known, not only hid the orchestra and its activities from audience view, but also brought the action on the stage closer to the audience. The maximum depth of this orchestra pit was 33 feet (10m). As Wagner had envisioned, the music now rose from the pit to surround the listeners instead of being played directly at them as before, and the physical distractions created by the conductor and the musicians were out of the audience's view. (Some time after the successful introduction of the orchestra that could not be seen, Wagner quipped that inasmuch as he had devised an invisible orchestra, now he could make theater even better if he could design an invisible stage.) Although Wagner has received rightful credit and distinction for the utilitarian design of the musicians' playing space, and dramatic use of the invisible orchestra, he cannot rightfully be credited as the originator of that significant concept. Such acknowledgement must go to André Grétry (1741–1813), a distinguished Belgian essayist, and the foremost composer of French light opera of his time. In the lengthy account of his numerous musical compositions Grétry wrote:

> I would wish to have a small theater, one which seats at most a thousand persons....I would have the orchestra hidden, out of sight, so that neither the musicians nor the lights on their music stands could be seen by the audience. The effect would be magical because no one would suspect that the orchestra was so placed. I believe that it is necessary to isolate the orchestra in the theater, and to that end a sound-wall should be built in order that the music reverberate up and throughout the theater.[2]

Wagner knew of Grétry and his music (the Belgian receives at least two

---

[2] *Memoires, ou Essais sur la Musique.* Paris: L'Imprimerie de la Republique, 1797. Vol. III, 32–33. Grétry also presents some details about his ideal theater, a depiction that could readily become a serviceable generalized blueprint for Wagner's Bayreuth Festspielhaus!

Orchestra pit in the Festival Theater

mentions in Cosima Wagner's *Diaries*), but he never indicated that he had read any of the composer's prose writings.

By 1876 Wagner had built his Festival Theater, and in that same year it housed the first performance of his Nibelung music drama. However, despite his indefatigable determination and the ceaseless efforts of a small group of dedicated workers, economic uncertainty hovered ever present over Bayreuth. At the close of the first festival the deficit was so large (almost 150,000 marks) that Wagner was very anxious about the necessary repayment. In a sincere effort to, satisfy this debt, he conceived no less than three plans to raise the needed funds: (1) the Bavarian government would acquire all properties and production rights and then, in conjunction with the Munich Opera, would determine performance schedules; (2) a worldwide society of patrons would be established to support the festival; and/or (3) he would declare bankruptcy, sell all the Bayreuth properties including his home, and make an arrangement to emigrate to the United States, with all funds received to be applied to the debt. Ludwig quickly rejected the suggestion that the government acquire the Wagner properties. The proposed society of patrons failed to produce the needed subscribers. (In August of 1882, six years after the premiere of the *Ring*, the *Patronatverein* was officially dissolved and the Festival Theater was then to be controlled by an administrative committee.) However, even if Wagner had considered seriously the idea of leaving Germany and settling on foreign soil, such a possibility greatly grieved his royal friend. Ludwig would not be parted from Wagner and the Wagnerian art. In a final magnanimous gesture of financial support, the "Dream King" made arrangements to satisfy the entire deficit. In late March 1878 yet another contract was drawn up among Ludwig, Wagner, and the festival management: The royal court would pay all festival debts, and repayment of the interest-bearing loan would be made on a regular basis. (The total cost of the theater and the *Ring* premiere was approximately 1,300,000 marks, with some 175,000 marks for the artists.)

In the end, then, it was Ludwig who saved Bayreuth for the world. (Of the total sum expended for the entire Bayreuth project, the king of Bavaria provided some eighty percent.) If his generosity allowed the properties to remain under Wagner's hand, indirectly it also permitted the founding of a now-popular artistic reality, the summer-festival concept. Although Ludwig's final loan preserved Bayreuth for posterity, it did not relieve Wagner of a large debt. The composer worked diligently to meet this financial obligation. He pledged personal income from his royalties and his conducting fees while Cosima volunteered the inheritance she had received through her mother. As late as 1900, seventeen years after the composer's death, the Wagner family was still doing everything possible to reduce the debt.

Upon Wagner's death in 1883, the property and the administration of the festival passed to Cosima. A devoted disciple of her husband's ideas, it was she—more than anyone else—who developed the tradition of the Bayreuth Festival and nursed it into the institution it is today. Although Cosima lived until 1930, her poor health forced her more and more to turn to their son Siegfried, who administered the festival from 1906 until his death in 1930. Upon Siegfried's death, his wife, the English-born Winifred Williams (1897–1980), assumed control of Bayreuth. In 1945, as a consequence of World War II and partly because of Winifred's association with Adolph Hitler, the American military government took over the properties. Several years with much litigation followed, and in 1949, after three years of trials and appeals, the Allied forces, working with the Bavarian government and the council at Bayreuth, agreed to restore the properties and the administration of Bayreuth to the Wagner family. A condition of the arrangement was that Siegfried's widow could no longer participate in any manner in festival matters. On February 28, 1949, Siegfried's sons and Richard Wagner's grandchildren, Wieland and Wolfgang, became executive directors of the festival and the property. Two years later, after being inoperative for seven years, the festival was revived, the Festival Theater was opened, and the *Ring* was again performed in Bayreuth. Wieland died on 17 October 1966, and, in accordance with the terms of the court agreement, his younger brother, Wolfgang, became the executive director of the Bayreuth Festival. In 1973, both the theater and Wahnfried were purchased from the Wagner family by the Richard Wagner Foundation, which consisted of numerous groups as members, including the Federal Republic of Germany, the city of Bayreuth, and Friends of Bayreuth and members of the Wagner Society. The Foundation now chooses the Director of the Festspielhaus and its programs, with preference to be given to a member of the Wagner family provided that the individual has the relevant qualifications. The Director retains artistic independence, but also assumes financial responsibility. The Foundation is governed by an overall principal factor: Only the works of Richard Wagner may be performed in the Festspielhaus. Three years later the festival celebrated its centenary with a controversial production of the *Ring* in the Festspielhaus, which, except for some structural strengthening and regular maintenance, was still the theater that Richard Wagner had built for the first performance of his *Ring*. In that same year Wahnfried, which upon the death of Wieland had ceased to be the principal residence of the Wagner family, was opened to the public as the Richard Wagner Museum and as a center for study and research on matters Wagnerian.

In 1979, Wagner's library was donated to the Richard Wagner Archive in Bayreuth. This was the library that Wagner had begun in 1843, and which he was forced to abandon in 1849 when he fled into exile. This library, which contained the work of numerous classical, medieval, and contemporary authors as well as source material of the German epic, had been reassembled over time, and once together, was placed in the large library room of Wahnfried, a room that looks out across the rear yard to the gravesite of Cosima and Richard Wagner.

Performances of Wagner's works in the Festival Theater are regularly sold out. In an average year, the administration of the Theater will receive some 250,000 requests from over seventy countries for tickets to the performances that are usually scheduled for the last two weeks of July and the month of August. Throughout the year there are some 50 regular employees, most of whom work for prestige rather than for high wages.

Richard Wagner conceived and built the Festspielhaus and established the festival at Bayreuth. In so doing, he literally set the stage for an artistic tradition that today stands firm in the mind and heart of every devotee of the composer and his art. The international public's enthusiasm for Bayreuth is, perhaps, puzzling to the Wagner initiate who senses, but as yet does not comprehend the magnetism of the man and his art, which after more than one hundred years enigmatically continues to draw followers to the Wagnerian fold. Albert Schweitzer, philosopher, physician, music scholar, humanitarian, Nobel Prize winner (1952), and ardent student of the Wagner art, summed up most succinctly what Bayreuth and Wagner have meant to the world. In a letter addressed to Wieland and Wolfgang in 1951 shortly after the resumption of the festival, Schweitzer wrote:

> Bayreuth is not music, but the experience of emotion and exaltation through the ideas above earthly existence, ideas which have been given form in the dramas of Richard Wagner.[3]

---

[3] Quoted in Skelton, *Wagner at Bayreuth*, 164.

Chapter Seven

First Performances of the *Ring*

7.1 BAYREUTH

On 13 August 1876, at 5:00 P.M., the curtain rose in the Festival Theater in Bayreuth, Germany, on the first performance of Richard Wagner's *Der Ring des Nibelungen*. Before the month had ended, three complete cycles would be presented: August 13–17, August 20–23, and August 27–30. For some twenty-eight years Wagner had struggled to give form to his artistic ideas, first in the composition of the monumental drama, then in its music, then in the construction of a theater in which the work could be performed. With his music drama and his theater essentially in hand, he had then labored to instruct, to train, and to rehearse the enormous staff of singers, musicians, and technicians. The fruits of his arduous labors, at last, had come before the public eye.

Wagner had begun active work on the production some four years before the premiere. Long before he had completed the composition of the music of the last of the four dramas, he had started to scour Germany for singers. During this extensive search he often invited artists to Bayreuth for testing to ascertain to what extent they would be able to meet his exacting and very distinct vocal and dramatic standards. Wagner had long been concerned with the matters of performance. He believed that the artistic standards for singers in Germany were atrociously low, that singers' training, if any, had been diffuse and of a more harmful than beneficial kind. He considered them to be even

Bühnenfestspielhaus
in Bayreuth.

Aufführungen am 13.—17., 20.—24. u. 27.—30. August

von

Richard Wagner's Tetralogie
Der Ring des Nibelungen.

Erster Abend: Rheingold.

Personen:

Wotan,		Herr Betz von Berlin.
Donner,	Götter	„ Eilers v. Coburg.
Froh,		„ Unger v. Bayreuth.
Loge,		„ Vogl v. München.
Fasolt,	Riefen	„ Eilers v. Coburg.
Fafner,		„ Reichenberg v. Schwerin.
Alberich,	Nibelungen	„ Hill v. Schwerin.
Mime,		„ Schlosser v. München.
Freia,		Frl. Grün von Coburg.
Freia,	Göttinnen	Frl. Haupt von Cassel.
Erda,		Frl. Jaide v. Darmstadt.
Woglinde,		Frl. Lehmann I v. Berlin.
Wellgunde,	Rheintöchter	„ Lehmann II v. Berlin.
Flosshilde,		„ Lammert v. Berlin.

Nibelungen
Ort der Handlung: 1. In die Tiefe des Rheines.
2. Freie Gegend auf Bergeshöhen a. Rhein.
3. Die unterirdischen Klüfte Nibelheims.

Zweiter Abend: Walküre.

Personen:

Siegmund		Herr Niemann von Berlin.
Hunding		„ Niering von Darmstadt.
Wotan		„ Betz von Berlin.
Sieglinde		Frl. Scheffzky von München.
Brünnhilde		Fr. Materna von Wien.
Frida		Fr. Grün von Coburg.

Acht Walküren.
Ort der Handlung: 1. Das Innere der Wohnung Hundings.
2. Wildes Felsengebirge.
3. Auf dem Brünnhildenstein.

Dritter Abend: Siegfried.

Personen:

Siegfried		Herr Unger v. Bayreuth.
Mime		„ Schlosser v. München.
Der Wanderer		
Alberich		„ Hill v. Schwerin.
Fafner		„ Reichenberg v. Schwerin.
Erda		Fr. Jaide v. Darmstadt.
Brünnhilde		Fr. Materna von Wien.

Ort der Handlung: 1. Eine Felsenhöhle im Walde.
2. Tiefer Wald.
3. Wilde Gegend am Felsenberg.

Vierter Abend: Götterdämmerung.

Personen:

Siegfried		Herr Unger v. Bayreuth.
Gunther		„ Gura von Leipzig.
Hagen		„ Kögl v. Hamburg.
Alberich		„ Hill v. Schwerin.
Brünnhilde		Fr. Materna von Wien.
Gutrune		Frl. Weckerlin von Berlin.
Waltraute		Fr. Jaide v. Darmstadt.
Die Nornen.		
Die Rheintöchter.		

Mannen. Frauen.
Ort der Handlung: 1. Auf dem Felsen der Walküren.
2. Gunther's Hofhalle am Rhein.
Der Walkürenfelsen.
3. Vor Gunther's Halle.
4. Waldige Gegend am Rhein.
Gunther's Halle.

Eintritts-Karten (⅓ Patronatschein) zu beziehen durch den

Kölner Richard Wagner-Verein.

Newspaper announcement
First performances of *Der Ring des Nibelungen*, 1876
(after a photocopy)

100

less qualified as actors. As early as 1834, when he was only twenty-one years old, he was already commenting on the ineffectiveness of the performer in opera. He believed that the singer, in his or her desire to be heard, would undertake any vocal assignment without due attention to the physical and artistic limitations of his or her vocal capabilities. Wagner echoed the same sentiment in 1837 when he wrote that singers thrust themselves into performances too quickly, without having given the necessary attention to technique. Lack of preparation, in a total sense, he maintained, accounted not only for less-than-acceptable performances, but also for early voice deterioration. Wagner believed that singers, in concentrating on voice and vocal distinction, had lost their grasp of the importance of the words in a performance, both the meaning those words conveyed and their intimate relationship with the music. Even if such was the state of the vocal side of operatic art, the blame, Wagner believed, did not lie fully with the singers. Audiences, he believed, were essentially the culprits through their lack of artistic concern. In his view, the public was undemanding; it had set no standards, or at least only minimal ones. In its undiscerning approach to drama and to music, public taste had become accustomed to frivolousness; it was more attuned to fad and fancy, to vocal gymnastics, than to great art. At this level of public expectation singers were called upon to perform an inordinate number of roles, often hurriedly and without adequate preparation, giving little consideration to the artistic demands of these roles. Such performances, then, could only be mechanical and perfunctory.

It was for the improvement of singers and their techniques that Wagner envisioned his "music school." Under his training, singers would learn the proper use of their voices, the relationship between the words and the music, the objective of acting in opera, in short, the true role of the singer in the musico-dramatic performance. Wagner achieved the first step in the foundation of his music school in 1865 when Ludwig II decreed that such an institution would be built in Munich. It did not come to fruition, however, because Wagner's less than acceptable life style had forced the king to remove him from that city; and now, in 1872, still firmly holding onto his beliefs, he was searching Germany for singers who, under his personal training, could undertake the complex interpretations of the *Ring*.

During the next four years Wagner would spend much time with many singers. Such was his stature as a composer, combined with the growing interest in the massive project of the *Ring* production, that there was no dearth of interested performers. This interest prevailed despite the fact that Wagner had made it known that his singers would receive no fee for their services. He had stated that only living costs in Bayreuth would be assumed by the festival because he believed that any artist who demanded a fee would not have the proper temperament to accept the training he required, and without this schooling such persons would be unsuitable for any role of the drama. Wagner held that enthusiasm for one's work and the right temperament were requirements, particularly for the *Ring*, this music drama that was essentially a national work of art. Compensation would come in the form of the pleasure and the honor of participation. Few of the prominent singers of the day hesitated to comply with Wagner's demands, and one of the Bayreuth traditions was established: Bayreuth became, and remains today, the mecca for singers of Wagner's works for whom the fee was and is secondary.

Wagner's training procedure was relatively simple. The first requirement was that the artist carefully study the complete drama to learn what lay in the character of the role to be interpreted. The composer opposed mere memorization of the text. Rather, he wanted his singers to know the meaning of the words, to understand their vital part in the drama, and to feel their full impact. Once the singer had reached the point of total comprehension and understanding, he would then feel "natural"; he and his role would become one and the same; each would be part and parcel of the other. Then, but only then, the singer was the character. Once this state had been achieved, attention could then be given to the music. The singer began the second phase of study with work on diction and enunciation. Wagner demanded that every word be sung; there was to be no recitative, no declamatory singing. Every word was to be sung cleanly and clearly, every syllable was to receive precise and accurate pronunciation. To accompany this mode of delivery and to facilitate it, careful attention must be given to each and every note of the music as written. There was no leeway for personal modification of the music. If some notes were of less importance in the music than others, each had its role in the total music; and, Wagner maintained, attention to these minor notes would permit the major ones to come more naturally, more easily.

As a person of total theater, Wagner also had ideas regarding acting. He objected strongly to what had become acceptable acting in the productions of his day. He denounced the "singer-aria-ego" and the false and artificial physical gesture that was the result of such an approach. He believed that his insistence on comprehension of the text and understanding of the music, and the requirement of clear diction, permitted the singer to become an integral part of the drama, a participant in the drama, not merely an actor in a play. If a player understood thoroughly the essence of a role as revealed through text and music, there was no need "to act" because movement, gesture, and expression would be spontaneous and natural, all arising out of the player and, hence, an accurate portrait of the character. This form of acting, this physical expression that was to be totally integrated and fused with the drama and the music, became known as the Bayreuth Style. After the composer's death, Cosima, so desirous to comply with her husband's directions, converted Wagner's ideas into a rigid and almost inflexible code of prescribed movement for every musical aspect of the music drama.

By 1874 work on the festival was well underway. Wagner concerned himself with every detail of the project, physical as well as artistic. The constant supervision of the construction of the theater required much of his time as did the endless labors of raising funds. He worked at some length with his scene and costume designers. He was in constant contact with the designers and the manufacturers of the elaborate equipment and machinery so essential to a successful production. He supervised the work of a group of devoted musicians, humorously known as the *Nibelungenkanzlei* (Nibelung Chancery), who were copying the music of the *Ring* and preparing the instrumental scores for the orchestra. (The group was also known by a term that Wagner conceived: *Kopisterei* [copyistery].) He was busy engaging singers and personally guiding, instructing, and teaching the intricacies of his score to them and to the musicians who, at their own expense, came to Bayreuth to receive their indoctrination from the master himself. Having firmly settled the point in his own mind that he could go forward, Wagner then announced that scheduled rehearsals of the *Ring* would commence the following summer.

During the first months of 1875 Wagner conducted several concerts as a means of raising funds. As he traveled, his eye and ear were always alert for potential singers. Upon his return to Bayreuth he again became active in the training of several singers who, at his invitation, had traveled to Bayreuth. In midyear, as scheduled, the rehearsals began. On June 24 the huge assembly of singers, musicians, technicians, and craftsmen gathered, first to view the scenery and equipment that was to bring about the unusual effects called for in the drama, then to get on with the work for which they had been selected. The month of July was devoted to a read-through of the *Ring*, which was then followed by a piano study of the numerous roles. On the first day of August the orchestra, which consisted of the finest of Germany's musicians, entered Wagner's "mystical abyss" to test the acoustics of the theater. Wagner's design had worked well; all marveled at the superb sound that flooded the theater. Cosima, in her diary of that date, recorded that Franz Betz, the Wotan of the drama, reacted with these words, "Vollendet der Bau" ("The structure is finished"). Betz's words were a paraphrase of those sung by Wotan in *Das Rheingold* when he sees the magnificent Valhalla for the first time: "Vollendet das ewige Werk" ("The eternal work is achieved"). These initial rehearsals continued through August 12, and fifteen days later Wagner announced the schedule of dates for the festival program of the following year.

The summer had been long and tiring for Wagner. However, he lost no time in turning to other aspects of the Bayreuth project. Casting for the *Ring* was still incomplete, and the matter was further complicated by the necessity of certain changes in the cast already engaged. All the while, work continued on the still unfinished theater. The scenery, the costumes, and the machinery were in varying stages of completion, and the numerous concerns natural to such conditions took much of Wagner's time. Clouded money matters continued to plague him.

During the last months of 1875 and in the Spring of the following year, Wagner was again engaged in fund-raising tours. As a means of stimulating interest, his concerts included music from the fourth music drama of the *Ring* which he had completed the year before. He also supervised a production of *Tannhäuser* and one of *Lohengrin* in Vienna and later one of *Tristan und Isolde* in Berlin. As usual, during these travels he was doing all possible to round out the still incomplete cast of the *Ring*. Time was short; the pace was maddeningly fast; the responsibilities were awesome.

As of May 1876, the festival was in a state of chaos. As preparations for full rehearsals were being concluded, additional problems began to surface. The anxiety stimulated by the approach of the scheduled performance magnified the seriousness of even the slightest of unresolved matters. Yet, there were major festival concerns that did demand attention: The auditorium was unfinished; much work was yet to be done on the stage; the roof leaked; the scaffolding throughout the interior of the building was still in place; some of the stage machinery did not function properly; some of the equipment was not yet on hand (the neck of the Dragon would never arrive, having been shipped by its manufacturer, Richard Keene of Wadsworth, England, to *Beirut*, Lebanon); the gas lighting was inoperative; the matters of the company's lodging and food service were still to be resolved; some of the roles in the drama had not yet been assigned; some of the cast members were having difficulty in securing leave from their home companies or release from their contractual commitments; illness caused some singers and musicians to withdraw, and there was one death. As is seemingly customary among performing artists, there were the usual ego drives, bickering, displays of temperament, jealousies, and even one love-affair, all of which contributed to the physical and mental chaos. Serious matters, separate from the festival, threatened the entire project: The press continued its diatribe against Wagner and the festival; there was concern that the townspeople were going to overcharge the visitors for goods and services; fear of impending war was growing; the chronic shortage of funds became more serious because of confusion over a reevaluation of the national currency, in spite of Ludwig's relaxation of the terms of his loan contract against the income derived from the sale of patron's certificates; the rumor of a typhoid epidemic among the soldiers stationed at Bayreuth was quickly seized upon by the press and used to stifle the festival, the result of which was a sudden decrease in the sale of certificates, a sale that even before the rumor's circulation had been moving slowly.

Despite the shadow of cancellation that shrouded Bayreuth, the rehearsals of the *Ring* began. During May there were tests of whatever equipment and machinery were on hand. Certain of the artists arrived at Bayreuth to undertake preliminary work on their roles. During this period, Wagner worked at great length, almost daily, with his Siegfried. On June 3, with most of the company now present, the first of the full orchestra rehearsals was held. Two days later, on 5 June 1876, the rehearsals of the music drama began. The work schedule included four phases:

June 5–July 12	First run-throughs with blocking and much interpretative direction and instruction from Wagner. (Two or three days were devoted to each act as the dramas were studied in the order of their intended presentation.) These rehearsals were usually carried out with piano, but occasionally the orchestra, which was rehearsing separately, was used.
July 14–26	More intense rehearsals of the dramas, generally with orchestra, one act each day, starting with *Das Rheingold*.
July 27–August 3	Costume fitting, followed by rehearsal with orchestra, costumes, and some scenery, one drama each day.
August 6–9	Final, full rehearsals, one drama each day with full orchestra, scenery, and costumes.

The preparations for the *Ring* performances had begun with a large, enthusiastic staff. As the days passed and the intensity of the work increased, the strains and pressures began to take their toll. Conflicts surfaced. Members of the cast set upon one another; friction was rampant as tempers flared and arguments, some quite violent, broke into the open. Wagner continuously argued, fought, yelled, cursed, jested, mocked, jibed, and cajoled, never relaxing his strict demands that his standards of performance be met. Almost miraculously, the rehearsals continued through June and July.

On July 23, the committee of local citizens that had been appointed to manage the theater advertised that a dress rehearsal with full sets and costumes would be held and that the public was invited. Entrance tickets were priced quite minimally, and all had been sold within an hour's time. Needless to say, Wagner, who had been unaware of the plan, was furious. The banker Feustel was quite pleased with the idea and even more delighted with the sum of money that would come into the operating fund.

The final rehearsals of the *Ring* began on August 6. These rehearsals were essentially much like actual performances, complete in every detail. Wagner had intended it to be so, for however much he desired that all aspects of his work be ready for public presentation, he was also concerned for a single figure whom he had allowed to enter the theater and who sat quietly alone in the royal box. To avoid both public and publicity, King Ludwig II of Bavaria had arrived in the early hours of that morning; his attachment to the art of Richard Wagner would no longer be denied. This meeting of Wagner and the King was their first since 1868. (At these rehearsals, the king was the only audience during the performance of *Das Rheingold*. The acoustics of the empty house were less than satisfactory, and the audience of local citizens was admitted to the rehearsals of the three remaining music dramas.) Friedrich Nietzsche, who was long an admirer of Wagner's music, but who soon was to decry both the man and his art, had been present for much of the last rehearsal.

On August 9 all preparations came to an end. The *Ring*, in whatever form it now existed, was to have its opening curtain in four days. A long and trying time was at an end. Through it all, however, there was Wagner who, if always an irritant, was the creative genius for all at hand. His mind, his thought, his talent, his insight, and his art lay at the root of everything, and in the end he prevailed. The hundreds of persons charged with the execution of this unprecedented project were not unmindful of their roles in this historic event and of the singular honor that was theirs through their participation. Richard Wagner was indeed the *Meister*, and it was for him and with him that they closed ranks as they approached the final goal.

On the eve of the premiere, Wagner, ever the teacher, posted his last memo to the company:

Last Request
to my faithful artists
¡Distinctness!

The big notes will take care of themselves; the little notes and their text are the chief thing. Never say anything to the public [audience], but always look at each other; in the monologues look either up or down, but never directly in front of you.

Last Wish:
Be good to me, you dear children.[1]

The following night, 13 August 1876, the world witnessed the rising of the first curtain of *Der Ring des Nibelungen*. The original schedule had announced that the music dramas would be presented on four consecutive evenings, but this program was not followed. After the performance of *Die Walküre* on the second night, the *Ring*'s Siegfried stated that he was suffering from hoarseness and the program had to be postponed one day. On August 17 the curtain was lowered on the first *Ring* Cycle, and Wagner's dream of twenty-eight years was now reality. (The cast and principals of the premiere performance of the *Ring* are provided in Table 6.)

The audience at this first complete *Ring* Cycle was an illustrious mixture of prominent figures. Among those first viewers of the drama were assorted royalty, dignitaries, diplomats, writers, painters, critics, actors, singers, composers, and intellectuals. Heading the list of celebrities of national importance was Emperor Wilhelm, who was amazed at the miracle that Wagner had wrought, despite the refusal of the German government to offer any financial aid. Also present were the king of Württemberg; Prince Liechtenstein; Prince Wilhelm of Hessen; the grand dukes of Weimar, Schwerin and Micklenburg; the grand duchess of Baden; and the duke of Anhalt. Foreign leaders in the audience included Dom Pedro II, emperor of Brazil, and Prince Wladimir of Russia. (The kedive of Egypt and Sultan Abdul Azir of Turkey had purchased patron's certificates, but the former did not attend, and the sultan had been deposed nine weeks before the premiere.) The composers who witnessed the premiere of the *Ring* included Franz Liszt, Peter Ilyich Tchaikovsky,

[1] Quoted in *The Story of Bayreuth as Told in the Letters of Richard Wagner*. Trans. Kerr, 249.

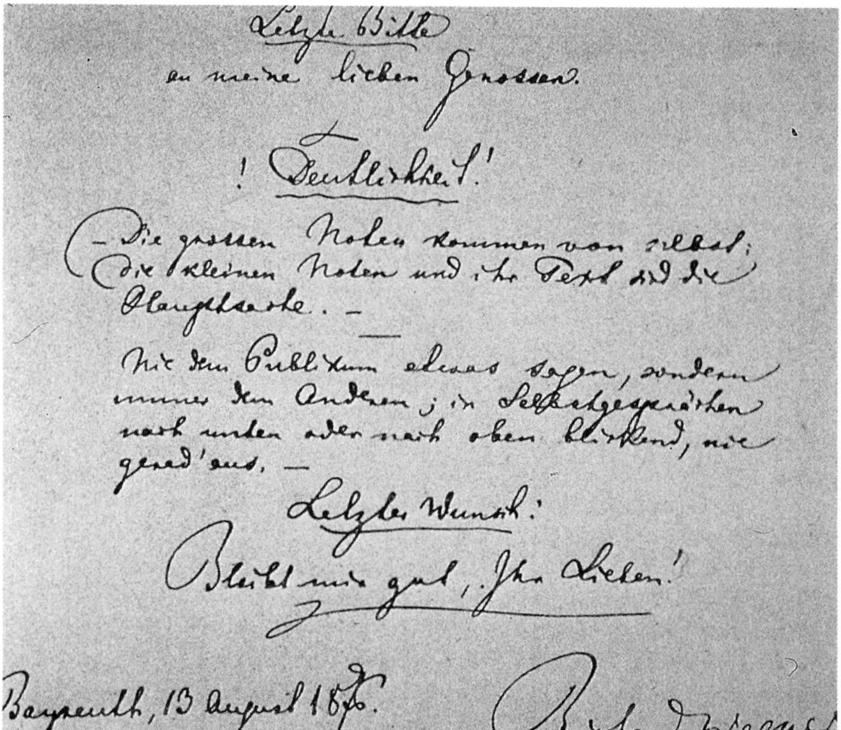

Letzte Bitte
an meine lieben Genossen.

! Deutlichkeit !

— Die grossen Noten kommen von selbst; die kleinen Noten und ihr Text sind die Hauptsache. —

Nie dem Publikum etwas sagen, sondern immer dem Anderen; in Selbstgesprächen nach unten oder nach oben blickend, nie gerad' aus. —

Letzter Wunsch:
Bleibt mir gut, Ihr Lieben!

Bayreuth, 13 August 1876. Richard Wagner

Wagner's *Last Request*

Table 6
Cast and Principals—Premiere Performance—*Der Ring des Nibelungen* August 13, 14, 16, 17, 1876 —Festival Theater—Bayreuth, Germany

	Das Rheingold	Die Walküre	Siegfried	Götter- dämmerung
Lilli Lehmann	Woglinde	Helmwige	—	Woglinde
Marie Lehmann	Wellgunde	Ortlinde	—	Wellgunde
Marie Lammert	Flosshilde	Rossweisse	—	Flosshilde
Karl Hill	Alberich	—	Alberich	Alberich
Friederike Sadler-Grün	Fricka	Fricka	—	3rd Norn
Franz Betz	Wotan	Wotan	Wanderer	—
Marie Haupt	Freia	Gerhilde	Forest Bird	—
Albert Eilers	Fasolt	—	—	—
Franz von Reichenberg	Fafner	—	Dragon	—
Georg Unger	Froh	—	Siegfried	Siegfried
Eugen Gura	Donner	—	—	Gunther
Heinrich Vogl	Loge	—	—	—
Karl Schlosser	Mime	—	Mime	—
Luise Jäide	Erda	Waltraute	Erda	Waltraute
Albert Niemann	—	Siegmund	—	—
Josephine Scheffzky	—	Sieglinde	—	2nd Norn
Josef Niering	—	Hunding	—	—
Amalia Materna	—	Brünnhilde	Brünnhilde	Brünnhilde
Antoinie Amann	—	Siegrune	—	—
Hedwig Reicher-Kindermann	—	Grimgerde	—	—
Johanna Jachmann-Wagner	—	Schwertleite	—	1st Norn
Gustav Siehr	—	—	—	Hagen
Mathilde Weckerlin	—	—	—	Gutrune

Chorus of 28 men and 9 women

Conductor	Hans Richter
Scenery	Josef Hoffmann
	Executed by Max and Gotthold Brückner
Costumes	Karl Emil Döpler
Stage Machinery	Karl Brandt
Choreography	Richard Fricke
Concertmaster	August Wilhelmj
Music Assistants	Franz Fischer
	Emmerich Kastner
	Demetrius Lalas
	Felix Mottl
	Josef Rubenstein
	Anton Seidl
	Hermann Zimmer
	Hermann Zumpe

Note: For brief notes on cast and principals, see Appendix B.

Camille Saint-Saëns, Edvard Grieg, and Anton Bruckner. Saint-Saëns attended the second cycle that summer and later wrote a series of articles for a French publication. The French composer also attended a reception in Wagner's home on August 24, at which he played several piano selections. (Saint-Saëns also attended the premiere in 1882 of Wagner's last music drama, *Parsifal*.) Others who were in attendance included Eduard Hanslick, a Viennese lawyer and influential music critic who had little good to say about the *Ring*, and Sir Charles Villiers Stanford, Irish composer and Professor of Composition at the Royal College of Music. Also in the audience were Otto and Mathilde Wesendonck; it was Otto who had befriended Wagner rather generously in earlier years while Wagner carried on an affair with the wealthy merchant's wife. Ludwig II returned for the third cycle and later inquired if a fourth cycle could be given!

The audience, which did not entirely match Wagner's artistic ideal, nevertheless was generous with its ovation. After the final curtain, Wagner came on-stage to speak briefly. He proclaimed that what the audience had seen and heard was a work of true national German art, one that he had created for the fatherland. He added that it was now a concern for the State and the people to nurture that art. Following the premiere, numerous banquets and receptions were held as the talk about Wagner, the *Ring*, and Bayreuth spread beyond the limits of the Bavarian city into all of Germany and then throughout the world.

On the negative side, the arrangements surrounding the *Ring*'s introduction to the world were by no means ideal. Although the town of Bayreuth had bedecked itself to welcome the distinguished audiences, it had not prepared itself in other ways: guests were inconvenienced by inadequate lodging facilities, food service was minimal, transportation to the theater was almost nonexistent, and the return to town in the dark along a barren, unlighted roadway irritated many people. The Festspielhaus itself, the most talked-of theater in the world, was less than ready to receive people. There was no foyer and the audiences were forced to remain outside before the performances and during intermissions. (This feature remains today as part of the Festival Theater.) No water was available inside, and the lighting failed repeatedly. The performances, too, had their weak moments: Some of the scenery was inadequate; stage hands erred in some of the scene transformations; equipment was lacking, and some machinery failed to function; at times some of the singers experienced vocal failure. At the same time, the audience's deportment did not meet Wagner's expectations. If he had anticipated behavior that was different from that of other audiences of his time, he was disappointed. It was apparent that many people were interested in viewing those in attendance as well as in being seen by others; there was incessant talk and laughter; and, in violation of Wagner's standards of proper audience etiquette, they committed the sin of sins against art when *they applauded during the performance!* Many of the singers became angry when no curtain calls were allowed.

If there were imperfections in this first performance of the *Ring*, they were those natural to new theatrical productions. What stands above any detail of criticism is an historic moment in the annals of creative man, an occasion when a masterpiece is presented to the world. Bayreuth is the symbol of one such moment. But in 1876 more than memorable music and drama were introduced; a tradition was born. Today, after more than one hundred years during which both the *Ring* and the traditions it established have been tried in numerous ways, each reflective of the interpretations of ever-changing cultures and societies, the music drama and the traditions of Bayreuth remain intact. Wagner's *Ring* is, in the modern era, a reflection of all that is Bayreuth, and Bayreuth is the symbol for Richard Wagner.

7.2 EUROPE

Within very few years after the premiere of the *Ring*, the music drama would be performed extensively in Europe. These many productions and their successes would come about essentially from the efforts of one person. However, immediately after the first performance in Bayreuth, Wagner announced that he wished to contract for a second festival the following year. Within a short time of this announcement, he realized that his plan could not be carried out. There were several reasons that convinced the composer of that reality, the principal one being the large debt that still remained from the 1876 festival. It has been estimated that the first *Ring* festival incurred a debt of approximately 150,000 marks, a sum that did not include the 200,000 marks that were needed to repay Ludwig for his earlier loan. (In 1878, and again in 1880, Ludwig modified some of the terms of the loan, in Wagner's favor, as usual.) To alleviate his financial problems, Wagner agreed immediately after the festival to conduct a series of concerts in London's Prince Albert Hall. Originally, twenty programs were contracted for May 1877, but only eight were realized. Wagner had brought with him a large retinue of musicians and singers from Bayreuth. If there was a profit of some 700 pounds, the venture turned into a loss because of Wagner's overdraft of some 1200 pounds! (As history would show, the Festival Theater was to remain closed until the premiere of *Parsifal* in 1882, and the *Ring* would not be produced there again until 1896, then under the guidance of Wagner's widow.)

During the first months of 1877, as he prepared for his London concerts, Wagner was occupied with requests from numerous cities throughout Europe for production rights to his *Ring*.[2] The composer was quite cautious as he sought to place his *Ring* where it would be financially advantageous. After rejecting a number of requests, he decided that he would grant production rights for the drama to three cities: to Vienna, to Munich for southern Germany, and to Leipzig for northern Germany. Wagner looked upon Vienna with a certain nostalgia. He remembered that it was in that city in 1861 that he had heard his *Lohengrin* for the first time since he had completed it thirteen years earlier. He also recalled the resounding ovation he had received and how that enthusiasm had been contained only when he addressed the audience from his box. (If Vienna had clamored for the *Ring* for its Staatsoper, its production of the tetralogy was something less than immediate, and then, not in cyclic form: *Die Walküre*, 1877; *Das Rheingold* and *Siegfried*, 1878; *Götterdämmerung*, 1879.) Munich, which witnessed its first *Ring* cycle in 1878, was a logical choice for the tetralogy because it was the capital city of Bavaria and the seat of the government of Ludwig II. Although Leipzig, which saw its first production of the *Ring* during the first week in January 1878, was the city of Wagner's birth, the choice of that location for exclusive production of his music drama was more directly the result of the work of the spirited impresario Angelo Neumann (1838–1910).

In 1876, the Austrian-born Neumann, a baritone formerly with the Vienna Opera and an admirer of Wagner, had produced *Lohengrin* in Leipzig where he had served as Director of the Leipzig Opera. Neumann's production was well received by both the critics and the public. Neumann then approached Wagner regarding the production rights to the *Ring*. Wagner, aware of Neumann's work on *Lohengrin*, soon saw in the young producer a man of his own stamp; he admired Neumann's administrative abilities as well as the artistic talents he had shown as a director. The *Ring* went to Neumann and to Leipzig.

---

[2] The copyright laws of Wagner's day were at best a confusing jumble of numerous conditions that varied from region to region. However, in the main, a principal element consisted of a permanent right that a composer granted to a specific theater to produce a given work. Whatever payment by the two parties agreed upon for this right was a single payment! This irrevocable "right" permitted the theater to produce the work when, and for whatever number of performances, the theater administration deemed appropriate, without consulting the composer and with no further payments of money.

Neumann wasted no time in mounting the Nibelung music drama. He presented *Das Rheingold* and *Die Walküre* in April 1878, and the remaining two dramas followed in September. During the first four months of 1879, he produced three complete cycles. Neumann's productions were quite successful, and Wagner was pleased. After the Leipzig performances Neumann proposed that he take the *Ring* to Berlin. Wagner was hesitant, not because of any doubt regarding Neumann, but rather because of the entangled situation he had created through previous concessions of various rights, especially to Ludwig. Neumann's plan did not materialize immediately. However, as the individual music dramas began to gain the attention of numerous directors throughout Germany and because Neumann persisted in his request, Wagner finally consented, although his agreement came only after extensive negotiations. In May 1881, Berlin applauded its first production of the *Ring*. Wagner as well as Kaiser Wilhelm attended the last of the four cycles performed in that city.

Wagner was delighted with Neumann's work, and his confidence in the man's talents as a producer of the *Ring* had grown. Neumann had proved not only that the *Ring* could be produced in existing theaters but also that it could be produced with both critical and financial success. When Neumann then approached Wagner with another idea, the composer listened with interest. Neumann wished to form a touring company that would take the *Ring* throughout the Continent. In addition to the potential income, which could be applied to the Bayreuth debt that still existed, Wagner viewed the Neumann plan as advantageous because other directors could learn about the production of his works. Wagner granted Neumann the necessary rights and on 5, 6, 8, and 9, May 1882, the Neumann company, now known as the "Richard Wagner Theater," gave the first London performance of the *Ring*, in Her Majesty's Theatre. In September, Neumann took the tetralogy to Breslau, Poland.

During the remaining months of 1882, Neumann made some alterations in his production, and the opening of the next year found the director and the 134 members of his troupe, along with much of the original Bayreuth equipment and machinery (which had been purchased from Wagner), offering a series of some thirty-six cycles in the Netherlands, Belgium, Italy, Switzerland, Hungary, and Austria. The *Ring* performances under Neumann's directorship were received with much acclaim, and his fame as a producer was firmly established. By the end of 1883, Neumann's troupe and theaters throughout Europe had presented 140 performances of the *Ring*, and an additional fifty-eight concerts of Wagner's music. Under Neumann's guidance, *The Ring of the*

Nibelung became well-known in England and throughout the Continent. Five years later Neumann was invited to St. Petersburg where he introduced the *Ring* in Russia. (Neumann's book, *Personal Reflections of Richard Wagner*, was published in German in Leipzig, in 1907, and an English translation was published in New York, in 1908, and in London the following year.)

7.3 THE UNITED STATES

The premiere of the *Ring* as a cycle in the United States took place only after each of the four music dramas had received separate first performances. In 1877, one year after Bayreuth, *Die Walküre* premiered on April 2 at the New York Academy of Music. Seven years later it made its first appearance at the recently founded Metropolitan Opera in New York, then in its second season. Within five years, the Metropolitan had presented United States premieres of each of the other three dramas: *Siegfried* — 9 November 1887, *Götterdämmerung* — 25 January 1888, and *Das Rheingold* — 4 January 1889.

The first mounting at the Metropolitan Opera of the *Ring* as a cycle was an abbreviated version (*Das Rheingold* was not performed) performed on 30 January and 1 and 3 February 1888. This premiere was followed a year later by production of the cycle of four dramas on 4, 5, 6, and 11 March 1889. (The Norn Scene and that of Waltraute and Brünnhilde in *Götterdämmerung* were deleted.) These performances were followed by a second cycle that month, after which the company took the *Ring* on tour. Between March and May 1889, the tetralogy was given first performances in five more American cities: Philadelphia, Boston, Milwaukee, Chicago, and St. Louis. Ten years later, on 12, 17, 19, and 24 January 1899, again at the Metropolitan Opera, the first uncut version of the *Ring* in the United States was performed, and later that year the company took this production to San Francisco for the first production in that city.

The *Ring* as a cycle has been quite successful in the United States. From the season of its premiere (1888–1889) to the midpoint of the twentieth century, the Metropolitan Opera alone performed the *Ring* cycle no less than sixty-four times, and the work was produced in forty-six of those sixty-three seasons.

If the *Ring* has remained a stalwart component of the operatic repertoire at the Metropolitan, so too have the separate performances of the individual music dramas. Of the four pieces, *Die Walküre* is more often played than any of the three others, and from the date of its premiere with that company in the 1883–1884 season through the 1950–1951 season, it was performed in that house no less than 260 times during fifty-seven of those sixty-eight seasons. On the tours of the Metropolitan to various cities of the United States, between 1884 and 1950, *Die Walküre* was performed 105 times in eighteen major cities.

7.4 THE *Ring* TODAY

Since 1950 the *Ring* has continued as successful operatic fare in houses throughout the world. As a cycle it is regularly produced in Bayreuth where, in 1976, it celebrated its one hundredth anniversary. The *Ring* is staged regularly in Berlin, and it is produced frequently in Hamburg, London, Leipzig, and Stockholm. In recent years it has received new productions in the European cities of Cologne, Munich, Vienna, and Warsaw. In the early 1970s, the English National Opera began its regular performances of the *Ring* in English. In 1972 the San Francisco Opera mounted its new production of the tetralogy, which was soon followed by a new production of the cycle at the Metropolitan Opera. Each of these two cities again mounted yet new productions, San Francisco in 1985, and the Metropolitan Opera in 1988. So popular were the performances that cycles were again presented, in San Francisco in 1990 and in New York in 1993. The first radio broadcast of the *Ring* as a cycle was achieved by the British Broadcasting Company when it aired the third cycle from Covent Garden in 1950.

In 1975 the Seattle Opera initiated a unique premiere of Wagner's *Ring*. In July of that year, within a two-week period, two cycles were presented. The first was sung in the original German, and the second was given in an English translation. These performances were the first in which a German and then an English version were performed together, and the latter was the premiere performance of the *Ring* in English in the United States. The Seattle festival was attended by persons from thirty-five states of the United States and from nineteen other countries. Known as the Pacific Northwest Wagner Festival, the Seattle summer *Ring* productions in the two languages continued each summer until 1983, and in 1985 a new cyclic production, in German and very much in contrast to its conservative predecessor, was premiered.

7.5 THE *Ring* IN TRANSLATION

After Neumann's tour of the *Ring* throughout Europe and the introduction of the tetralogy in Russia and in the United States, the popularity of the music drama was such that there began to emerge a demand for performances in languages other than German. In 1893 the first non-German-language *Ring* was performed in Hungarian, in Budapest. Ten years passed before the Cycle was performed in a language other than German, this time in French, in Brussels in 1903. During the following eight years, the *Ring* received its first performances in six additional languages: Swedish (Stockholm, 1907), English (London, 1908), Italian (Lisbon, 1909), Danish (Copenhagen, 1909), Flemish (Antwerp, 1910), and Polish (Lemberg, 1911). The United States had to wait almost one hundred years after the premiere in Bayreuth to hear the *Ring* in English, the first such production being given in the Seattle Opera House on 22, 23, 25 and 27 July 1975. The translation was that of Andrew Porter, and the Cycle was under the direction of the late George London, a famed Wotan of earlier days.

The four music dramas of the *Ring* are often presented as separate works and have been heard in several languages other than German. In addition to the Cycle productions cited above, other non-German performances include *Das Rheingold* in Croatian, Czech, Finnish, and Russian; *Die Walküre* in Catalan, Croatian, Czech, Dutch, Finnish, Lettish, Rumanian, Russian, and Slovenian; *Siegfried* in Catalan, Croatian, Czech, Finnish, and Russian; and *Götterdämmerung* in Finnish and Russian.

Chapter Eight

The Poetry and the Drama of the *Ring*

8.1 POETRY

In 1853 Wagner published a private edition of the *Ring* which he distributed to a small group of select friends. Other acquaintances were introduced to the tetralogy at small gatherings during which Wagner read aloud from his work. The initial reaction, both of readers and of those who heard Wagner's readings, was one of puzzlement. They were convinced that this Nibelung poem was not a libretto for opera, and these first readers and hearers concluded, most naturally under the artistic circumstances of the day, that rather than lend itself to operatic treatment, the poem actually defied such a setting.

One of the several aspects of the *Ring* which occasioned this negative reaction was the poetry of the drama. Operatic audiences of Wagner's day, even the most knowledgeable, were accustomed to a specific kind of poetry in opera. That poetry had six essential characteristics: (1) a relatively long verse line, (2) end word rhymes, (3) a romantic metaphor, (4) standard grammatical and syntactical structures, (5) a vocabulary whose meanings were contemporary to the audiences, and (6) frequent repetition of words, phrases, or lines. In its way, each of these poetic features allowed for a more elaborate musical development, at least for that development which was the accepted standard of the time; each permitted greater opportunity for individual vocal display in the form of arias, duets, and occasionally choruses. Those privy to the private edition of the *Ring* or to the composer's readings, steeped in the traditions of the Italian and French styles for libretti, were taken aback by Wagner's poem as text for opera. Few, if any, of the familiar poetic traits were to be found in the work; it had a distinct poetic structure of its own, and viewed beside the verse of standard mid-nineteenth-century operatic repertoire, it was a poetry that seemed nonconducive to opera. It could not be sung, they argued. It did not lend itself to "melody," and furthermore, no orchestration, regardless of the manner in which it was set down, could convert to accepted operatic form a poetry that did not accommodate itself naturally to expression in song.

Wagner was well aware of the reaction to the poetic structure of his drama and its assumed incompatibility with traditional operatic format. In mid-1853, shortly after the appearance of his private edition of the *Ring*, he wrote a letter in which he attempted to defend his poetry by discussing the state of the poetry of the day. Such poetry, he wrote, had developed into its own special art form, an artistic expression that was now completely divorced from music. Each of these art media, poetry and music, now trod different paths, and each had so developed that contemporary music and poetry had little concern for each other; each had become dissociated from the other. Wagner believed that this lack of association between music and poetry was especially noticeable when the poetry represented human speech, as it supposedly did in opera. He concluded that the time had come when it was no longer possible, in an artistic sense, to join contemporary music and the poetry of the time. These sentiments reinforced what he had written two years earlier in *Oper und Drama*, the essay in which he had stated that if music was to attain its full expressiveness, the words for that music must be equally expressive, equally sensuous, even if the traditional meanings of the words were occasionally altered. Thus, poetry in drama must not be forced to adhere to rigid rules, but rather must be unhampered by the inflexibilities of finite forms if the naturalness of speech was to be achieved.

If Wagner's views on contemporary poetry were instrumental in helping him avoid popular traditional verse structures for his drama, there was present an additional factor of equal persuasiveness. The argument of his *Ring* was mythological in substance; it dealt with and reflected an ancient past, a time far removed from whatever were the colorings of contemporary society and manners. Wagner found it impossible to blend the antiquity of his theme and the seriousness of its symbolic representations with a verse form that mirrored the life of a later day. He was convinced that such a combination of antiquity and modernity would convert the universality of myth into the dramatic trivia that he believed nineteenth-century operatic fare to be.

Wagner thus sought a distinct verse form for his work. He desired a poetic structure that would fulfill his dramatic needs as he envisioned them: That form must impart the nature of myth and it must reflect antiquity; it must mirror the naturalness of speech; it must lend itself to expression in music, in accordance with the totality of his artistic concepts. Such a verse form, he concluded, was *Stabreim*, a poetic structure long abandoned but prevalent in German poetry as early as the ninth century, and popular in English verse through the fourteenth century. Wagner had been much moved toward *Stabreim* by the work of a contemporary writer, Ludwig Ettmüller, who, in 1837, published his work *Lieder der Edda von den Nibelungen* (*Eddic Songs of the Nibelungs*). In his book Ettmüller translated the Eddic poems into modern German, attempting always to retain the original Eddic strophe.

The *Stabreim* structure offered more than historic relationship to the past. It had no fixed metrical pattern, a characteristic that freed Wagner from the limitations of a fixed line length and the related matters of number of syllables and stressed and unstressed syllables. With *Stabreim* he could determine his own verse length, a factor very important for individual emotional situations that were to be reached entirely through poetic dialogue. The flexibility of verse length also allowed him a means whereby the dialogue could incorporate the "purely human" elements that he considered so necessary to great drama. In Wagner's mind *Stabreim* offered yet another attribute that blended with his dramatic concepts—conciseness. It had a verse form that was essentially devoid of word elegance, and Wagner had long objected to the elaborate, exaggerated, metaphorical overstatements that he believed were so common in modern libretti. *Stabreim* freed him from that semantic maze by permitting him to determine whatever conciseness he deemed natural and relevant to any situation. *Stabreim* did not have end rhyme, an element mandatory in the operatic poetry of the nineteenth century; in its stead, this ancient verse form had an *internal alliteration* which, Wagner would write, lent itself naturally to the regular accents of German speech. Such a repetition of similar sounds in neighboring syllables or words appealed to Wagner not only because it provided literary distance from the rhyme of his day but also because he felt that with alliteration he could achieve a more strikingly sensuous quality in his words, a necessary attribute that he had described in *Oper und Drama*.

Wagner used the *Stabreim* poetics extensively in the *Ring*. Although it was his primary verse form, at times he added certain modifications that helped him to create a thoroughly pervasive ancient atmosphere. He made wide use of archaic vocabulary, employing words that were frequently used in medieval poetry but which had disappeared from the modern idiom. (During his intensive study of Germanic mythology, Wagner acquired a basic familiarity with the Old Norse language.) At other times, Wagner reverted to words in current usage, placed in such contexts that their meanings, at least in his mind, helped enhance the mythological flavor of his story. In addition, he adapted the German language compound-word form and thus created unusual compounds that often consisted of a word from the past joined to one of the present. And, unlike the librettists of his day, Wagner frequently employed unconventional, non-idiomatic grammar and syntax, a technique that he believed both created a more intense effect and contributed to rhythms more easily fused with the music he envisioned.

Wagner's *Stabreim* poetics, combined with those linguistic elements of his own design, created a unique "language." If it was not the cultural, social, and economic idiom of the German people, it was a new German, that of his day, refashioned and sprinkled with characteristics of another age. Thus, in Wagner's time it was only natural that readers of the *Ring* reacted strongly to its language and were unable to view it as poetry. In their minds, it was not the language of opera! Today, criticism is neither so rigid nor so severe, yet the language of the *Ring* remains unchanged and it is still, for many, a linguistic and semantic enigma.

8.2 Drama

By 1851 Wagner had arrived at definite conclusions about the many and varied artistic matters that he had been pondering and evaluating during the previous three years. His concepts and his ideas on drama and music, and their fusion into a single art form, were now fixed, and the application of these innovating principles was the next course of action. In the natural order of events, it was to drama that he would turn, to the libretti for his music drama *Der Ring des Nibelungen*.

Wagner's fundamental principle, that concept which underlay all else in his artistic thought and which he had discussed at length in his essays, was that of the "reality of existence" and its dramatization. He would not concern himself with the external world of incidents and situations, although he obviously realized that a minimum of that world must be present to set his drama in motion. Wagner's "reality of existence" was, rather, the internal world of the mind and of the heart, the unseen but sensed and felt nature of humanity. Drama, "true drama" as he called it, must mirror the truth of that interior world, and the dramatization of that truth was his artistic objective.

The *Ring* adheres faithfully to this dramatic principle. It is drama that shows little of humanity's external environment and is, instead, an expression of the human condition, a drama in which the deepest innermost reactions of the figures are of much greater import than the physical incidents that caused them and, indeed, are more important than the figures themselves. Wagner's dramatic probing into the inner reaches of the human experience revealed what was "realistic" by the standards he had set down, and his expressions were not simply those of a personal or individual nature but rather those of the infinite mind, the mind that is found in myths, the collective and substantial thought of mankind as filtered and refined through the ages.

Wagner clearly understood that even this kind of drama must be firmly set within the dramatic framework explicit to the genre itself. As drama, its form, its properties, and more importantly the technique of its elaboration, must include the necessities of tried dramatic construction. Under such an imposition, he could not avoid a situational facade, but in the light of his concepts, it would be only minimally situational, sufficient to serve as the step into what he deemed the substance of the "true drama." This dramatic foundation, then, this determinant of all succeeding matters would be substantial, but at the same time, this *vera causa* would be secondary to the total scheme. This, with one single incident, one bit of action that takes place during the first moments of the drama, that is, the theft of the gold in order to allow a prominent individual to renege on his given word, Wagner established the solid base for all that was to follow, the basis for the dramatic expression of the unconscious but universal realities that are so much the driving forces in mankind's existence. With his drama, Wagner realized his goal, yet those who only read the poem as drama are unaware of the second "dialogue," the other drama in which he couched all that he had written as words, the descriptive music that carried to a supreme end the expression that his poetry initially defined or depicted.

In a very real sense, the poem of the *Ring* as drama is a passive work. If there are events and actions, they are minimal and their presence is always overshadowed by the emotional aspects that they evoke. The drama of the *Ring* is not one of physical action in the accepted dramatic sense, but the presence of any action establishes a dramatic continuity that satisfies the mind, which then can suspend its disbelief to accept emotionally all else that happens. The quality of the *Ring* lies in this subjectivity, and to approach the *Ring* in any other state of mind is to strip it of its own reality and to disguise it with a conventional dress that hides its purpose.

The success of the *Ring* as drama is not found merely in the presence of subjectivity. Rather, the work succeeds because Wagner, proceeding from a single physical act, was able to detail the reactions of each of his figures to that stimulus or the resultant situations, and by means of these reactions to expose the inner self of man. If each of these reactions is individual yet natural, and thus very real to any who react in kind, in their totality they present a finely patterned mosaic of human emotions. These emotions, however, are not surface emotions, those that are neatly defined, pictured, and categorized in the course of routine societal intercourse. They are, rather, the emotions of a hidden conscience, those emotions that so secretly yet so forcibly drive, mold, shape, and even erode humanity's basic morale. Approached in these terms, the *Ring* becomes epical, not epical in a poetic or dramatic or—as Wagner had thought—a national sense, but epical in the sense that it brings to view both the positive and the negative aspects of subconscious human emotions and places them in relief on the plane of conscious ideals.

8.3 THE MEANING OF THE *Ring*

So extensive is the scope of the *Ring* and so inherently universal is its totality of thought, precept, and idea that its meaning must become one of personal interpretation. As the reactions of the figures of the drama to a stimulus are varied, so too are the human reactions to the stimulus of the *Ring*. It is thus most likely that no two minds will arrive at the same interpretative conclusion, yet in a most curious way each conclusion is appropriate for its interpreter, and for each of these interpreters that final, individual analysis is definitive in itself.

Studies, analyses, commentaries, and interpretations of the *Ring* have appeared with regularity since its premiere in 1876. These writings, as well as the productions of the *Ring* that some of these concepts have engendered, have placed on exhibit the thoughts of respected minds of the times, the thoughts of persons, both professionals and laypeople alike, of every intellectual school. Some of these writers have approached Wagner's poem as a condensed history of the world, while others, whose considerations run along a similar path, have concluded that the *Ring* is a portrait of the troubled world as it winds its way to inevitable destruction.

Other interpretations are as varied. Some followers of the *Ring* have viewed the drama as an accurate reflection of their own culture and their own society, the events in the *Ring* being the very events of their own day. There have been those who, without a regard for time or geography, have perceived the four dramas as the mirror of mankind's innate corruption, a moral corruption in the eyes of some and a political or even an economic corruption in the eyes of others. Some students of Wagner and his poem have appreciated the work as a thesis on behalf of socialism, as one that exposes a degenerate capitalism. In the extreme, there have been scholars who have regarded the *Ring* as a justification for the overthrow of society by revolution. Other interpreters have come to conclusions along more psychological lines. Some have deemed the *Ring* an example of the forces of humanity, ever divided against one another, the worlds of the gods and giants and dwarfs being but disguises for the dominant sectors of human society. There have been more than a few who propose the drama to be a picture of lust, not only a lust for power and a greed for wealth, but also a lust for death. At the same time, there have been analysts who insist that Wagner's poem pictures the defeat of lust and greed or is, at least, a pronouncement against those sins. Still other interpreters have viewed the message of the *Ring* as one in which the human spirit seeks a strength and a power that, when the full circle of civilization is drawn, will destroy those who have attained them. Others conclude that the *Ring* urges breaking the chains of societal bondage and then making independent determinations of a course of action. In yet other conclusions, the *Ring* has been made a sermon, an exhortation perhaps, in which the salvation of the world will come about only through love and sacrifice. Many minds have adjudged the *Ring* a study of fatalism, an insistence on the implacability of destiny. Also expressed has been the thought that Wagner's poem is a confirmation of the existence of *Will*. It is perhaps only natural that more recent times have given rise to studies that analyze the *Ring* in terms of Freudian thought and others that have scrutinized it according to Jungian concepts. Others have viewed the *Ring* as a depiction of the nineteenth-century industrial revolution, or as a space odyssey, while some have seen the drama as an exposé of the life of Wagner himself. Peter Wapnewski, a respected writer on the music dramas, stated that the *Ring* "is a great parable of life, which Wagner presents as innocent by nature and as encumbered with guilt by its history. It comprehends its own finite character, and yet it is not prepared to give up hoping against hope for the infinite."[1]

[1] "The Operas as Literary Works." *Wagner Handbook*, 41.

A second well-versed scholar of Wagner matters, Bryan Magee, offers a succinct but nevertheless substantial comment on the *Ring* when he writes that Wagner's drama "explores the irreconcilable conflict between the morality of the heart and social morality, and shows how those who live in accordance with the former are punished and destroyed by the guardians of the latter—who nevertheless themselves atrophy because of their denial of the former within themselves."[2]

As varied and extreme as are the numerous analyses of the *Ring*, when examined under the criteria by which each was made, all reflect a truth that is determined by the experiences of the respective writers. The arguments presented in order to reach a specific conclusion are usually logical in their own right, yet they are not guided by an accepted universal set of standards, but by an hypostasis that firmly determines each writer's emotional and intellectual concerns. Such richness of interpretation, each appropriate in the light of the measurements applied, is ample evidence of the universality to be found in the *Ring*, a universality that provides the many vantage points from which the work may be viewed, a universality that has withstood the shifts and changes of time and society.

8.4 WAGNER ON THE MEANING OF THE *Ring*

Although Wagner never assumed the role of analyst for purposes of interpreting *Der Ring des Nibelungen*, he commented occasionally on certain aspects of his drama. In 1854, two years after he had completed the poem, he wrote to August Röckel, who had been a close colleague in the revolutionary activities in Dresden in 1848; in his letter Wagner discussed what he termed "the most general and dominant features" of the work.[3]

Wagner contended that he had incorporated into the *Ring* three major themes. Although not referred to as such by the composer, these themes may be called: (1) death and learning "to die," (2) the Will, and (3) the laws of change.

On the theme of death and learning "to die," Wagner wrote:

We must all learn to die, in fact to die in the most absolute sense of the word; the fear of the end is the source of all lovelessness and it arises only where love itself has already faded. How did it come

[2] "Schopenhauer and Wagner," *The Opera Quarterly*, Vol. I, No. 3 (Autumn, 1983), 153.

[3] Quotations from this letter are the translations of Ford and Whitall, *Wagner: A Documentary Study*, ed. Barth, Mack, Voss, 184–195.

about that mankind so lost touch with this bringer of the highest happiness to everything living that in the end everything they did, everything they understood and established, was done solely out of fear for that end? My poem shows how.

(This theme clearly reflects those of Wagner's thoughts that parallel the concepts proposed by Arthur Schopenhauer in his principal work *Die Welt als Wille und Vorstellung* [The World as Will and Idea], 1818. Wagner came into contact with this work in late 1854, an event that he characterized as the most important of his life, and he immediately became a devoted disciple of the author, immensely influenced by the philosophy of renunciation.)

The second theme of the *Ring* to which Wagner made brief reference in his letter dealt with the Will, or more specifically, Wotan's rise "to the tragic height" of willing his own downfall. Of this aspect of the nature of man, a concern that occupied much of the composer's thought throughout the years, Wagner wrote:

This is everything we have to learn from the history of mankind: to Will the inevitable and to carry it out oneself. The product of this highest, self-destructive Will is the fearless, ever-loving man who is finally created: Siegfried.

The third of the *Ring* themes that Wagner deemed important was that of changeability, or more accurately, the lack of changeability in humanity. He approached this subject by means of the strained relationship that he had developed between Wotan and his wife, Fricka. On this subject, he wrote:

The rigid bond that unites them both, arising from love's involuntary mistake of perpetuating itself beyond the inescapable laws of change, of maintaining mutual dependence, this resistance to the eternal renewal and change of the objective world lands both of them in the mutual torment of lovelessness.

Wagner maintained that it was this state of affairs among the gods, this lack of the ability to change when confronted by the need for change, that made them "ripe for disaster" and, hence, was the "nub of the catastrophe" of their downfall. He believed his drama revealed the necessity for lending oneself to the changeableness of reality and of life, of the need to accept the diversity, the multiplicity, the eternal newness of existence.

Wagner was certain that the three themes that he had discussed, if only briefly, were those of major significance in his *Ring*. All else, he wrote, was "detail" although he did go on to mention some of that "detail" which, in the main, concerned what he considered to be the three major figures of his drama. The composer's references to Wotan, Siegfried, and Brünnhilde, if succinct, are basic to his intent in the *Ring* and are understandably related to the themes he considered so important. Of Wotan, he wrote, "He resembles us [mankind] to a tee; he is the sum of the intelligence of the present." Siegfried, he wrote, is "the man of the future," willed and sought by us [mankind], but who cannot be made by us and who must create himself through our *destruction*. Wagner's thoughts on Brünnhilde were of a different vein: She is "the suffering, self-sacrificing redeemer; for love is really 'the eternally feminine' itself."

However, if Wagner, in 1854, was specific regarding the meaning of the work he himself had created, he soon became somewhat less certain of his initial pronouncements. Two years later, on 23 August 1856, he wrote again to Röckel and again briefly revealed some of his thoughts on the *Ring*. On this occasion, Wagner wrote:

How can an artist expect that what he felt intuitively should be perfectly realized by others, seeing that he himself feels in the presence of the work, if it is true Art, that he is confronted by a riddle about which he too might have illusions just as another might.[4]

[4] Quoted by Shaw, *The Perfect Wagnerite*, 85.

Chapter Nine

The Music of the *Ring*

9.1 WAGNER AND ORCHESTRAS

Throughout his professional life Richard Wagner was much concerned with orchestral matters in theatrical productions. From an early date he began to argue in behalf of improvement in the state of the orchestral art. He held a firm belief that operatic productions of his day were of only mediocre artistic quality, and he was equally convinced that orchestras were culprits in this sad state of affairs. His efforts for change were consistent and continuous.

The first tangible display of Wagner's concern appeared in 1846. By this time he had served for three years as royal Kapellmeister in the Dresden Court Theater, a period that brought him into close professional contact with singers, actors, theater administrators, musicians, and their orchestras. His observations of the general conditions that existed in theaters, and specifically the level of artistic standards that prevailed, led him to conclude that serious thought and extended effort must be given to the theater if it was to go on, and that much change throughout was necessary for its survival as a viable artistic medium. Wagner saw the first step of this change as a thorough revitalization of the orchestra. Thus, in March of that year, after spending several months on its preparation, Wagner completed an unsolicited report that revealed the essence of his thought on the matters at hand.

"Die Königliche Kapelle betreffend" ("Concerning the Royal Orchestra") was a lengthy report in which the young composer discussed several aspects of theater operation, focusing on details for improvement of the orchestra. His specifics ran the gamut of considerations:

127

from the need for comfortable chairs on which the musicians could sit and appropriate stands on which they could place their music, to the salaries to be paid those musicians for their services; from the size of the orchestra pit, to the need for players of professional stature; from the need for more rehearsal time, to the number and balance of instruments and their placement within a harmonic whole.

Wagner's report, prompted and tendered by his own instigation, was given little consideration, and ultimately was rejected by the Dresden authorities. However, the substance of the ideas and suggestions that were included in the study persisted as an integral part of Wagner's total theatrical thought. During the ensuing years, as his renown as one of Europe's most celebrated conductors grew, he incorporated his musical requirements and directions into his works, thereby successfully establishing the primacy of the orchestra. Eventually these changes, with some of the innovations that he later introduced at Bayreuth, became standard practice in the world's opera houses. If Wagner was not alone among the ranking composers of history who gave serious attention to orchestral matters, he is among those few whose actions have resulted in the permanent revampings that are responsible for the greater regard bestowed on orchestras today.

9.2 The Orchestra of the *Ring*—Instruments

The total complement of instruments of an orchestra and the number of each kind of instrument were important matters to Wagner in his report of 1846. That concern remained with him through the years and was ever present in his artistic thoughts as he created the music for *Der Ring des Nibelungen*.

By all standards, current as well as past, Wagner's score for the *Ring* requires not only an orchestra uniquely varied in terms of the kinds and the distribution of its instruments, but also one quite large in terms of the number of its instruments. The original manuscript indicated a total of 107 instruments in the pit, including percussives (drums, cymbals, triangles, etc.). This number was increased to 119 for the premiere performance in 1876; twenty years later, for the second production of the *Ring* at Bayreuth, the number had been further increased to 124. (These total numbers do not include numerous instruments which varied for each music drama, but which were played offstage.) In addition to the orchestra of conventional instruments, Wagner's score called for the sounds of several instruments not ordinarily considered standard in orchestral composition. The score later included a musical sound for which no instrument existed at the time; therefore, Wagner himself had to design one. This instrument is known today as the "Wagner tuba." (The word *tuba* is really a misnomer in that it is an adaptation of the German word *tuben* ["tubing"]). This instrument is played by the horn players and its sound is similar to that of the French horn, although their physical resemblance is slight.

Wagner's call for such an imposing orchestra was, in his day, essentially a call for the impossible. In all of musical history there had never been an established first-ranked orchestra that could meet Wagner's musical demands. In 1783 the Dresden orchestra, considered one of the outstanding orchestras of Germany, numbered forty instruments. By 1842 the number had increased to fifty-five. Five years later that number had grown by only eleven. In Leipzig in 1781 the number of instruments in the Gewandhaus orchestra was thirty-one and this number was regularly thirty to thirty-five only a few years before Wagner began work on the *Ring*. Some sixty years later, at the turn of the century, that same orchestra had increased to a complement of only seventy to seventy-five pieces. Among the other orchestras of Wagner's day, one of forty-five to fifty musicians was looked upon as large and many numbered as few as twenty-five to thirty. (In 1838–1839, while serving as musical director in Riga, Wagner conducted an orchestra of twenty-four musicians in performances of six of Beethoven's symphonies!) Today a full symphony orchestra seldom consists of more than ninety instruments, a fair average being seventy-five to eighty-five, and that of a ranking opera house is usually much smaller.

Table 7 indicates the instrumentation called for in the scores of the *Ring* in 1874, 1876, and 1896, and, for purposes of comparison, the distribution of instruments in several *Ring* orchestras of recent times.

9.3 The Orchestra of the *Ring*— Seating Arrangement

In his report of 1846 Wagner stressed the need for a proper seating plan for the musicians of the orchestra. This concern persisted through the years, and finally, at Bayreuth, the composer was able to put into effect those ideas that he had developed with time and experience. His objective was to realize a more balanced arrangement of the musicians, one that not only grouped together like instruments, but also permitted all musical sound to reach both the other musicians and the audience in

Table 7
Instrumentation for the *Ring*

	*Original Score 1874	Bayreuth Festival 1876	Bayreuth Festival 1896	San Francisco Opera 1990	Seattle Opera 1991	**Metropolitan Opera 1993
First Violin	16	16	17	14	13	14
Second Violin	16	16	16	12	12	9
Viola	12	12	13	10	9	10
Cello	12	12	13	8	8	9
Bass	8	8	8	7	7	6
Flute	3	4	4	4	3	4
Piccolo	1	1	1	1	1	2
+English Horn	1	1	1	1	1	1
Oboe	3	4	4	4	3	4
Clarinet	3	4	4	4	3	4
Clarinet (Bass)	1	1	1	1	1	1
Bassoon	3	4	4	3	3	4
Bassoon (Double)	1	1	1	1	1	1
Horn	8	8	10	10	9	9
Trumpet	3	4	4	3	3	4
Trumpet (Bass)	1	1	1	1	1	1
Trombone	3	4	4	4	3	5
Trombone (Contrabass)	1	1	1	1	1	2
Tuba (Contrabass)	1	1	1	1	1	1
++Tuba (Bass)	-	2	2	2	-	2
++Tuba (Tenor)	-	2	2	2	-	2
Harp	6	8	8	2	4	2
Timpani (Pairs)	2	2	2	2	2	3
Drum (Tenor)	1	1	1	1	1	1
Cymbals, Triangle, Glockenspiel, Gong	1	1	1	1	2	2
	107	119	124	100	92	103

*In addition to the instruments listed, Wagner wrote into the score of the *Ring* the following instrumentation, to be played offstage:

1. *Das Rheingold*

18 anvils, notation on three octave Fs. (9 small, medium, large). The anvil sounds are heard in the transition music between scenes 2 and 3 as Wotan and Loge descend to and ascend from Nibelheim.

A hammer, whose sound is used to indicate the smithing of the Nibelungs in the transitions between scenes 2 and 3 and between 3 and 4.

1 harp, to accompany the Rhine Daughters in the final scene.

The Music of the *Ring*

2. *Die Walküre*

1 alpenhorn (alphorn), note of C. This instrument, used by herdsmen, is made of strips or staves of wood bound together to form a conical tube whose length varies from 4 to 15 feet. The bell curves slightly upward, and the hardwood mouthpiece is cupped. The alpenhorn can be used to play simple melodies.

Wagner indicated that this instrument was to be used to announce the arrival of Hunding in Act II, scene 5 as he chases the fleeing Siegmund.

1 thunder machine which is used several times throughout the music drama: in Act I, that music heard before the rise of the curtain; in Act II, scene 5, as Hunding bears down upon the fleeing Siegmund and Sieglinde, and again as Wotan causes the death of Hunding and then chases the escaping Brünnhilde; in Act III, scene 1, as the Valkyries gather at Valkyrie Rock and the angered Wotan swiftly rides down upon them and in scene 2 as the Valkyries flee Wotan's anger.

3. *Siegfried*

1 English horn. The English horn is spotlighted in the second act of *Siegfried* when it is played offstage to indicate the sounds that Siegfried makes as he attempts to play a reed flute.

1 horn

1 forging hammer, which is used by Mime in the first scene of Act I of this drama, and then later, in scene 3, by Siegfried.

1 thunder machine, heard in Act I, scene 2, as Wotan (Wanderer) approaches Siegfried's cave, and then again in that scene when he strikes the ground with his spear. The thunder is again heard in Act II, scene 1, as a "stormwind" is present when Wotan enters and when he leaves. The thunder machine is in action again in Act III, scene 1, as Erda and Wotan meet, and in the following scene, at that instant when Siegfried breaks Wotan's spear.

4. *Götterdämmerung*

4 harps

1 horn

3 steerhorns (cowhorns), note of C, D flat, and D. These instruments, like the alpenhorn of *Die Walküre*, are used by herdsmen. Originally, these instruments were the horns of cattle, removed, and allowed to dry. Once the proper state was reached, the horn was cleaned and a small hole was made in the tip. Sound was made by forcing air through tightly pursed lips into the tip of the horn. Steerhorns were used as signaling instruments rather than for the playing of melodies.

These horns are first used in *Götterdämmerung* in Act II, scene 3 by Hagen to summon the Gibichung vassals. Two horns, one left and one right, both offstage, answer Hagen's call.

A second use of the steerhorn occurs in the short musical prelude of Act III. The horn is heard twice, the sound representing the two groups of a hunting party calling to each other.

(The steerhorns that were used in the premiere of the *Ring* remained in Bayreuth until World War II, during which they were taken as souvenirs, apparently by the occupying forces of the United States Army.)

** The orchestra of the Metropolitan Opera was assisted, as necessary, by a complement of thirty-six *Associate Musicians*: 11 violins, 3 violas, 4 cellos, 2 basses, 1 flute, 1 oboe, 1 clarinet, 2 bassoons, 3 trumpets, 2 trombones, 1 tuba, 4 percussion, 1 harp.

+ In some passages of *Siegfried* and *Götterdämmerung*, Wagner felt that the English horn did not produce the intended tonal effect. For these special passages, he indicated that an alto oboe be substituted.

++ Wagner sought a tone that would be somewhat more brusque than that of the horn of his day, a tone between that of the horn and that of the trombone. The lack of an instrument that played such tones caused the composer to develop one of his own design. The main body of this instrument has the form of an ellipse. It is held upright, with the bell facing upward and the base resting on the player's lap. The *Wagner tuba*, the name used most frequently for this instrument, has four rotary valves that are pressed by fingers of the left hand. Built as a tenor (B flat) and bass (F), the Wagner tuba is also known as the *Waldhorntuba* ("hunting horn tuba"), the *Bayreuthtuba*, and the *Ringtuba*, the last name applied because of the introduction of the instrument in the Ring premiere in 1876 in Bayreuth. (As stated earlier, the word 'tuba' as a name for this instrument is a misnomer in that it is an adaptation of the German word *tuben*, whose translation is *tube*, or *tubing*.)

The original horns were made by the firm of Moritzh, of Berlin, although the firm of Alexander, of Mainz, took over their manufacture after 1900. Anton Bruckner and Richard Strauss have included these instruments in certain of their compositions.

In the *Ring*, these instruments are used as part of the Hunding music in *Die Walküre* and are played by the 5th, 6th, 7th, and 8th horn players. There is no indication of these instruments in the original score of the *Ring*. Until their introduction at the 1876 premiere, the music that would become the role of the Wagner tubas was played solely by horns.

---

an intelligible and harmonious manner. At the same time he was determined that the conductor be located so as to be seen at all times by the musicians and the singers. His objective in this last regard was to ensure the conductor's complete control of the performance at all times.

Wagner's seating arrangement for the orchestra of the *Ring* premiere (see Table 8) which essentially was duplicated in 1896, was a departure from the practice in German theaters in the mid-nineteenth century. Although his Bayreuth arrangement was later to undergo revision, Wagner's concepts were influential in the seating plans that eventually became the standard arrangement for modern orchestras.

Only the center row of instruments (harps, cellos, oboes, flutes, and English horn) in the "mystical abyss" was in uncovered space. The first two rows (1st and 2nd violins, violas, and basses) were covered by the top portion of the sounding board that separated the orchestra from the audience and which curved upward and inward toward the stage. The last two rows (horns, trumpets, bassoons, clarinet, tubas, trombones, timpani, and percussion) were covered by the projection of the stage. The conductor's sight line was at stage level; and the orchestra pit, from the conductor to the last row of instruments, descended seventeen feet.

Wagner incorporated into his seating arrangement of the *Ring* orchestra several of the ideas he had offered years before in his report:

1. In order to ensure maximum control by the conductor, the depth of the orchestra was to be one-half of the distance across its front.
2. The conductor was placed in the center-front position, facing the orchestra and the stage. In this location both the players and the singers could see the conductor, and the latter could also see the entire orchestra as well as the performers on the stage. (In earlier times, the conductor was frequently stationed against the center of the stage, facing the singers but presenting his back to the orchestra. Later, the conductor was moved from the front of the stage to the center of the pit where he was then surrounded on all sides by the orchestra.)
3. In order to achieve a total harmonic unity and thus form an ensemble, most of the members of an instrument group were seated together. Those instruments not placed with their group were located in such a manner that a greater harmonic balance would result.
4. Musicians were seated in such a manner that within an instrument group each could hear the other players of that group, and the groupings were so arranged that each could hear the other groups.
5. The string groups were seated in such a manner that the players could see and thus follow the bowing of the first chairs.

9.4 THE *Ring* MUSIC AND THE LEITMOTIF

The music of *Der Ring des Nibelungen* was developed around a framework of the *Leitmotiv* (leitmotif, "leading motive"). In the briefest of terms, a leitmotif is a short, uncomplicated musical phrase or theme, usually one to three measures, which is employed, and reused, by the composer when he deems it important to the composition. In the case of Wagner and his *Ring*, the leitmotif became a musical theme representative of a figure, an event, an emotion, a thought, an idea, or a concept in the drama, which theme he repeated, often in subtle but distinct, varying, and often tempered pitch, tone and/or intensity, according to the interpretative demands of his dramatic argument.

The origin of the leitmotif as a musical device is difficult if not impossible to uncover. The word itself was coined by Friedrich Wilhelm Jähns (1809–1888) in his musical analysis of the operas of Carl Maria von Weber (1786–1826), one of Germany's crusaders for the establishment of a German national opera, whose work Wagner held in great esteem. (Wagner was personally responsible for the return, in 1844, of von Weber's remains from London to Dresden where Wagner spoke eloquently at the interment.) It is possible that, as a device, the leitmotif

Table 8

Orchestra Seating Arrangement—*Ring* Premiere

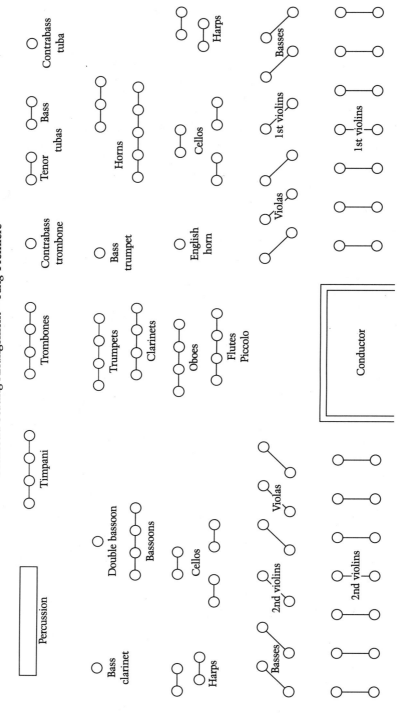

had functioned—if ever so subtly—in musical composition since that day when music came into its own as an art form. Before Wagner's time, Bach, Gluck, and Mozart had included musical references in certain of their works. Later, such composers as Mendelssohn, Schumann, Berlioz, Glinka, Meyerbeer, and particularly von Weber, interspersed their creations with recurrent musical themes. Some of the operas of Verdi contain music that scholars have related to the leitmotif concept. However, it remained for Wagner to develop this musical form of representation, to establish its importance, and to employ it almost entirely as the design of a complete work.

The permanent association of Wagner with the leitmotif was forged by Hans von Wolzogen (1848–1938). This well-to-do German country gentleman came to Bayreuth in 1877 to further the cause of Richard Wagner, who had selected him as the first editor of the *Bayreuther Blätter* (*Bayreuth Journal*), a publication devoted to the continuation and improvement of things Wagnerian, to which the composer was a frequent contributor. It was Wolzogen who, in his writings on the *Ring*, labeled its many musical themes *leitmotifs*, gave many of them names, and thus set the stage for a relationship between the composer and his music which has persisted into the modern day.

Although Wolzogen's work, in the main, was important in the total Wagnerian picture, it is unfortunate that his discussions of the musical aspects of the *Ring* caused many to believe that the leitmotif was really only a musical guidepost, a sign that Wagner had used in his composition at appropriate times merely to facilitate comprehension of the drama. Although a multitude of Wagnerites have devoted themselves to detailed studies of the leitmotif in the tetralogy, and there are many who continue to do so today, Wagner himself expressed little interest in the matter. If, more than any composer before him, he had made musical themes an integral part of his score, and more so in the *Ring* than in any other of his creations, he did not use them solely as a means of "identification" or of simple "association." In the leitmotif Wagner had found a means that was amenable to his musical concepts of *Gesamtkunstwerk*. It was not to the leitmotif in and of itself that he attached importance, but rather to how such musical fragments could serve as the base on which larger, more complete musical selections could be developed. The word *leitmotif* was not a part of Wagner's musical vocabulary, and it was only infrequently that he made reference to musical motifs or themes. In 1867, in a discussion of *Tristan und Isolde*, he wrote briefly of *Hauptmotiv* ("chief" or "leading motive"). On occasion he used the word *Grundthema* ("foundation theme") or the term *Gedächtnismotiv* ("remembrance" or "memory motive"). Yet such usage was isolated, and his public attention to this aspect of his music dramas was so scant as to be almost nonexistent. At such times when he referred to these musical bits, he preferred a name that was more descriptive than technical; he called them "melodic moments of feeling."

A study of Wagner's music reveals that during the composition of his early works he was exploring the techniques of musical phrases and themes. This experimentation can easily be noted by listening carefully to Wagner's operas in the chronological order of their composition (see Appendix A). In his first works Wagner developed musical fragments that essentially were merely leitmotifs of identification, usually that of the principal figures in a drama. He used these themes sparingly, and they were incorporated into the musical text at the appropriate points of the dramas only when their appearance did not detract from an even flow of the main body of the music. By 1845, with the completion of *Tannhäuser*, Wagner had begun to envision in the leitmotif something more than a simple musical tag of "identification." Three years later, in *Lohengrin*, he resorted to the motif device not only more extensively than in any previous work, but also in a manner much more complex than before. In this work about the knight of the Holy Grail, his musical themes had lost their "label" distinction; they had ceased "to announce"; they no longer served as an indication of the presence of a figure of the drama. In this composition, he recalled earlier motifs but in altered rhythms; he reshaped original motifs by means of distinct instrumentation and orchestral coloration. He had begun to overlap the motifs, to intertwine them, to fuse them, and to merge them. In *Lohengrin* the leitmotifs took on a more sophisticated musical character. They manifested a greater intensity of expression, and they exhibited shades of emotion that were uniquely appropriate to the respective dramatic situations. In *Lohengrin* the leitmotifs were no longer musical fragments separate from the musical text; they had become musical fabric itself.

After the composition of *Lohengrin*, Wagner composed no music for some six years. This was the period when his ideas on music, on drama, on myth, and on legend—in short, on what the world would later call music drama—took form. These years were a period of artistic and intellectual contemplation, a period in which he was molding and shaping his concepts and his theories and, at least in his mind, developing a number of musical themes. By early 1854 Wagner had completed the music of *Das Rheingold*, the first of the four parts of the *Ring*, a work which, when joined with the others yet to come, would demonstrate in a revolutionary manner the artistic conclusions he had reached regarding the musical phrase, the *Leitmotiv*, as Wolzogen would call it.

The music of *Der Ring des Nibelungen* was conceived and developed with the concept of individual musical themes as its technical framework. Since the first performance of the *Ring*, and Wolzogen's persuasive application of the term *leitmotif* to the Wagner method of composition, scholars have studied this music carefully to determine the composer's procedures in utilizing themes, and the manner in which he joined musical form and function to specific dramatic situations. These analysts have given names to the themes; they have numbered them, classified them, placed them in respective groups, determined them to be primary, secondary, or incidental; they have viewed them as single themes or have concluded that some are combinations of several themes or otherwise derivations, extensions, or transformations. In the main, each of these numerous studies has been distinctive in its approach, its presentation, and in the method of analysis used. The conclusions offered by each writer are a reflection of individual artistic and intellectual definitions of the basic term *leitmotif* in combination with the author's personal and often philosophic interpretation of a specific theme and its adequacy, efficacy, and artistic service within the total drama. In 1896 a French musicologist published a study of that year's *Ring* performance in Bayreuth and included in his work an inventory of the musical motifs, each titled and catalogued according to its initial and subsequent appearances throughout the tetralogy. The list included a total of 82 leitmotifs with the following breakdown in order of their first appearance: *Das Rheingold*—34; *Die Walküre*—22; *Siegfried*—18; *Götterdämmerung*—8. A later work cited a total of seventy motifs of which only thirty were considered to be "root" themes. Other studies that have since been published have shown numeric totals that ranged from 116 to 245, the latter including a quantity of ingenious, but nevertheless revealing interpretations. In 1991, the Mainz publisher Schott & Co. issued a libretto of the *Ring* in which each leitmotif is indicated, as well as its location in the music drama. The total number of motives cited in this work is 367, a number that included some musical variations of earlier musical themes as independent leitmotifs. These data were republished in the *Program* of the Vienna Staatsoper's production of the *Ring* in 1993.

The importance of the leitmotifs in the *Ring* does not lie in their numbers or in the arbitrary names attached to them, but rather in the musical and dramatic effectiveness achieved through their use. The utilization of the leitmotif as a musical device in any form, and its potential for technical modification, are essentially limitless; such developments depend only on the creative talent of the composer. However, it remained for Wagner to perceive the musical theme as a valid instrument of artistic expression and, having explored its possibilities, to use it as the foundation for an entire work. Wagner took the leitmotif in its simplest form and gave it a tonal coloration and a dynamics that ranged from a light, refreshing sound to one of intense majesty. He adapted the musical theme to all aspects of his poem, from the most subtle of emotional sensibilities to the most obvious of concrete realities. He molded the leitmotif to reflect the nuances of human thought and human action as well as those of the vast nature of the universe, in all its extremes. He combined his themes, blended them, fragmented them, and reshaped them in multiple ways. He made them appear, then fade, only to recall them, perhaps in a different guise, but he was always guided by the dramatic needs of his poem and the imagery of his argument. In Wagner's hand the leitmotif became something more than a musical label, much more than a simple sign or a tag. He made it a dramatic expression that articulated the "purely human" that he sought to portray. Some of his themes were fleeting; some were blatant; some were obvious; others were suggestive, more intuited than recognized or understood. But together they became a musical utterance that the logic of the human mind could accept as well as one that the sensitivity of the human heart could understand.

Wagner's leitmotifs, in all their hues, served as the detail of the *Ring*, and his method of weaving them into a musico-dramatic pattern was on a symphonic order. He did not allow his themes to exist independent of the whole; he did not place them in the appropriate sequence and then tie them together by means of incidental accompaniment. They were at once the detail and the whole itself. With the *Ring* Wagner forged a musical composition that was continuous and unfragmented, a music that was total and inclusive. To accomplish this artistic feat, Wagner laid aside the textbook laws of musical composition and created a symphonic structure that fused all the elements into an encompassing musical expression of his drama. His *Ring* was a cosmic music, energetic and charged to pair with the boldness of the drama, yet always a music that, through its intricacies and its variations, was a reflection of the shades and shadows that lay behind that boldness. The *Ring* music also displayed delicacy and intimacy. It was a sound that coursed its way almost as a single *melos* (song), infinite because it had neither genesis nor finis. It was, at the same time, a music that somehow entered and inundated the far reaches of the human conscience, a music that bared the unconscious and made its hidden and concealed secrets into conscious reality. It was a music that explored the totality of the human experience. Wagner's music was, in the end, all he had said it would be. In a letter to Franz Liszt he had written: "The thing shall 'sound' in such fashion that people shall hear what they cannot see."

9.5 A MUSICAL SAMPLER OF THE *Ring*

One can fully appreciate the drama of the *Ring* only if one thoroughly understands its argument, and an individual can greatly increase enjoyment of its music by becoming familiar with the themes that Wagner conceived and developed in the musical dramatization of the poem. However, it is also possible that much of the music of the *Ring* can be pleasurable simply as music.

The selections cited here will serve both as an introduction to the techniques of Wagner's art and as a demonstration of that art which has set him apart in the world of music. The selections are listed in the order of their appearance in the *Ring*. The overall lack of arias, duets, and choruses, so much a part of traditional opera, makes it difficult to state precisely either the exact beginning or end of many of the selections; hence, the textual indications given are approximations only. The playing time shown for each selection is also approximate. If any selection is generally known by a specific title, that name is given in parentheses after the short description of the scene.

1. *Das Rheingold*

    a. Scene 1   26'
        FROM: Opening music
        TO: Scene 2, Fricka—"Wotan, Gemahl! Erwache!"
        As the three Rhine Daughters frolic in the waters of the Rhine, Alberich enters the river from his home in Nibelheim. Lustfully, he pursues the nymphs, who reject him. The Dwarf then learns the secret of the Gold, forswears love, and steals the magic Treasure. (This selection includes the transition music as the scene changes from the waters of the Rhine to a mountain top where Wotan and Fricka lie sleeping.)

    b. Scene 2   6'
        FROM: Loge—"Mich kümmert's minder"

TO: Beginning of scene 3
Wotan finally resolves to win the Gold from Alberich. The King of the Gods and Loge then descend to Nibelheim, home of the Nibelung Dwarfs. (Includes "Descent into Nibelheim")

   c. Scene 4   24'
FROM: Erda—"Weiche, Wotan, weiche!"
TO: End of the drama
Erda warns Wotan of the impending doom if he does not rid himself of the cursed Ring. The King of the Gods gives the last of the Treasure to the Giants, who then quarrel over their shares. Fafner kills Fasolt and leaves with the Gold. Wotan, filled with dread, is cheered by his wife who encourages him to enter his new fortress. Donner sweeps the sky clear of the mists, and Froh calls forth the Rainbow Bridge over which the gods pass in order to enter Valhalla. (Includes "Wotan's Greeting to Valhalla" and "Entrance of the Gods into Valhalla")

2. *Die Walküre*

   a. Act I   5'
FROM: Opening music
TO: Scene 1, Siegmund—"Wes Herd dies auch sei"
This is the orchestral prelude of violent, stormy music that introduces scene 1.

   b. Act I, scene 3   15'
FROM: Siegmund—"Keiner ging"
TO: End of Act I
Siegmund and Sieglinde discover who they are, and as they give expression to the love they have found, Siegmund finds the sword promised him long ago by his father, a sword that he names Notung. (This scene includes the music that is known as the "Spring Song," a name that Cosima Wagner gave to the piece, and which was her favorite music of the *Ring*.)

   c. Act II, scene 1   5'
FROM: Opening music
TO: Wotan—"Der alte Sturm"
Wotan commands Brünnhilde to prepare for the battle between Siegmund and Hunding and orders that the latter shall fall. Brünnhilde gives her greeting of the Valkyries and leaves. (Includes "Hoyotoho")

d. Act II, scene 5   10'

Siegmund, with Sieglinde nearby, awaits the arrival of Hunding with whom he then does battle. Brünnhilde disobeys her father's order and attempts to protect Siegmund. Wotan appears and, through his godly powers, Siegmund is killed. Brünnhilde recovers the pieces of the Volsung's shattered sword and then helps Sieglinde to her horse and the two flee. Wotan, filled with contempt, waves his Spear, and Hunding falls dead. The King of the Gods, in great wrath, storms after Brünnhilde, vowing that she will suffer dreadful punishment for her disobedience.

e. Act III, Scene 1   8'

FROM: Opening music

TO: Waltraute—"Nach dem Tann lenkt sie"

The Valkyries arrive at Brünnhildenstein (Brünnhilde's Rock) on their journey from the battlefield to Valhalla. ("The Ride of the Valkyries")

f. Act III, scene 3   20'

FROM: Wotan—"In festen Schlaf"

TO: End of drama

Wotan bids farewell to his favorite daughter whom he must banish from the World of the Gods because of her disobedience when she ignored his command to allow Siegmund to die. He leads her to the top of Brünnhilde's Rock where he kisses away her godhead and brings upon her a magic sleep from which she can be awakened only by a fearless mortal. The King of the Gods then surrounds the rock with a great wall of flame. (Includes "Wotan's Farewell" and "Magic Fire Music")

3. *Siegfried*

a. Act I, scene 1   9'

FROM: Opening music

TO: Entrance of Siegfried

Mime sits on an anvil in his forest cave. The Dwarf laments how useless have been his labors to forge a sword that Siegfried cannot break. If he can forge the pieces of Notung, then Siegfried can slay the Dragon with it and Mime will be able to have the Gold and its powers for himself. ("Mime's Lament")

b. Act I, scene 3   15'

FROM: Siegfried—"Notung! Notung!"

TO: End of Act I

Mime cannot reforge the pieces of Notung. Because the Dwarf has promised to teach him to fear by leading him to the Dragon, Siegfried grabs the fragments, applies the bellows to the fire, and reforges Notung himself. ("Forging Scene")

c. Act II, scene 2   8'

FROM: Siegfried—"Dass der mein Vater nicht ist"

TO: Siegfried—"Er schweigt und lauscht"

In the forest near the Dragon's cave, Siegfried stretches out under a linden tree. Mime has left, and the Volsung is alone. Siegfried wonders aloud what his father looked like and says that he would like to see his mother. Gradually, the youth finds delight in the sounds of nature which surround him. ("Forest Murmurs")

d. Act III, scenes 2–3   55'

FROM: Wanderer—"Kenntest du mich"

TO: End of drama

Wanderer (Wotan) attempts to prevent Siegfried from finding the fire-girded rock on which Brünnhilde sleeps. Wanderer holds out his Spear to bar the way. Siegfried splinters the Spear with his sword, Notung. Wanderer, now without his power, turns away as the youth makes his way to Brünnhilde's Rock. The Volsung penetrates the wall of flame and makes his way to the top where he finds the sleeping maid. He removes her armor, and drawn by Brünnhilde's beauty, he kisses her tenderly. Brünnhilde awakens. The joys of first love are soon stirred in the two. Their rapture becomes more intense, and as the act ends, they pledge themselves to each other, both in life and in death. (Includes "Awakening Scene" and "Love Duet")

4. *Götterdämmerung*

a. Prelude   12'

FROM: Opening music

TO: First Norn—"Dämmert der Tag?"

It is night as the three Norns attempt to resume spinning the Cord of Destiny. They discuss the World Ash Tree, Wotan, and his Spear. They tell how Siegfried shattered the Spear, thus putting an end to Wotan's divine rule and how, now, the gods sit forlornly in Valhalla awaiting their doom. (Fragment of the "Norn Scene")

b. Prelude   21'
FROM: First Norn—"Hinab!"
TO: Beginning of Act I
Brünnhilde and Siegfried vow anew their love and bid farewell to
each other as the new bride sends her husband away to seek new
adventures and deeds of glory. (Includes "Siegfried's Rhine Journey")

c. Act II, scene 3   11'
Hagen summons the vassals to welcome the return of Gunther
and his bride, Brünnhilde.

d. Act II, scene 4   11'
FROM: Siegfried—"Achtest du so"
TO: End of scene
Siegfried swears on a spear that he has not dishonored Brünnhilde
and dedicates the spear to his death if he has acted falsely. Brünnhilde also swears on the same spear that Siegfried has betrayed
every vow he has taken and that he has sworn falsely. She then
dedicates the spear to his death for his treachery. Siegfried, weary
of the argument, then invites all to go on with the wedding
ceremony. (Includes "Spear Oath")

e. Act II, scene 5   14'
Brünnhilde reveals Siegfried's vulnerable spot to Hagen as she and
Gunther, urged on by Hagen, seek revenge for their dishonor. The
three then vow that Siegfried shall pay for his act of betrayal with
his life as Hagen schemes to seize the Ring. ("The Great Trio")

f. Act III, scene 2   16'
FROM: Siegfried—"Rasch ohne Zögern"
TO: End of scene
As Siegfried tells the Gibichung vassals how he penetrated the
flames and then awakened Brünnhilde, Hagen buries his spear in
the Volsung's back. Siegfried gives a final greeting to Brünnhilde
and dies, and his body is then borne away by the vassals. (Includes
"Siegfried's Farewell" and "Funeral March")

g. Act III, scene 3   21'
FROM: Brünnhilde—"Starke Scheite"
TO: End of drama
Brünnhilde gives praise to the dead Siegfried. She removes the
Ring from his hand and places it on her finger, promising it to
the Rhine Daughters, once it has been cleansed by the fire. She

lights Siegfried's pyre and, with her horse, enters the fire. The flames spread and reach into Valhalla, to the gods. The Rhine overflows and floods the scene as the Rhine Daughters rush in to retrieve the Ring from the ashes. Hagen scurries to retrieve the Ring for himself and is pulled into the waters by the nymphs. (Includes "Brünnhilde's Immolation" and "Destruction of the Gods")

Chapter Ten

The *Ring* in Recordings

It is only in recent years that *Der Ring des Nibelungen* has been available to the public in audio-recorded form, and even newer is the availability of the music drama in recorded form for television. Until the introduction of the tape recorder and the long-playing record, the length and musical format of the *Ring* ruled out, for all practical purposes, the possibility of a complete audio recording. The first commercial audio recording of the *Ring* was not completed until 1965. However, the artistic and financial success of that first *Ring* recording on long-playing disk prompted others, and within the next few years several complete recordings of the drama came onto the market. The majority of these later recordings were taken from live performances that had been recorded as early as 1950. In more recent times, some of these complete recordings have been transferred electronically to Compact Disk, and a few have also been recorded for viewing on laser disk and VHS television format. (Several of the audio recordings listed have been transferred to commercial audio cassettes, although these recordings are not listed in this book.)

The information that follows pertains only to *complete* recordings of the *Ring*.[1] (There have been numerous recordings of the individual dramas.) The presentation of data is in the chronological order determined by date of each original recording.

CD – Compact disks
LD – Laser Disk

---

[1] The casts for most of these recorded cycles are listed in *Wagner Companion*, 236–254.

LP – Long playing records
TV – VHS television tape cassettes

A. Peerless Murray Hill

11 LP
One boxed set without libretti or notes
Monaural
Wilhelm Furtwängler, conductor
Orchestra and Chorus of Teatro alla Scala, Milan
Recorded: Teatro alla Scala, Milan, 1950
    Live performances
        Das Rheingold—4 March 1950
        Die Walküre—9 March 1950
        Siegfried—22 March 1950
        Götterdämmerung—2 April 1950

(This audio recording was also issued by Arkadia, 12 CD, and in 1984 the original was remastered by the Italian firm Fonit-Cetra. The remastered recording is available only as a complete *Ring*, 18 LP, libretto in German with some notes in English.)

B. "Bruno Walter Society"

11 LP
Four Albums

(This recording is a private issue of 10-A.)

C. Melodram (Italy)

16 LP
Four albums, with libretti
Monaural
Joseph Keilberth, conductor
Orchestra and Chorus of the Bayreuth Festival Theater
Recorded: Bayreuth Festival Theater, 1952
    Live performances

(These recordings were made in 1952, but were not released commercially until 1984.)

D. Foyer Imports

17 LP
Four albums, no libretti
Monaural
Clemens Krauss, conductor
Orchestra and Chorus of the Bayreuth Festival Theater
Recorded: Bayreuth Festival Theater, 1953
   Live performances

E. Seraphim

18 LP; transferred to 13 CD
Four albums with libretti and notes included
Monaural
Wilhelm Furtwänger, conductor
Orchestra and Chorus of RAI Rome Symphony
Recorded: Studios of RAI Radiotelevisione Italiana, Rome, October–
   November 1953.

The LP recording of *Das Rheingold* was made in its entirety in one session. The remaining music dramas were recorded one act at a time with a few days between each recording session. These LP recordings were carried out before an invited audience, each of whom had to attest that he did not suffer from any illness that might force him to cough. The broadcasts of these recordings were first made on Rome Radio on four separate evenings.

(This Seraphim LP recording is now out of print, but the set was reissued by EMI, 1972. 18 LP with libretti.)

F. Opera Live Cetra

18 LP
Four albums without libretti or notes
Monaural
Hans Knappertsbusch, conductor
Orchestra and Chorus of the Bayreuth Festival Theater
Recorded: Bayreuth Festival Theater, 1957
   Live performances
      Das Rheingold—14 August 1957
      Die Walküre—15 August 1957
      Siegfried—16 August 1957
      Götterdämmerung—18 August 1957

G. London

19 LP; transferred to 15 CD
Available as individual albums and as a cased set of four albums, each with notes and libretti.
Stereo
Sir Georg Solti, conductor
Vienna Philharmonic Orchestra and the Chorus of the Vienna State Opera
Recorded: the Sofiensaal, Vienna, 1958–1965
Das Rheingold—22 September–9 October 1958
Die Walküre—29 October–November 1965
Siegfried—16–17 May; 21 October–5 November 1962
Götterdämmerung—May–June; 26 October–5 November; 5–26 November 1964

(An abridged version of this recording is available in a four-record LP album with notes.)

The original boxed set of LP disks included a copy of *Ring Resounding* in which John Culshaw, the author and director of the recording, recounts the interesting story of this recorded cycle.

(Telefunken (Germany) has repressed this *Ring* by the Teledec direct-metal process and has reissued the recording on 14 LP.)

Selections from this recording, coupled with some re-recorded excerpts, form the musical basis of the recording "An Introduction to *Der Ring des Nibelungen*." Narration is by Deryck Cooke.

H. Phillips

16 LP; 14 CD
One album with notes and libretti
Stereo
Karl Böhm, conductor
Orchestra and Chorus of the Bayreuth Festival Theater
Recorded: Bayreuth Festival Theater, 1966–1967
Live Performances
Das Rheingold—July 1966
Die Walküre—July 1967
Siegfried—July 1966
Götterdämmerung—July 1967

I. Deutsche Grammophon

19 LP; 15 CD
Available as individual LP albums or as a cycle in a presentation case
with a fifth album that contains notes and libretti.
Stereo
Herbert von Karajan, conductor
Berlin Philharmonic Orchestra and Chorus of the Deutsche Oper
Recorded: Berlin, 1967–1970
Das Rheingold—1968
Die Walküre—1967
Siegfried—1969
Götterdämmerung—1970

(An abridged version of the recording is available in a four-record LP
album with notes.)

J. Westminister Gold Series

19 LP
Four albums
Stereo
Hans Swarowsky, conductor
Suddeutsche Philharmonie Orchestra and Chorus of the Vienna State
Opera

A record magazine, published in Italy, requested that certain parts of
the *Ring* be recorded in order that a disk of excerpts could be prepared
and then distributed to its subscribers. When the conductor, musicians, and singers gathered in Munich to discuss their work, they
ultimately decided to record the entire tetralogy. The work was reviewed world-wide in 1974.

K. Angel (EMI) Sung in English

20 LP
Four albums with libretti and notes
English translation by Andrew Porter
Stereo
Reginald Goodall, conductor

Orchestra and Chorus of the English National Opera (Sadler's Wells Opera Orchestra)
Recorded: The Coliseum, London, 1973–1977
Live performances
The Rhinegold—10, 19, 25, 29 March 1975
The Valkyrie—18, 20, 23 December 1975
Siegfried—2, 8, 21 August 1973
Twilight of the Gods—6, 13, 27 August 1977

L. Philips

16 LP, 12 CD, 11 LD, 7 TV
Available as a cycle with libretti and a special illustrated booklet in a carrying case.
Stereo/Digital. (The first three parts of this recording are digital recordings, while *Götterdämmerung* is an analogue recording.)
Pierre Boulez, conductor
Orchestra and Chorus of the Bayreuth Festival Theater
Recorded: Bayreuth Festival Theater.
Live performances
Das Rheingold—1980
Die Walküre—1980
Siegfried—1980
Götterdämmerung—1979

This recording, both audio and visual, is that of the 1976 Centenary Anniversary production at Bayreuth. The LD and TV albums include "The Making of the *Ring*," with an Introduction by Friedlind Wagner, granddaughter of Richard Wagner.

M. RCA/Eurodisk

19 CD (Not available on LP)
Stereo
Marek Janowski, conductor
Orchestra and Chorus of Dresden State Opera
Recorded: 1985 (?)

N. EMI

14 CD
Stereo

Bernard Haitink, conductor
Orchestra and Chorus Bayerischen Rundfunks
Recorded: (Date unavailable)

O. Deutsche Grammophon

15 LP, 11 LD, 15 CD, TV
Available in four LP and CD albums with notes and libretti, and as a
set in a deluxe collectors edition slipcase.
Stereo
James Levine, conductor
Orchestra and Chorus of the Metropolitan Opera
Recorded: 1988–1992

P. [Not released]

The Bayreuth Festival performances of 1951, Hans Knappertsbusch,
conductor, were recorded in monaural sound and intended for reproduction on records for public distribution. These master tapes, however, have never been used for commercial recordings, and the reasons
for this failure have never been made public.

Appendix A

A Chronological Summary of Wagner's Operatic Works

The dates shown on the following table, except those under the heading "PREMIERE," are those of completion.

The column headed *Premiere* includes the name of the conductor of that first performance as well as the city in which the premiere was held.

Table 9

	Sketch/ Scenario	Poem	Musical Sketches	Score	Premiere
Die Feen	Fall 1832	Jan. 1833	Dec. 1833	Jan. 1834	29 June 1888 Hermann Levi Munich
Das Liebes- verbot oder die Novize von Palermo	June 1834	Oct. 1834	Jan. 1836	Jan. 1836	29 March 1836 Richard Wagner Magdeburg
Rienzi, der Letzte der Tribunen	July 1837	Aug. 1838	Oct. 1840	ACT I—Feb. 1839 ACT II— Apr. 1839 ACTS III, IV, V—Nov. 1840	20 Oct. 1842 Karl Reissiger Dresden

Table 9 cont.

Table 9 (continued)

	Sketch/ Scenario	Poem	Musical Sketches	Score	Premiere
Der fliegende Holländer	May 1840	May 1841	Aug. 1841	Nov. 1841	2 January 1843 Richard Wagner Dresden
Tannhäuser und der Sängerkrieg auf Wartburg	July 1842	Apr. 1843	ACT I— Jan. 1844 ACT II— Oct. 1844 ACT III— Dec. 1844	Apr. 1845	19 Oct. 1845 Richard Wagner Dresden
Lohengrin	Aug. 1845	Nov. 1845	ACT III— Mar. 1847 ACT I— June 1847 ACT II— Aug. 1847	Apr. 1848	28 August 1850 Franz Liszt Weimar
Tristan und Isolde	Sept. 1857	Sept. 1857	ACT I— Dec. 1857 ACT II— July 1858 ACT III— July 1859	Aug. 1859	10 June 1865 Hans von Bülow Munich
Die Meistersinger von Nürnberg	Nov. 1861	Jan. 1862	Mar. 1867	Oct. 1867	21 June 1968 Hans von Bülow Munich
Das Rheingold*	Mar. 1852	Nov. 1852	Jan. 1854	May 1854	22 Sept. 1869 Franz Wüllner Munich
Die Walküre*	May 1852	July 1852	Dec. 1854	Mar. 1856	26 June 1870 Franz Wüllner Munich
Siegfried*	June 1851	June 1851	ACT I, II— June 1857 ACT III— Aug. 1869	ACT I— Mar. 1857 ACT II— Aug. 1857 ACT III— Feb. 1871	16 August 1876 Hans Richter Bayreuth

Table 9 cont.

Appendix A

Table 9 (continued)

	Sketch/ Scenario	Poem	Musical Sketches	Score	Premiere
Götter-dämmerung *	Nov. 1848	Nov. 1848	ACT I— June 1870 ACT II— Nov. 1871 ACT III— Apr. 1872	Nov. 1874	17 August 1876 Hans Richter Bayreuth
Parsifal	Feb. 1877	Apr. 1877	PRELUDE— Sept. 1877 ACT I— Jan. 1878 ACT II— Oct. 1878 ACT III— Apr. 1879	Jan. 1882	26 July 1882 Hermann Levi Bayreuth

*For a more detailed review of dates, see Tables 4 and 5.

Appendix B

Notes on the Cast and Principals of the 1876 Premiere of the *Ring* at Bayreuth

BETZ, FRANZ (1835–1900)

This German baritone, who had sung mostly Italian and French operas in his early days, eventually became a superior performer of Wagnerian roles. Betz was one of the soloists in the performance of Beethoven's Ninth Symphony at the laying of the cornerstone of the Festival Theater on May 22 (Wagner's birthdate), 1872 in Bayreuth. In time, in addition to his role in the *Ring*, Betz sang those of Telramund, King Marke, Kurvenal, Wolfram, and the Dutchman. Betz's favorite role, however, was that of Hans Sachs, a role that he had created at the premiere of *Die Meistersinger von Nürnberg* in Munich in 1868, and which he sang no less than 100 times in Berlin alone. After Wagner's death, he sang the same role under the directorship of Cosima Wagner at Bayreuth.

BRANDT, KARL (1828–1881)

Brandt's previous work as a technical director at Darmstadt earned him an appointment at Bayreuth. Although it is reputed that Brandt was a difficult and demanding supervisor, he was very active in the construction of the Festival Theater as well as in the premiere production of the *Ring*. Brandt died before he had completed the machinery required for the premiere of *Parsifal* at Bayreuth in 1882, and his work was carried out by his son, Fritz (1854–1895). (It was Brandt's brother, Friedrich Carl [1846–1927] who had been chief machinist for the initial performances of *Das Rheingold* and *Die Walküre*, in Munich, in 1869 and 1870 respectively. These productions had come about by royal orders of Ludwig II and were very much opposed by Wagner.

BRANDT, MARIANNE (Born: Marie Bischoff) (1842–1921)

Brandt, a mezzo-soprano from Austria, had been singing in Berlin since 1868 and had become the understudy to Luise Jaïde who was to sing the *Götterdämmerung* Waltraute. Brandt stepped in when the later became indisposed. In time, Brandt established herself as a foremost performer of the Wagnerian roles. She sang Brangäne in the first performance of *Tristan und Isolde* in London in 1882 and shared the role of Kundry with Amalia Materna and Therese Malten in the premiere at Bayreuth of *Parsifal* in 1882. In 1886 Brandt sang the first Brangäne in the United States as well as the first Kundry, a concert performance that raised some concern because of the possible infringements upon the copyright of the music drama.

BRÜCKNER BROTHERS

Max (1839–1919) and Gotthold (1844–1892) were employees of the Court Theater in Coburg who executed Josef Hofmann's scenic designs for the *Ring* after the latter and Wagner fell into disagreement. Ironically, Wagner engaged them at Hofmann's recommendation. The pair also prepared the scenery for the 1882 premiere of *Parsifal* at Bayreuth and continued to work there after the composer's death.

DÖPLER, KARL EMIL (1824–1905)

Döpler was the costume designer for the Court Theater in Weimar, 1868–1870. In March 1876, Cosima Wagner writes in her *Diaries* of Döpler's "lovely costumes for the *Ring*." However, by July of that year she had changed her mind completely, writing that Döpler's figurines reveal "an archaeologist's fantasy to the detriment of the tragic and mythical elements [of the *Ring*]." No doubt Cosima's reactions to Döpler's work were much influenced by those of her husband who did not like the designer's illusory concepts of Nordic life to represent the characters that Wagner insisted came from the *Nibelungenlied*. In the end Döpler became quite an irritant to the Wagner family.

Döpler's recollections of matters during the *Ring* project were related to P. Cook and were published in book form, *A Memoir of Bayreuth, 1876*, in English, in London, 1979. The work includes illustrations of his costume designs for the premiere of the *Ring* in 1876.

EILERS, ALBERT (1830–1896)

Eilers was originally scheduled to sing the roles of Fasolt and Hunding, but was replaced in the latter role by Joseph Niering. (It was Eilers who, in 1878, translated into German the zarzuela *La conquista de Madrid* [*The Conquest of Madrid*]. This Spanish musical drama, by the talented composer Joaquín Gaztambide y Garbayo, was performed in Coburg, 25 December 1878, and became the first work of its type to be performed in Germany.)

FISCHER, FRANZ (1849–1918)

Fischer was a cellist from Munich who became a member of the *Nibelungenkanzlei*[1]. He conducted at Munich from 1879, and also conducted performances of *Parsifal* at Bayreuth, to which he frequently returned.

FRICKE, RICHARD (1818–1903)

A respected ballet master from Dessau, Fricke first met Wagner in 1872; the composer was much impressed with his talents in grouping and movement, as well as with his personality and character. The two became close friends. Portions of Fricke's diary, sections that dealt with his life and work while in Bayreuth, were translated into English and published in serial form in *Wagner*, the publications of the Wagner Society in London, in 1990–1991.

GURA, EUGEN (1842–1906)

Gura made his debut in Munich in 1865 and later sang in Breslau, Hamburg, and Leipzig, returning to Munich in 1883–1895. It was Gura who introduced the roles of Hans Sachs (*Die Meistersinger*) and King Marke (*Tristan und Isolde*) to English audiences with the first performances of these works in London in 1882. Gura continued at Bayreuth until 1892, singing these roles as well as that of Amfortas (*Parsifal*). In 1905 he published his memoirs, *Erinnerungen aus meinem Leben* (*Recollections of My Life*).

HAUPT, MARIE (?)

It is possible that Haupt was contracted for the Bayreuth *Ring* through

---

[1] *Nibelungenkanzlei* ("Nibelungen Chancellery") A humorous name given to a group of skilled and talented artists whose principal first assignment was to prepare the parts of the Ring for each of the instruments of the orchestra, for the 1876 premiere. Because of this work, Wagner and his wife also called the group the *Kopistery* ("copyistery"). Later, during the rehearsals and performances, the members of this group assisted in any manner that contributed to an efficient production.

the intervention of her fiance, Unger, the 1876 Siegfried. Unger frequently absented himself from his instruction and his training for this role in order to visit with Marie. After the Bayreuth premiere of the *Ring*, the two were married.

HILL, KARL (1831–1893)

Although born in Nassau, the German baritone spent most of his life in Germany where his first major position was that of postal official in Frankfurt am Main. He made his operatic debut in Schwerin, in 1868. Wagner heard Hill in a performance of *Der fliegende Holländer* in 1873 and asked him to sing the *Ring*'s Alberich. He sang Klingsor at the 1882 premiere in Bayreuth of Wagner's last work, *Parsifal*.

HOFMANN, JOSEF (1831–1904)

Hofmann was a landscape artist and court painter in Vienna when he was engaged by Wagner to prepare the scenic designs for the *Ring*. Although he had designed sets for Mozart's *The Magic Flute* and Weber's *Der Freischütz*, both Wagner and his wife soon became disillusioned with Hofmann's talents in theatrical matters, and the situation worsened when personal friction developed between the painter and the Wagners. In 1874 Wagner contracted with the Brückner brothers to execute the designs, a move that angered Hofmann, who then attempted to exercise his rights over his work. In October of that year Wagner wrote Hofmann that the decision was final and that he was certain that appropriate compensation could be negotiated. Hofmann's drawings for the *Ring* have been preserved, and are in the archives maintained in Wagner's home in Bayreuth.

JACHMANN-WAGNER, JOHANNA (1826–1894)

Johanna became the adopted daughter of Wagner's brother, Albert, when the latter married her mother in 1828. She had a celebrated singing career through which, at the age of eighteen, she created the role of Elizabeth in 1845 in the first production of *Tannhäuser*. In 1862 her voice failed and she turned to acting. When she regained her voice, she returned to vocal roles and was a soloist in Beethoven's Ninth Symphony at the laying of the foundation stone of the Festival Theater in Bayreuth in 1872. In 1926 her son, Hans Jackmann [*sic*], wrote in his biography that Wagner had created the role of Brünnhilde for his mother.

JÄIDE, LUISE (1842–1914)

Jäide became indisposed for the second cycle of the *Ring* (1876) and was replaced as Erda by Hedwig Reicher-Kindermann and by the Austrian Marianne Brandt as the *Götterdämmerung* Waltraute. Jäide slipped from public view, but Brandt became one of the most celebrated of Wagnerian singers.

KASTNER, EMERICH (1847–1916)

Kastner was employed by Wagner as a copyist despite the fact that he was much disliked by Cosima Wagner. Kastner began work in September, 1872, and was dismissed in January, 1873. During the next few years, and with little regard for Wagner's protestations, he prepared a *Wagner-Katalog*, a catalogue of Wagner's works and letters. Cosima wrote in her *Diaries* in April 1878, that Kastner's catalogue had many incorrect entries and that the work was of no value whatsoever!

LALAS, DEMETRIOS STERGIOU (1844–1911)

In the 1876 *Ring* program this Wagnerian's name is spelled "Demetrius Lallas." He was recommended to Wagner by Hans Richter, and joined the *Nibelungenkanzlei* in 1874. Lalas was born and died in Macedonia, but he moved to Thessaloniki (Greece) in 1856, and then to Athens in 1859 where he studied music, music history, and music composition. After the Bayreuth *Ring*, and because of his successful work in Bayreuth, Lalas was named Musical Director of the conservatory in Athens. (In 1917 Lalas's family gathered an extensive library of his compositions and sent them to Italy, on an Italian ship. During the journey, the ship was sunk by a German U-Boat.)

LAMMERT, MARIE (1852–?)

Lammert was a company singer at the Berlin Opera from 1873 to 1896.

LEHMANN, LILLI (1848–1929)

Lilli, a sister of Marie Lehmann, took her vocal training from her mother, Marie Lowe (1807–1883), a prominent musician and singer and a friend of Wagner. Lehmann gained an international reputation as one of the foremost Wagnerian singers of her time. In 1896 she sang Brünnhilde in the Bayreuth *Ring* (the first time there since the premiere); she also sang the first Isolde, in 1886, in the United States (she had been offered the role of Brangäne, but had refused the offer). She also was the first *Götterdämmerung* Brünnhilde in that country, in 1888. In 1913 she published a book, *Mein Weg (My Path)*, in which she gives an interesting account of the summer of 1876, with direction under Wagner himself. It can be said that Lilli Lehmann was the first international

Wagnerian diva. (During her career, Lehmann sang 170 roles in 119 operas.)

LEHMANN, MARIE (1851–1931)

Like her sister, Lilli, Marie received her vocal training from her mother, and made her debut in Leipzig in 1867. She was a soloist in Beethoven's Ninth Symphony at the laying of the foundation stone of the Festival Theater in Bayreuth in 1872 and was a member of the Vienna Opera from 1881 to 1902.

MATERNA, AMALIA (Amalie) (1844–1918)

This Austrian soprano, whose last name is sometimes given as Friedrich-Materna, made her debut in 1864 and became one of the great Wagnerian singers of her day. She sang in the Wagner concerts in London in 1877 and shared the role of Kundry with Marianne Brandt and Therese Malten in the premiere of *Parsifal* at Bayreuth in 1882. During the 1884–1885 season at the Metropolitan Opera in New York, Materna sang the first Brünnhilde (*Die Walküre*) in that house, and Elizabeth (*Tannhäuser*).

MOTTL, FELIX (1856–1911)

Upon the recommendation of Franz Liszt, Mottl was appointed to the *Nibelungenkanzlei* in May 1876. After the Bayreuth premiere of the *Ring*, Mottl became a conductor and a composer. None of his three operas created much excitement in artistic circles. He achieved renown, however, as a Wagnerian conductor in London (where he conducted the *Ring* in 1898), Munich, New York, and Bayreuth where he served until 1906. Neither Wagner nor his wife became too friendly with Mottl, principally because he was quite fond of the music of Hector Berlioz!

NIEMANN, ALBERT (1831–1917)

The German tenor made his operatic debut in Dresden, in 1849, and he was a member of the Berlin Opera 1866–1889. Niemann sang the title role in 1861 in the first Paris production of *Tannhäuser*. (He sang the three performances that were given before Wagner withdrew the work because of audience jeering in what has been called the musical scandal of the century.) He also was a soloist in 1872 at the laying of the foundation stone of the Festival Theater in Bayreuth. Niemann wanted to sing the roles of Loge, Siegmund, and Siegfried in the Bayreuth premiere of the *Ring*, but Wagner was against any singer undertaking two major roles in one cycle. Niemann continued as Siegmund

in 1882 in the first London cycle and in 1886 the first *Götterdämmerung*
Siegfried in the United States.

NIERING, JOSEF (?–1891)

Niering was a last-minute replacement as Hunding for Albert Eilers.
Niering had been a company singer at Breslau, Danzig, and at Darmstadt
before his appearance at Bayreuth. After Bayreuth, Niering moved on
to Bremen.

REICHENBERG, FRANZ VON (1885–1905)

Reichenberg, from Mannheim, auditioned for Wagner in 1875 and was
engaged two months later.

REICHER-KINDERMANN, HEDWIG (1853–1883)

When Louise Jäide became indisposed during the second cycle of the
1876 *Ring*, Reicher-Kindermann substituted as Erda. She later joined
the Neumann company to sing the roles of Fricka, Brünnhilde, and
Waltraute in 1882, in the first London cycle. She continued with Neumann's group as it toured Europe with the *Ring* in 1883. Reicher-
Kindermann was the daughter of August Kindermann, celebrated
German bass-baritone who created the role of Wotan in the Munich
premieres of *Das Rheingold* and *Die Walküre*, in 1869 and 1870 respectively.

RICHTER, HANS (1843–1916)

Wagner employed this Austro-Hungarian in 1866 as a copyist for the
score of *Die Meistersinger*. Three years later the former horn player at
the Vienna Opera was appointed conductor for the contended premiere
of *Das Rheingold* in Munich, a production ordered by King Ludwig II.
Loyal to the composer, Richter resigned this position at Wagner's request. Richter later conducted Wagner's music dramas extensively, including in 1870 the Belgium premiere of *Lohengrin*, the first production
in London of *Tristan und Isolde* and *Die Meistersinger* in 1882, and
London's first *Ring* in English, in 1908. He remained associated with
Bayreuth as principal conductor until 1912, the year in which he conducted his last performance in the Festspielhaus, *Die Meistersinger*.
Richter was considered the foremost interpreter of Wagner during his
lifetime.

RUBENSTEIN, JOSEF (1847–1884)

The son of a wealthy Jewish family in Kharkov, Russia, Rubenstein studied with Franz Liszt, and went on to become an accomplished pianist. In 1872, in Lucerne, he sought out Wagner to ask assistance in order to cope with his Jewishness! Later Wagner employed him as a member of the *Nibelungenkanzlei*. Rubenstein became somewhat of a regular guest in the Wagner home in Bayreuth where he frequently played piano music for the family, some of which was his arrangement of parts of the *Ring*. Rubenstein was the author of an infamous literary attack on the composer Robert Schumann, an essay that was published in Wagner's monthly journal *Bayreuther Blätter*. Rubenstein became quite unpopular with the others who were associated with the *Ring* project in Bayreuth; his colleagues asserted that he monopolized Wagner. When Wagner died in 1883, Rubenstein became quite depressed and the following year, in Lucerne, he took his own life.

SADLER-GRÜN, FRIEDERICKE (1836–1917)
Hans Richter had heard Sadler-Grün sing Elvira in a production of *Don Giovanni* and recommended her to Wagner as a Valkyrie. She auditioned for the composer in July, 1874. She desired to sing the role of Brünnhilde, but her voice was not adequate for that role, and in November of that year it was decided that she would sing the role of Fricka and that of the Third Norn.

SCHEFFZKY, JOSEPHINE (?)
A singer in Munich from 1871 to 1879, she was assigned the role of Sieglinde when Wagner's first choice, Therese Vogl, became pregnant.

SCHLOSSER, KARL (Max) (1835–1916)
Schlosser had been unsuccessful as a singer in his earlier years. After a period as a baker, her returned to singing, going on to become a celebrated tenor. He was a member of the Munich Opera company during the years 1868–1904. This tenor from Augsburg created the role of David in the 1868 premiere of *Die Meistersinger* in Munich, and the following year he became the first Mime in Ludwig II's command premiere of *Das Rheingold* in the same city. He sang the same role in 1882 in the London premiere of the *Ring*. He toured with Neumann as Mime in 1880–1882.

SEIDL, ANTON (1850–1898)
Seidl, from Pest, Hungary, was recommended to Wagner by Hans Richter, to serve as a copyist and he became one of the several copyists who, as a group, acquired the name of *Nibelungenkanzlei*. Seidl went on to conduct in Leipzig, and then joined the Neumann company to

conduct the first London performance of the *Ring* in 1882, and also that city's first *Rienzi*. He then toured Europe with the Neumann company and its *Ring* performances in 1883. Seidl lived in the United States (1885–1889) where he became a celebrated conductor of Wagner's works, particularly at the Metropolitan Opera in New York. It was at the Metropolitan that he conducted the first American performances of five of the composer's operas: *Die Meistersinger*, 1886; *Tristan und Isolde*, 1886; *Siegfried*, 1887; *Götterdämmerung*, 1888; and *Das Rheingold*, 1889. *Das Rheingold* was a part of the first performance of the *Ring* Cycle in the United States, also conducted by Seidl. All in all, during the period 1885–1897, Seidl conducted 340 performances of Wagner's music dramas at the Metropolitan Opera. A year before his death he conducted *Parsifal* at Bayreuth.

SIEHR, GUSTAV (1837–1896)
Siehr, from Wiesbaden, so pleased Wagner with his 1876 performance as Hagen that the composer planned for him to sing Wotan in the 1877 Bayreuth production of the *Ring*, a production that never materialized. Siehr was a second Gurnemanz in the 1882 premiere of *Parsifal* at Bayreuth, where he continued to sing until 1889.

UNGER, GEORG (1837–1887)
Unger made his debut in 1867, in Leipzig, and although he was originally appointed to sing the role of Loge in the *Ring* premiere, he ultimately became the first Siegfried and thus the first *Wagnerheldentenor* (Wagner heroic tenor). For his 1876 appearance in the *Ring*, Unger studied the role several months in Munich and then spent much time in Bayreuth under Wagner's tutelage. In addition to his Siegfried role, Unger also sang Froh in the first of the three cycles of 1876. Although he never appeared again at Bayreuth, Unger sang in the Wagner concerts in London in 1877, and in 1878 sang Siegfried in the Neumann production in Leipzig.

VOGL, HEINRICH (1845–1900)
Vogl was the leading tenor of his day. This German singer (and composer) made his debut in Munich, in 1865, as Max in *Der Freischütz* (*The Freeshooter*), and he was a member of the Munich Opera from that date until his death. Vogl created the role of Loge in the 1869 premiere of *Das Rheingold*, ordered by Ludwig II, and the following year he and his wife, Therese Thoma (1845–1921), became the first Siegmund and Sieglinde in the premiere of *Die Walküre*, also a production ordered by Ludwig. Vogl was Wagner's choice to create the role of *Parsifal* for the

premiere at Bayreuth in 1882, but the singer insisted that his wife sing the part of Kundry, a condition that Wagner could not accept. Vogl became the favored Tristan of his day, and his wife was equally known for her roles as Isolde, Elsa, and Brünnhilde. Vogl sang the roles of Loge, Siegmund, and Siegfried in the one cycle of the first Berlin *Ring* in 1881 and those of Loge and Siegfried in the first London *Ring*—his wife sang Sieglinde in the London production—and he toured Europe with the Neumann *Ring* in 1883. In 1889 Vogl sang Siegfried in the Russian premiere of the tetralogy. Vogl was also popular in the United States, singing at the Metropolitan Opera in 1890. During that season, he sang the roles of Lohengrin, Tannhäuser, Tristan, Loge, Siegmund and the two Siegfrieds. He continued to sing at Bayreuth until 1897. In 1890, in Munich, he sang the role of Baldur in his own unsuccessful opera, *Der Fremdling (The Stranger)*. Four days before his death, he sang the role of Canio in *Pagliacci*.

WECKERLIN, MATHILDE (1848–1928)
Weckerlin was first considered for both the role of Sieglinde and that of Gutrune, the latter actually being her assignment when Scheffzky proved more acceptable vocally and dramatically as Sieglinde. After the *Ring* premiere Weckerlin continued as a singer with the Munich opera.

WILHELMJ, AUGUST (1845–1908)
Wilhelmj was already a celebrated violinist when he entered the Bayreuth picture. Wagner engaged him as temporary director of the orchestra in July 1872, and his charge was to execute Wagner's plans for that group. Wilhelmj remained close to the Wagner family after 1876, even though from 1894 until his death he worked as a music teacher in London.

ZIMMER, HERMANN (?)
Zimmer was from Karlsruhe and had written Wagner in 1872 expressing his desire to be involved in the Bayreuth project. Three years later Wagner appointed him to the *Nibelungenkanzlei*.

ZUMPE, HERMANN (1850–1903)
Zumpe had studied music at Leipzig before he was invited to join the *Nibelungenkanzlei*, the group that was working on *Ring* matters. He also studied conducting and eagerly accepted coaching from Wagner himself. After Bayreuth, he went on to become one of the most celebrated conductors of Wagner's music. He is known especially for a series of concerts of Wagner's music that he gave in Munich in 1900.

Appendix C

Notes on the Cast and Principals of the 1869 and 1870 Premieres of *Das Rheingold* and *Die Walküre* in Munich

Upon royal orders from Ludwig II, *Das Rheingold* was performed for the first time on 22 September 1869, at the Hof- und Nationaltheater (Munich Court Opera), in Munich. Ludwig then commanded the initial performance of *Die Walküre*, which took place on 26 June 1870, in the same theater. (Wagner was very much opposed to these performances.) Following is the cast of each of these first performances, with brief notes on some of the principals.

The majority of those involved in these two command-performances were *company* singers and workers, staff employed by the Munich Court Theater. Each participated, according to his talents and skills, in each production offered throughout the season. In the main, the singers were members of the chorus. Few of such members remained any length of time with the company, departing when it became evident that their future as a principal singer was doubtful. There were some, however, whose talent carried them beyond the chorus status and who, in one manner or another, established themselves in the operatic field. Following are brief notes relative to those singers and major staff.

166

Appendix C

Table 10
Premieres

	Das Rheingold	Die Walküre
August Kindermann	Wotan	Wotan
Karl Samuel Heinrich	Donner	
Franz Nachbaur	Froh	
Heinrich Vogl	Loge	Siegmund
Toni Petzer	Fasolt	
Kaspar Bausewein	Fafner	Hunding
Karl Fischer	Alberich	
Karl Schlosser	Mime	
Sophie Stehle	Fricka	Brünnhilde
Henriette Müller	Freia	Ortlinde
Therese Seehofer	Erda	Schwertleite
Anna Kaufmann	Woglinde	Fricka
Wilhelmine Ritter	Flosshilde	Grimgerde
Therese Vogl	Wellgunde	Sieglinde
Karoline Leonoff		Gerhilde
(?) Hemauer		Waltraute
Anna Possart-Deiner		Helmwige
Walburga Eichheim		Siegrune
(?) Tyroler		Rossweisse

Conductor	Franz Wüllner
Producer	Reinhard Hallwachs
Designers	Christian Jank
	Heinrich Döll
	Angelo Quaglio (Das Rheingold)
Costumes	Franz Seitz

BRANDT, FRIEDRICH CARL (1846–1927)

Brandt was Chief Machinist at the Munich Court Theater during the years 1865–1876. He was active in the premiere performances of not only *Das Rheingold* (1869) and *Die Walküre* (1870), but also in that of *Die Meistersinger von Nürnberg* (1868). In 1876, he began a similar position with the Berlin Opera. Friedrich Carl was a brother to Karl Brandt who served as Chief Machinist for the *Ring* premiere in Bayreuth.

DÖLL, HEINRICH (?)

Döll was a member of the staff of the Munich Court Opera for several years, during which time he worked with Angelo Quaglio and Christian Jank on the scenery and lighting for the premiere of *Die Meistersinger*

Appendix C

von Nürnberg (1868), followed by work on the premieres of *Das Rhein-gold* (1869) and *Die Walküre* (1870). Döll was also involved in other scenic matters for Wagner's music dramas in Munich: *Der fliegende Holländer* (1864), *Tristan und Isolde* (1867), and *Rienzi* (1871).

HALLWACHS, REINHARD (1833–1872)
This stage director was brought to Munich to direct the premiere of *Die Meistersinger von Nürnberg*. Wagner was pleased with Hallwachs's work and, despite his opposition to the project, recommended him to King Ludwig as producer of the 1869 *Das Rheingold*. Hallwachs proved to be a loyal admirer of Wagner and the success of his Wagner work prompted others to see him as a ranking director. On 26 June 1870, on the afternoon of the premiere of *Die Walküre*, and for reasons unknown, Hallwachs replaced Franz Grandaur (1822–1886) as resident stage director of the Munich Court Opera.

JANK, CHRISTIAN (?)
Jank was a member of the Munich Court Opera staff and had worked at length with Angelo Quaglio and Heinrich Döll on numerous scenic and lighting matters. In 1868, he worked with them on the scenic and lighting work for the initial performance of *Die Meistersinger von Nürnberg*. (Wagner liked Jank's work.) Later, Ludwig II commissioned Jank and Angele Quaglio to develop themes and lighting for certain rooms in the castle that he had ordered built (Neuschwanstein).

KINDERMANN, AUGUST (1817–1891)
This German bass baritone had no formal voice training, yet his musical sensitivity and his powerful voice catapulted him onto the operatic scene. Kindermann served in the chorus of the Berlin Opera, moving on to Leipzig (1839–1846), followed by a long tenure in Munich (1846–1890), where he sang a wide repertory of operatic works. In addition to his creation of Wotan (*Das Rheingold* and *Die Walküre*), he also sang the first Titurel in the Bayreuth premiere of *Parsifal* in 1882. Kindermann was the father of Hedwig Reicher-Kindermann who sang Grimgerde in the 1876 premiere of the *Ring* at Bayreuth.

NACHBAUR, FRANZ IGNAZ (1835–1902)
This German tenor from Württemberg made his operatic debut in Passau, in 1857, after which he sang in Meiningen (1858), Hanover (1859), Prague (1860–1863), Darmstadt (1863–1869), and then to Munich Court Opera where he remained until 1890 and where he was appointed principal tenor. Nachbaur created the role of Walther in the premiere

168

Appendix C

of *Die Meistersinger von Nürnberg* (1868), a performance much to Wagner's pleasure. In addition to his role of Froh in the 1869 first performance of *Das Rheingold*, Nachbaur also sang the Wagnerian roles of Rienzi, Lohengrin, Siegmund, and Tannhäuser while with the Munich company. (At his farewell performance, which took place on 13 October 1890 and which was his 1001st appearance on the Munich stage, he sang the role of Chapelou in Adolphe Adam's popular *Le Postillon de Lonjumeau* [The Postilion of Lonjumeau].)

POSSART-DEINET, ANNA (?)

The singular significant factor in the career of Anna Deinet was that she married Ernst Ritter von Possart (1841–1921) who, in 1864, began an appointment as actor and stage director at the Munich Court Opera. In time, he rose to the position of General Director. It was von Possart who, after Wagner's death, revived the idea of a Richard Wagner Festival Theater to be held in Munich. (The theater would be constructed using the plans that had been drawn up in 1869 by the architect Gottfried Semper.) This idea, which seriously worried Cosima and the backers of the Bayreuth festival, never really became a serious threat. The theater was built, the Prinzregententheater, and the productions that came about would hardly rival what Bayreuth had to offer.

QUAGLIO, ANGELO (1829–1890)

Although Cosima Wagner writes in her *Diaries* that Quaglio is a "scene painter," this Munich-born staff designer was a member of the Italian, later German, family of illustrious stage designers that originated in 1765 and continued on into the twentieth century. Angelo, actually the second in the family to bear that name, worked at the Munich Court Opera with his father Simon (1795–1878) on numerous first productions of Wagner's works in Munich: *Der fliegende Holländer* (1864), *Tannhäuser* (1855), *Lohengrin* (1858) *Rienzi* (1871). In addition to his work for the world premieres of *Das Rheingold* (1869) and *Die Walküre* (1870), Quaglio was a principal in the world premieres of *Tristan und Isolde* (1865) and *Die Meistersinger von Nürnberg* (1868). Heinrich Döll worked with Quaglio, as did Christian Jank with whom Quaglio was commissioned by Ludwig II to design certain rooms at the Neuschwanstein castle after settings of acts of Wagner music dramas. Quaglio's son Eugen (1857–1942) carried on his father's work on the Wagner operas with designs for *Tannhäuser* (1890), *Lohengrin* (1891), *Rienzi* (1895), and *Tristan und Isolde* (1903).

Appendix C

SCHLOSSER, KARL
See Appendix B.

SEITZ, FRANZ (1817–1883)

Seitz, a costume designer and technical director at the Munich Court opera, designed the costumes for the world premiere there of *Tristan und Isolde*, 1865. Wagner liked Seitz' work and recommended him as a costume designer for the 1868 world premiere in Munich of *Der Meistersinger von Nürnberg*. Perhaps Wagner's pleasure with Quaglio's work is explained, at least in part, because Seitz followed Wagner's instructions to the letter!

STEHLE, SOPHIE (1838–1921)

Stehle, who was born in Hohenzallern-Sigmaringen, made her debut at the Munich Court Opera in 1860. (She sang the role of Emmeline in Weigl's *Die Schweizerfamilie* [*The Swiss Family*].) In addition to her creation of the roles of Fricka and Brünnhilde, she also sang the other Wagner roles of Senta, Elsa, Elizabeth, and Eva. Stehle was offered the role of Brangäne, but declined the offer.

VOGL, HEINRICH
See Appendix B.

VOGL, THERESE (1845–1921)

This wife of Heinrich Vogl created the role of Sieglinde, a role that Wagner wanted her to sing in the *Ring* premiere. Her pregnancy forced her to withdraw, although she later sang Brünnhilde in Munich (1878) and with Neumann's company in the first complete *Ring* in London (1882). Vogl also sang Elsa and Isolde, often performing with her husband, Heinrich Vogl. (See Appendix B).

WÜLLNER, FRANZ (1832–1902)

A conductor and composer of some repute, Wüllner was brought to Munich in 1869, as successor to Hans von Bülow, then the husband of Cosima Liszt von Bülow. Wüllner's original appointment was to develop a department of choral singing for a music school, but factors in the daily relationships of Richard Wagner, Ludwig II, and von Bülow soon cast him into the role of conductor of the command performance of *Das Rheingold*. Wüllner faced many problems as he developed the musical plan for the opera, not the least of which was Wagner himself. Wagner was unconditionally opposed to the production. A letter that he wrote to Wüllner, reproduced many times since it became public, clearly reveals Wagner's feelings on the matter. Among other things, Wagner wrote: "Hands off my score,—that is my advice to you, sir, or may the Devil take you! Beat time for glee clubs or amateur choirs." Despite Wagner's admonition, Wüllner continued at his task, the result of which was a quite successful production of the Wagner music drama. The following year, 1870, he enjoyed another success when he conducted the premiere of *Die Walküre*, again very much opposed by Wagner. This duo of artistic triumphs induced Ludwig to appoint Wüllner to the position of Court Conductor (1871).

A Selected Bibliography

<hr style="width:25%">

PART I. BOOKS

B.1 CRITERIA FOR INCLUSION

The titles included in this first section of selected bibliography represent works that, in the main, conform to most if not all of the following criteria:

1. A book-length publication (except those of Richard Wagner) whose theme and development correspond to the context of this handbook.
2. A work that does not necessarily require an extensive knowledge of music, opera, or Wagner to be appreciated.
3. A work written in or translated into English.
4. A work generally available either in better libraries or through publishers or book dealers in the United States.

Bibliographical Entries

1. If a work has had one or more reprints, the year of the original publication is shown in parentheses immediately following the pertinent title information. The bibliographical entry that follows (city, publisher, date) is automatically a reprint of the original publication.
2. For those works that have enjoyed several printings, only the data of the most recent printing known to the compiler is given.
3. A revised and/or enlarged edition of a work is so indicated.
4. If a work has been published by two publishers in the same year (usually one in the United States and one abroad), only an entry for the publisher in the United States is given.

B.2 GENERAL WORKS

Adorno, Theodor W. *In Search of Wagner (Versuch über Wagner)*. Translated by Rodney Livingston. (1981). New York: Verso, 1991.

Barth, Herbert, Dietrich Mack, and Egan Voss, eds. *Wagner: A Documentary Study*. Preface by Pierre Boulez. Translation of *Wagner, sein Leben, sein Werk, und sein Welt in Zeitgenössischen Bildern und*

Texten by P.R. Ford and Mary Whittall. New York: Oxford University Press, 1975.

An interesting reproduction of photographs, letters, drawings, scores, documents, and translations of Wagner and Wagner-related publications. Arranged in chronological order to illustrate the life and works of Wagner.

Burbridge, Peter, and Richard Sutton, eds. *The Wagner Companion.* New York: Cambridge University Press, [1979].

This work should not be confused with another publication (data relative to the premieres of Wagner's works) with the same title.

Chancellor, John. *Wagner.* Boston: Little, Brown and Company, [1978].

The life and works of Wagner "written for those who have, perhaps inadvertently, in their intellectual and spiritual journeyings, passed Wagner by."

Culshaw, John. *Wagner: The Man and His Music.* New York: E.P. Dutton, [1978].

A short bibliography of Wagner, profusely illustrated with photographs pertinent to each of his operas. An appropriate first adventure into the world of Wagner.

Deathridge, John, and Carl Dahlhaus. *The New Grove Wagner.* New York: W. W. Norton & Company, [1984].

A short biography derived from *The New Grove Dictionary of Music and Musicians.* 6th edition. 20 vols. Washington, D.C.: Macmillan Publishers Ltd., 1980.

Ellis, William Ashton. *The Life of Richard Wagner.* 6 vols. (1900–1908). New York: Da Capo, 1977.

Volumes I–III are translations of Carl Friedrich Glassenapp's biography of Wagner (*Richard Wagner, Leben und Wirken.* [1876–1877]). This latter work was called, at the time, the "first scientific biography," probably because the author had access to Wagner and his wife, and to much material that was kept in the Wagner home. In light of the idealized Wagner that is presented, factual accuracy is frequently questioned. Ellis's three volumes take Wagner's story down to 1859!

Gregor-Dellin, Martin. *Richard Wagner, His Life, His Work, His Century.* (*Richard Wagner: Leben, Werk, sein Jahrhundert*). Translated by J. Maxwell Brownjohn. San Diego, CA: Harcourt, Brace, Jovanovich, 1983.

Gutman, Robert W. *Richard Wagner: The Man, His Mind, and His Music.* (1968). San Diego, CA: Harcourt Brace Jovanovich, 1990.

A "Special Edition" of Gutman's work, which consisted of the text and additional material, including some four hundred pictures, photographs, drawings, and charts, was published in 1972, in New York by Time-Life Records.

Hodson, Phillip. *Who's Who in Wagner.* New York: Macmillan Publishing Co., [1984].

"An A-to-Z Look at his Life and Work."

Mack, Dietrich, and Egan Voss. *Richard Wagner: Life and Works in Dates and Pictures.* Translated by Patricia Crampton. Frankfurt am Main: SDV Saarbrücher Druckerei, und Verlag GmbH, 1983.

A shortened version of *Richard Wagner. Leben und Werk in Daten und Bildern.* Frankfurt am Main: Insel Verlag, 1978.

Mayer, Hans. *Portrait of Wagner (Richard Wagner in Selbstzengnissen und Bildokumenten).* Translated by Robert Nowell. New York: Herder and Herder, 1972.

———. *Richard Wagner in Bayreuth, 1876–1976 (Richard Wagner in Bayreuth 1876–1976).* Translated from the German by Jack Zipes. New York: Rizzoli International Publications, 1976.

A handsome volume with individual essays on Richard Wagner and members of his immediate family. Numerous photos accompany each essay.

Millington, Barry. *Wagner.* (1984). Revised edition. Princeton, NJ: Princeton University Press, 1992.

———, ed. *The Wagner Compendium.* New York: Schirmer Books, [1992].

An extensive collection of essays and articles by numerous authors on many aspects of Wagner, his life, and his works.

Müller, Ulrich, and Peter Wapnewski, eds. *Wagner Handbook (Richard Wagner Handbuch).* Translated by John Deathridge. Cambridge, MA: Harvard University Press, 1992.

This work is a rich collection of substantive essays and articles on Wagner's life and works. The original book, which was published in 1986, includes the following as part of the subtitle "...*unter Mitarbeit zahlreicher Fachwissenschaftliches herausgegeben.*"

Newman, Ernest. *The Life of Richard Wagner.* 4 vols. (1933–1946). New York: Cambridge University Press, 1976.

A thorough and detailed account of much of Wagner's life with valuable information about his works. Volume 1 covers the years 1813–1848; Volume 2, 1848–1860; Volume 3, 1859–1866; Volume 4, 1866–1883. Indispensable for the serious reader, despite the fact that research after the publication of the volume has rendered several of Newman's statements, if not totally incorrect, at least partially so.

Osborne, Charles. *Wagner and His World*. New York: Charles Scribner's Sons, [1977].

An informative work appropriate as a first encounter with Wagner's life and works.

Raphael, Robert. *Richard Wagner*. New York: Twayne Publishers, [1969].

Sabor, Rudolph. *The Real Wagner*. London: A. Deutsch, 1987.

Skelton, Geoffrey. *Richard and Cosima Wagner: Biography of a Marriage*. Boston: Houghton Mifflin Company, 1982.

Taylor, Ronald. *Richard Wagner: His Life and Thought*. New York: Taplinger Publishing Company, [1979].

Wagner, Cosima. *Cosima Wagner's Diaries—1869–1883*. Translation of *Die Tagebücher*, which were published in 1976–1977, with an introduction by Geoffrey Skelton. Edited by Martin Gregor-Dellin and Dietrich Mack. Vol. I—1869–1877; Vol II—1878–1883. New York: Harcourt Brace Jovanovich, 1978–[1980].

Although perhaps of more interest to advanced scholars of Wagner, these volumes reveal much of the personal lives of Cosima and Richard Wagner, and offer interesting information about the *Ring*.

Wagner, Richard. *My Life*. (1911). St. Clair Shores, MI: Scholarly Press, 1976.

Scholars have serious questions regarding the factualness of numerous statements and are equally concerned regarding the sometime romantic, or at least emotional, depiction given to certain elements in this work.

————.————. Edited by Mary Whittall. Translated by Andrew Gray. (1983). New York: Da Capo Press, [1992].

This volume purports to include matters not contained in the first translation (see above) as well as amplification of certain topics which were avoided in the earlier work. (Originally published in 1963 in German as *Mein Leben*.)

————. *Wagner Writes from Paris*. Edited and translated by Robert L. Jacobs and Geoffrey Skelton. New York: The John Day Company, [1973].

Stories, essays and articles written by the young composer.

————. *Selected Letters of Richard Wagner*. (1987). Edited and translated by Stewart Spencer and Barry Millington. New York: W. W. Norton, 1988.

A selection of 500 letters written by the composer.

————.*The Diary of Richard Wagner 1865–1882. The Brown Book*. Presented and Annotated by Joachim Bergfeld. Translated by George Bird. New York: Cambridge University Press, 1980.

Originally published as *Das braune Buch: Tagebuchaufzeichnungen 1865 bis 1882*. Zürich, 1975.

Watson, Derek. *Richard Wagner: A Biography*. (1979). New York: Schirmer Books, 1981.

Westernhagen, Curt von. *Wagner: A Biography*. Translated by Mary Whittall. Vol. I—1813–1864; Vol. II—1864–1883. New York: Cambridge University Press, [1978].

An extensive work that contains some data and information gathered from documents previously unavailable.

White, Chappell. *An Introduction to the Life and Works of Richard Wagner*. Englewood Cliffs, NJ: Prentice Hall, [1967].

B.3 WAGNER'S PROSE WORKS

Throughout this handbook references are made, both directly (by specific title) and indirectly, to several of the prose writings of Richard Wagner. These works are included as entries in the individual chapter bibliographies, each accompanied by an indication of where that title may be found in the following printings of the composer's collected writings.

Wagner, Richard. *Richard Wagner's Prose Works*. Translated by William Ashton Ellis. 8 vols. (1892–1899). St. Clair Shores, MI: Scholarly Press, 1972.

Vol. 1 *The Art of the Future* (1892)
Vol. 2 *Opera and Drama* (1893)
Vol. 3 *The Theater* (1894)
Vol. 4 *Art and Politics* (1895)
Vol. 5 *Actors and Singers* (1896)
Vol. 6 *Religion and Art* (1897)
Vol. 7 *In Paris and Dresden* (1898)
Vol. 8 *Posthumous, etc.* (1899)

B.4 CHAPTER BIBLIOGRAPHIES

Each of the works cited in the following listings contains information that is pertinent to the specific subject that is discussed in the corresponding chapters of this book.

Chapter 1. The Art of Richard Wagner—An Overview

Barzun, Jacques. *Darwin, Marx, Wagner—Critique of a Heritage*. (1941). Revised edition, 1958. Chicago: University of Chicago Press, 1981.

Bekker, Paul. *Richard Wagner: His Life in His Work*. Translation of *Richard Wagner: Das Leben im Werk* by M[ildred] M[ary] Bozman. (1931). Westport, CT.: Greenwood, [1971].

Dahlhaus, Carl. *Richard Wagner's Music Dramas*. Translation by Mary Whittall of the original title *Richard Wagners Musikdramen*. (1971). New York: Cambridge University Press, 1979.

Furness, Raymond. *Wagner and Literature*. New York: St. Martin's Press, [1982].

    Contains a number of parodies and spoofs of the *Ring*.

Hueffer, Frances (Franz). *Richard Wagner and the Music of the Future*. (1874). Freeport, NY: Books for Libraries Press, [1971].

    The Appendix of this work contains "An Account of the Festival at Bayreuth on the Occasion of the Foundation Stone of the Wagner Theatre Being Laid."

Magee, Bryan. *Aspects of Wagner*. (1968). Revised and enlarged. New York: Oxford University Press, [1988].

Mann, Thomas. *Essays of Three Decades*. (1937). Translated by H. T. Lowe-Porter. New York: Alfred A. Knopf, 1947.

    (First published as *Freud, Goethe, Wagner*.)

Newman, Ernest. *Wagner as Man and Artist*. (1924). New York: Limelight Editions, 1985.

Pourtales, Guy de. *Richard Wagner: The Story of an Artist*. Translation of *Histoire d'un Artiste* by Lewis May. (1932). Westport, CT: Greenwood, 1972.

Stein, Jack M[adison]. *Wagner and the Synthesis of the Arts*. (1960). Westport, CT: Greenwood, 1973.

Wagner, Richard. Works. [See B.3]

    "Actors and Singers," Vol. 5.

    "Art and the Revolution," Vol. 1.

    "Art Work of the Future," Vol. 1.

    "The Destiny of Opera," Vol. 5.

    "Music of the Future," Vol. 3.

    "On the Application of Music to the Drama," Vol. 6.

    "On the Name 'Musikdrama,'" Vol. 7.

    "Opera and Drama," Vol. 2.

    "Opera and the Nature of Music," Vol. 2.

Chapter 2. Der Ring des Nibelungen—An Overview

Branston, Brian. *Gods of the North*. (1955). Paperback with revisions. New York: Thames and Hudson, 1980.

Cord, William O. *The Teutonic Mythology in Richard Wagner's "Der Ring des Nibelungen."* Vol. I—*Nine Dramatic Properties;* Vol. II—*The*

Family of Gods; Vol. III—(Parts 1 and 2) *The Natural and the Supernatural Worlds.* Lewiston, NY: The Edwin Mellen Press, [1989–1991].

————. *201 Questions (and Answers) on Richard Wagner's "Der Ring des Nibelungen."* San Francisco: The Wagner Society of Northern California, 1993.

Cooke, Deryck. *I Saw the World End: A Study of Wagner's "Ring."* New York: Oxford University Press, 1979.

> This volume contains a section of the text of the *Ring* and several studies of the first two dramas. Cooke's death prevented the additional research, study, and composition that had been planned.

Culshaw, John. *Reflections on Wagner's "Ring".* New York: Viking Press, 1976.

Davidson, H[ilda] R[oderick] E[llis]. *Scandinavian Mythology.* (1969). Revised edition. New York: Peter Bedrick Books, 1986.

————. *Gods and Myths of Northern Europe.* (1964). New York: Bell Publishing Co., 1981.

Dumézil, Georges. *Gods of the Ancient Northmen.* (1973). Edited by Einar Haugen. Introduction by C. Scott Littleton. Paperback edition. Berkeley, CA: University of California Press, 1977.

> Each chapter of this work (*Les dieux des Germains*) was translated from French by one of four of the editor's students.

Fay, Stephen. *The "Ring": Anatomy of an Opera.* (1984). Dover, NH: Longwood Press, 1985.

Magee, Bryan. *Aspects of Wagner.* (1968). Revised and enlarged. New York: Oxford University Press, [1988].

Magee, Elizabeth. *Richard Wagner and the Nibelungs.* New York: Oxford University Press, 1990.

Magnusson, Magnus. *Hammer of the North.* Photographs by Werner Forman. New York: G. P. Putman's sons, 1976.

Richardson, Herbert, ed. *New Studies in Richard Wagner's "The Ring of the Nibelung."* Lewiston, NY: The Edwin Mellen Press, [1991].

Wagner, Richard. *Works.* [See B.3] "Music of the Future," Vol. 3.

Weston, Jessie L[aidlay]. *Legends of the Wagner Dramas.* (1896). New York: AMS Press, 1978.

————."Legends of the Wagner Trilogy." In *The Volsunga Saga.* (1906). London: Norreona Society, 1907.

> Also contains "Legends Kindred to those of the Volsungs."

Chapter 3. The Format of the "Ring"

3.5 Major Properties

Cord, William O. *The Teutonic Mythology of Richard Wagner's "The*

Ring of the Nibelung." Volume I, *Nine Dramatic Properties*. Lewiston, NY: The Edwin Mellen Press, [1989].

Donington, Robert. *Wagner's "Ring" and Its Symbols*. (1963; 2nd ed. 1969; 3rd ed. 1974). New York: Da Capo Press, 1991.

Chapter 4. The Composition of the "Ring"

4.1 The Dramas

Benvenga, Nancy. *Kingdom of the Rhine*. Harwich, Essex: Anton Press, 1983.

Cord, William O. *The Teutonic Mythology in Richard Wagner's "Der Ring des Nibelungen."* Vol. I—*Nine Dramatic Properties*; Vol. II—*The Family of Gods*; Vol. III—(Parts 1 and 2) *The Natural and the Supernatural Worlds*. Lewiston, NY: The Edwin Mellen Press, [1989–1991.

Lippert, Woldemar. *Wagner in Exile, 1849–1862*. Translated by Paul England. (1930). New York: AMS Press, 1974.

Wagner, Richard. *Works*. [See B.3]
    "The Nibelungen Myth," Vol. 7.
        This composition is the *Sketch* of 1848 which Wagner had intended to use as the compositional guide for the creation of one drama, but which eventually became a literary understanding for the four dramas of the *Ring*.
    "Preface to the *Ring* Poem," Vol. 3.
————. "The Legend of the Nibelungen." (The 1848 *Sketch*). In *Art, Life, and Theories of Richard Wagner*. Selected writings translated by Edward L. Burlingame. (1875). New York: Henry Holt and Company, 1904.

4.2 The Music

Wagner, Richard. *Works*. [See B.3]
    "On the Completion of *Siegfried*, August 25, 1870," Vol. 4.
————. *Letters from Richard Wagner to Mathilde Wesendonck*. Translated with a preface by William Ashton Ellis. (1905). New York: Vienna House, 1972.

Chapter 5. The Origins and the Sources of the "Ring"

5.3.1 *Edda Saemundar*

The Elder Eddas [sic] *of Saemund Sigfusson*. Translated from the original Old Norse by Benjamin Thorpe. Viking Edition. London: Norroena Society, 1906.

Also contains *The Younger Eddas* [sic] *of Snorri Sturlson*, translated from the Icelandic by I. A. Blackwell.

The Elder or Poetic Edda. Translated and edited by W. C. Collingwood. Viking Translation Series, Vol. II. (1908). New York: AMS Press, [1982].

Icelandic and English texts on opposite pages.

The Poetic Edda. Translated from the Icelandic by Henry Adams Bellows. (1923). Introduction by William O. Cord. Lewiston, NY: The Edwin Mellen Press, 1991.

The Poetic Edda. Translated by Lee M. Hollander. (1928). Austin, TX: University of Texas Press, 1977.

Textbook issued from the second edition, 1962.

The Poetic Edda. Edited by Ursula Dronke. Fairlawn, NJ: Oxford University Press, 1969.

Poems of the Vikings—The Elder Edda. (1969). Translated from the Old Norse by Patricia Terry. Introduction by Charles W. Dunn. Revised edition. Philadelphia, PA: University of Pennsylvania Press, 1990.

Norse Mythology: The Elder Edda. Prose translation from the Old Norse by Gudbrand Vigfusson and F. York Powell. Edited by Lawrence S. Thompson. [Hamden, CT]: Archon Books, 1974.

5.3.2 *Völsungasaga*

The Volsunga Saga. Translated from the Icelandic by Eirikr Magnusson and William M. Morris. (1906). Totowa, NJ: Cooper Square Publisher, 1980.

An edition published in London in 1907 also contains "Legends of the Wagner Trilogy" by Jessie L. Weston and "Legends Kindred to those of the Volsungs."

Volsunga Saga. Translated by Eirikr Magnusson and William M. Morris. (1906). Edited by Robert W. Gutman. New York: Collier Books, 1962.

The Saga of the Volsungs. Edited, translated, and introduced with notes and appendices by R. G. Finch. [London]: Nelson, [1965].

The Saga of the Volsungs. Translated from the Old Norse by Margaret Schlauch. (1930). New York: AMS Press, 1978.

Contains *The Saga of Ragnar Lodbrok* and *The Lay of Kraka.*

The Saga of the Volsungs. Translated and annotated by George K. Anderson. Newark, NJ: University of Delaware Press, 1982.

The Saga of the Volsungs. Introduction and translation by Jesse L. Byock. Berkeley, CA: University of California Press, [1990].

5.3.3 *Nibelungen Nôt und die Klage*

Grimes, Heilan Yvette. *The Legend of the* Nibelungenlied. Wolfeboro, NH: Longwood Academic, 1989.

The Nibelungenlied. Translated from the German by Margaret Armour. Illustrated by Edy Legrand. Introduction by Franz Schoenberner. (1897). New York: Heritage Press, 1961.

The Nibelungenlied. Translation by William Nanson Lettsom. Introduction by William H. Carpenter. (1901). Folcroft, PA: Folcroft Library Editions, 1977.

The Song of the Nibelungs. Verse translation from the Middle High German by Frank G. Ryder. (1962). Detroit: Wayne State University Press, 1982.

Nibelungenlied. Translated by D. G. Mowath. New York: E.P. Dutton & Co., 1962.

The Nibelungenlied. Translation by Helen M. Mustard. In *Medieval Epics*. New York: Modern Library, 1963.

The Nibelungenlied. Translated by A[rthur] T[homas] Hatto. (1965). Middlesex: Penguin Books, 1973.
    Fourth printing of the 1969 edition.

The Nibelungenlied. Translated and introduced by Robert Lichenstein. Lewiston, NY: The Edwin Mellen Press, 1991.

5.4.1 *Deutsche Mythologie*

Grimm, Jakob. *Teutonic Mythology*. Translated from the fourth German edition (1875–1878) by James Steven Stallybrass. 4 vols. (1966). Magnolia, MA.: Peter Smith, 1976.

5.4.3 *Deutsches Heldenbuch*

"Book of Heroes." Translated from the German edition of Kaspar von der Roen. In *Poets and Poetry of Europe*, edited by H[enry] W[adsworth] Longfellow. Philadelphia, PA: Q. Por, 1871.

5.4.4 *Heimskringla*

Heimskringla. Translated by Robert Michael Ballantyne. London: J. Nisbet, 1872.

Heimskringla. Translated from the Icelandic by William Morris and Eirkir Magnusson. 6 vols. London: B. Quaritch, 1891–1905.

Heimskringla or The Lives of the Norse Kings. Edited by Erling Monsen and translated from the Old Norse with the assistance of A. H. Smith. Introduction by Gudmund Sandvik. (1932). New York: Dover, 1990.

The Heimskringla or Sagas of the Norse Kings. Translated from the Old Norse by Samuel Laing. Revision of the 1906 edition with introduction and notes by Peter Foote. (1930). New York: AMS Press, 1979.

Heimskringla, History of the Kings of Norway. Translated from the Icelandic by Lee M. Holland. Minneapolis, MN: American-Scandinavian Foundation, 1964.

Heimskringla. A History of the Norse Kings. 3 vols. New York: Gordon Press, 1977.

Chapter 6. Bayreuth

Bertram, Werner. *A Royal Recluse. Memories of Ludwig II of Bavaria.* Translated by Margaret McDonough. Munich: Martin Herpich & Son, n.d.

Blunt, Wilfrid. *The Dream King: Ludwig II of Bavaria.* (1970). Baltimore: Penguin Books, 1973.
Contains a chapter on Ludwig and the arts by Michael Petzet.

Burg, Katerina von. *Ludwig II of Bavaria: The Man and the Mystery.* [Windsor]: Windsor Publications, 1989.

Channon, Henry. *The Ludwigs of Bavaria.* New York: Methuen Inc. 1933.

Chapman-Huston, Desmond. *Bavarian Fantasy: The Story of Ludwig II.* (1955). New York: n.p., 1956.

Gerard, Frances A. *The Romance of King Ludwig II of Bavaria: His Relations with Wagner and His Bavarian Fairy Palaces.* (1901). New York: AMS Press, 1974.

Hartford, Robert. *Bayreuth, The Early Years.* New York: Cambridge University Press, [1980].
"An account of the early decades of the Wagner Festival as seen by celebrated visitors and participants."

Hueffer, Francis (Franz). *Richard Wagner and the Music of the Future.* (1874). Freeport, NY: Books for Libraries Press, [1971].
An appendix contains the following: "An Account of the Festival at Bayreuth on the Occasion of the Foundation Stone of the Wagner Theater Being Laid."

Magee, Bryan. *Aspects of Wagner.* (1968). Revised and enlarged, New York: Oxford University Press, [1988].

Mayer, Hans. *Richard Wagner in Bayreuth, 1876–1976.* (*Richard Wagner in Bayreuth 1876–1976*). Translated from the German by Jack Zipes. New York: Rizzoli International Publications, 1976.

McIntosh, Christopher. *The Swan King, Ludwig II of Bavaria.* London: A. Lane, 1982.

Richter, Werner. *The Mad Monarch.* Translated by William G. Schlamm. Chicago: Henry Regnery, 1955.
Originally entitled *Ludwig II: King of Bavaria.*

Skelton, Geoffrey. *Wagner at Bayreuth*. Foreword by Wieland Wagner. (1965). Reprint of a 1976 revised edition. New York: Da Capo Press, 1983.

Turing, Penelope. *New Bayreuth*. St. Martin, Jersey, C.I.: Jersy Artists, 1969.

Wagner, Friedelind, and Cooper, Page. *Heritage of Fire*. (1945). Westport, Conn.: Greenwood, 1974.

Wagner, Richard. *Works* [See B.3]

"End of the Patronat-Verein," Vol. 6

"The Festival Playhouse at Bayreuth with an Account of the Laying of its Foundation Stone," Vol. 5.

"Final Report on Circumstances that Attended the Execution of *Der Ring des Nibelungen* down to the Founding of the Wagner Societies," Vol. 5.

"A Music School for Munich," Vol. 4.

"To the Presidents of the Wagner-vereins," Vol. 6.

"Preface to the *Ring* Poem," Vol. 3.

"Proposed Bayreuth 'School,'" Vol. 6.

————. "The Opera House at Bayreuth." In *Art, Life, and Theories of Richard Wagner*. Translated by Edward L. Burlingame. (1875). New York: Henry Holt and Company, 1904.

————. *The Story of Bayreuth as Told in the Bayreuth Letters of Richard Wagner*. Translated and edited by Caroline V. Kerr. (1912). New York: Vienna House, 1972.

Zarek, Otto. *Tragic Idealist: Ludwig II of Bavaria*. Translated by Ella Goodman and Paul Sudley. New York: Harper, 1939.

Chapter 7. First Performances of the "Ring"

7.1 Bayreuth

Appia, Adolphe. *Staging Wagnerian Drama*. Translation of *La mise en scène du drama Wagnerien*. Boston, MA: Birkhauser, 1982.

Bauer, Oswald Georg. *The Stage Designs and Productions from the Premieres to the Present*. Foreword by Wolfgang Wagner. New York, n.p. 1983.

Originally published in Frankfurt am Main, 1982, as: *Richard Wagner: Die Bühnenwerk von der Urauffuhrüng bis heute.*

Gollancz, Victor. *The* Ring *at Bayreuth and Some Thoughts on Operatic Production*. "Afterword" by Wieland Wagner. London: [Camelot Press], 1966.

On the 1965 *Ring* produced by Wieland Wagner.

Millington, Barry, and Stewart Spencer, eds. *Wagner in Performance.* New Haven, CT: Yale University Press, 1992.

Porges, Heinrich. *Wagner Rehearsing the "Ring."* Translated by Robert L. Jacob. New York: Cambridge University Press, 1983.
> "An eye-witness account of the stage rehearsals of the first Bayreuth Festival." Originally published in Leipzig, 1877, under the title: *Die Bühnenproben zu den Bayreuther Festspielen des Jahres 1876.*

Wagner, Richard. *Works.* [See B.3]
> "End of the Patronat-verein," Vol. 6.
> "Epilogue to the Nibelung's *Ring,*" Vol. 3.
> "Retrospect of the Stage Festival of 1876," Vol. 6.

7.2 Europe

Neumann, Angelo. *Personal Reflections of Wagner.* Translation of *Erinnerungen aus Richard Wagner* by Edith Livermore. (1908). New York: Da Capo Press, 1976.
> Reprint of a translation of the fourth edition.

7.5 The *Ring* in Translation

This listing of the translations of the complete *Ring* into English is presented in alphabetical order according to the surnames of the translators. References to audio and/or visual recordings are to those that are listed in Chapter 10.

Armour, Margaret. Illustrated by Arthur Rackham. 2 vols. 1910–1911). New York: Abaris Books, [1976].

Cochrane, Peggie. (This translation of the *Ring* is the one that was offered as four libretti in the albums of the London recording, 10-G.)

Corder, H[enrietta] and F[rederick]. Boston, MA: Oliver Ditson, 1904.
> This is a reprint of the original 1882 translation that was used in the first publication of the German-English vocal score.

Finck, Henry T. Cincinnati, OH: John Church Co., 1903. (Accompanied a vocal score.)

Forman, Alfred. London: Schott, 1877.
> Forman intended that this translation, which is made in alliterative verse, be used for study rather than for singing. Nevertheless, Wagner called Forman's work a "monument." Cosima Wagner makes reference in her diary to Forman's "fine translation" of *Die Walküre,* which he had published privately in 1873.

Fynes, Randall. 2 vols. (1899). London: Smith Elder, 1913. (Blank verse).

Henderson, Getrude. New York: Alfred A. Knopf, 1932. (Prose).

Huckel, Oliver. New York: Thomas Y. Crowell, 1907–1911. 4 vols. (*The Rhinegold*, 1907; *The Valkyrie*, 1909; *Siegfried*, 1910; *The Dusk of the Gods*, 1911).
English only and freely translated into poetic narrative form.

Jackson, John P. New York: F. Rullman, 1877.
A line-for-line, non-metrical translation.

Jameson, Frederick. London: Schott, 1896.
This translation, reprinted in 1900 and 1904, was a part of the vocal score that was used for the first production of the *Ring* in English at London's Covent Gardens in 1908. The work is subtitled *An Accurate Translation*.

Le Massena, C.L. New York: Grossman-Roth, 1930. (Prose).

Mann, William. 2 vols. (1964). London: Friends of Covent Garden, 1970.
This translation, originally published in 1964 in four volumes, is the libretti that accompanied the Seraphim recording of the *Ring* [10-E]. The translation of *Die Walküre* is the libretto that accompanied the Deutsche Grammophon recording of the *Ring* [10-I].

Newman, Ernest. London: Breitkopf & Härtel, 1914. Included as part of the vocal score.

Porter, Andrew. New York: W. W. Norton & Company, 1976.
This paperback edition was first published in 1976 as a two-volume boxed set. In 1977 the work was published in both hardback and paperback editions. Numerous printings of the latter have been made. The translation was used by the Seattle Opera in 1975 for the first production of the *Ring* in English in the United States. Porter's translation was also used for the first recording of the *Ring* in English. (Angel, 10-K).

Rankin, Reginald. London: Longmans Green, 1899–1901. 2 vols. (Blank verse).

Robb, Stewart. Introduction by Edward Downes. New York: E. P. Dutton & Co., 1960.
English only, in one volume. This translation was published the same year by G. Schirmer as individual libretti, each with German-English text.

Salter, Lionel. (The translations of *Das Rheingold*, *Siegfried*, and *Götterdämmerung* were prepared as libretti to accompany the Deutsche Grammophon recording of the *Ring* [10-I]. The libretto of *Die Walküre* in that recording was William Mann's translation.)

Spencer, Stewart. *Wagner's* Ring of the Nibelung. Subtitled: "A Companion." Commentaries by Warren Darcy, Roger Hollinrake, Elizabeth Magee, Barry Millington. New York: Thames and Hudson, 1993.

Updike, John. New York: Alfred A. Knopf, 1964.
   Translated as a children's story.

Chapter 8. The Poetry and the Drama of the Ring

8.1 Poetry and 8.2 Drama

Barzun, Jacques. *Darwin, Marx, Wagner—Critique of a Heritage.* (1941). Revised edition, 1958. Chicago: University of Chicago Press, 1981.
Garten, H[ugh] F[rederick]. *Wagner the Dramatist.* (1977). Totowa, NJ: Rowman and Littlefield, 1978.
Krehbiel, Henry E. *Studies in the Wagnerian Drama.* (1891). Brooklyn, NY: Haskell House, 1977.
Schuler, John. *The Language of Richard Wagner's* Der Ring des Nibe-lungen. Lancaster, PA: Steinman & Faltz, 1909.
Stein, Jack. *Richard Wagner and the Synthesis of the Arts.* (1960). Westport, CT: Greenwood Press, 1973.
Wagner, Richard. *Works.* [See B.3]
   "The Arts of Poetry and Tone in the Drama of the Future," Vol. 2.
   "Opera and Drama," Vol. 2.
   "The Play and the Nature of Dramatic Poetry," Vol. 2.

8.3 The Meaning of the *Ring*

Aberbach, A.D. *The Ideas of Richard Wagner.* (1984). Revised edition. Lanhan, MD: University Press of America, 1988.
Barzun, Jacques. *Darwin, Marx, Wagner—Critique of a Heritage.* (1941). Revised edition, 1958. Chicago, IL: University of Chicago Press, 1981.
Culshaw, John. *Reflections on Wagner's* Ring. New York: Viking Press, 1976.
DiGaetani, John L., ed. *Penetrating Wagner's* Ring. *An Anthology.* (1978). New York: Da Capo, 1991.
Donington, Robert. (1963; 2nd ed. 1969; 3rd ed. 1974). *Wagner's* Ring *and Its Symbols.* New York: Da Capo Press, 1991.
Rather, L.J. *The Dream of Self-Destruction.* Baton Rouge, LA: Louisiana State University Press, [1979].
   "Wagner's *Ring* and the Modern World."
Shaw, George Bernard. *The Perfect Wagnerite: A Commentary on* The Nibelung's Ring. (1898).
   Numerous printings of this work have appeared since the original publication in 1898 in London, by Henry S. Stone & Co.
Skelton, Geoffrey. *Wagner in Thought and Practice.* (1991). Portland, OR: Amadeus Press, 1992.

Winkler, Franz E. *For Freedom Destined*. Grader City, NV: Waldorf Press, [1974].

8.4 Wagner on the Meaning of the *Ring*

Cleather, Alice Leighton, and Basil Crump. *"The Ring of the Nibelung":* *An Interpretation Embodying Wagner's Own Explanation."* (1924). 7th ed. Folcroft, PA: Folcroft Library Editions, 1977.

Wagner, Richard. *Richard Wagner's Letters to August Röckel.* (1897). Translated by Eleanor C. Sellar. New York: AMS Press, 1974.

> These letters, written to his good friend who, at the time, was serving a prison sentence, include some of Wagner's most detailed and elaborate thoughts regarding *Ring* matters.

Chapter 9. The Music of the Ring

9.1 Wagner and Orchestras

Bekker, Paul. *The Orchestra.* (1936). New York: W. W. Norton & Company, 1963. Paperback edition.

> Originally published under the title *The Story of the Orchestra.*

Berlioz, Hector. *Mozart, Weber, and Wagner.* "The Art of Music and other Essays." Translation of *A travers chants* by Edwin Evans. (1918). Bloominton, IN: Indiana University Press, 1994.

9.4 The *Ring* Music and the Leitmotif

Abraham, Gerald. *A Hundred Years of Music.* (1938). London: Duckworth & Co., 1974.

Brown, H[ilda] M[eldrum]. *Leitmotif and Drama.* New York: Oxford University Press, 1991.

Cooke, Deryck. *"An Introduction to* Der Ring des Nibelungen." Three twelve-inch LP records and text. London: Decca Recording Company, 1969.

> An explanation and an analysis of Wagner's system of leitmotifs with musical examples, the majority of which were taken from the *Ring* recording of Georg Solti, conductor, and the Vienna Philharmonic Orchestra [10-G].

Dickinson, A[lan] E[dgar] F[rederic]. *The Musical Design of the* Ring. London: Oxford University Press, 1926.

Donington, Robert. (1963; 2nd ed. 1969; 3rd ed. 1974). *Wagner's* Ring *and Its Symbols.* New York: Da Capo Press, 1991.

Hanslick, Eduard. *The Beautiful in Music.* Translation of *Vom Musikalisch-Schönen* by Gustav Cohen. (1854). 8th revised edition, 1891. Indianapolis, IN: Hackett Publishing Co., 1986.

Hutcheson, Ernest. *A Musical Guide to* The Ring of the Nibelung. (1940). New York: AMS Press, 1972.

Jacobs, Robert L[ouis]. *Wagner.* Master Musicians Series. (1935). Revised edition. Totowa, NJ: Littlefield, Adams, & Co., 1977.

Kobbe, Gustav. *How to Understand Wagner's* Ring of the Nibelung. (1916). 7th ed., revised and enlarged. New York: AMS Press, 1976.

This work presents the story and a descriptive analysis of the *Ring*, with musical examples of the leading motives of each of the four dramas.

Magee, Bryan. *Aspects of Wagner.* (1968). Revised and enlarged. New York: Oxford University Press, [1988].

The Seraphim Guide to the Ring. One twelve-inch LP record without text. Hollywood: Capitol Records, 1972.

A brief synopsis illustrating motives of the *Ring* with musical examples played by the Rome Symphony Orchestra, William Fürtwangler, conductor, recording 10-E.

Spencer, Stewart, and Barry Millington. *Wagner's "Ring of the Nibelung."* Subtitled: "A Companion." Commentaries by Warren Darcy, Roger Hollinrake, Elizabeth Magee, Barry Millington. New York: Thames and Hudson, 1993.

Presents sixty-seven leitmotives and indicates their use throughout the text of the *Ring*.

Westernhagen, Curt von. *The Forging of the* Ring. Translation of *Die Enstehung des* Ring. by Arnold and Mary Whittall. 2 vols. New York: Cambridge University Press, 1976.

Wolzogen, Hans von. *Thematic Guide for the Music of Richard Wagner's Festival Play* Der Ring des Nibelungen. Translated by E[rnst] von Wolzogen. (1876). New York: G. Schirmer, 1895.

Originally published as *Thematischer Leitfaden durch die Musik zu Richard Wagners Festspiel* Der Ring des Nibelungen, this work is the celebrated study that firmly, and permanently, associated Wagner and his music with the *leitmotif* manner of composition.

Chapter 10. The Ring—*Recordings*

Culshaw, John. Ring *Resounding.* (1967). New York: Limelight Editions, 1987.

An account of the recording of the *Ring* [10-G] by the Decca Recording Company as told by the director. A "Special Edition" of Culshaw's work was published in 1972, in New York by Time-Life Records.

Mander, Raymond, and Joe Mitchenson. *The Wagner Companion.* (1977). New York: Hawthorn Books, 1978.

A Selected Bibliography

A compilation of the data relative to the first performances of each of Wagner's musical works. (Not to be confused with another publication with the same title.)

Russell, Anna. *The Anna Russell Album.* One twelve-inch LP record. Columbia Records, 1972.

A humorous resumé of the *Ring* argument that was issued originally as *Anna Russell Sings.*

Appendix A. A Chronological Summary of Wagner's Operatic Works

Dahlhaus, Carl. *Richard Wagner's Music Dramas.* Translation of *Richard Wagners Musikdramen* by Mary Whittall. (1971). New York: Cambridge University Press, 1979.

Gilman, Lawrence. *Wagner's Operas.* (1937). New York: Somerset Publishers, 1986.

Guerber, H[elene] A[deling]. *Stories of the Wagner Operas.* (1977). Boston, MA: Longwood Press, 1978.

Mander, Raymond, and Joe Mitchenson. *The Wagner Companion.* (1977). New York: Hawthorn Books, 1978.

Newman, Ernest. *The Wagner Operas.* (1949). Princeton, NJ: Princeton University Press, [1991].

There have been several reprints of this work which was originally published in London under the title *Wagner Nights.*

Osborne, Charles. *The Complete Operas of Richard Wagner.* (1990). New York: Da Capo Press, 1993.

———. *The World Theater of Wagner.* New York: Macmillan Publishing Co., [1982].

A textual and pictorial review of 150 years of Wagner productions.

PART II. JOURNALS

During the course of Wagner's later life, and indeed down to the present day, there have been numerous periodicals committed solely to studies of the composer and his music dramas. The contents of these publications, originating in numerous countries and written in any of several languages, vary greatly in style and interest, as well as in aptness of theme or topic, and thoroughness of discussion. The publications that are mentioned here appear primarily because of their overall significance in the story of Richard Wagner and his musical works, and because they can also serve a most useful end for those Wagnerians who wish to know more about the composer and his works but cannot or do not wish to become involved in serious academic research. At the same time, such periodicals give further evidence of the qualitative import of Wagner in the history of musico-dramatic art. The older periodicals cited here are available only in libraries, and the more current publications are available in libraries or by individual subscriptions. (There have also been numerous publications that are more the *newsletter* type of periodical which, if important in their own right, in the main purposefully do not include articles of an essentially serious nature.)

Some of the more relevant periodicals, primarily the learned type, past as well as present, are listed below with some brief data pertinent to their individual history. These publications are listed chronologically.

1. [Untitled issues]. Wiener akademischer Wagners-Verein. (Viennese Academic Wagner Society). Vienna, Austria; 1872–1915.

   The early publications of this Society, which was one of the first to be founded, included reports of the number of certificates that were sold through the *Patronatverein*, whose sale was intended to aid Wagner in his efforts to build his festival theater and to present the premiere of his *Ring* there. Later publications of this journal apparently are unavailable.

2. *Bayreuther Blätter* (*Bayreuth Journal*). Bayreuth, Germany; 1878–1938.

   This periodical, which became a house organ for all things Wagnerian, was the idea of Wagner himself. In October 1877, the composer invited Baron Hans Paul von Wolzogen (1848–1938), a rich country-gentleman from Schwerin, to be its editor. Von Wolzogen accepted the offer and served in that capacity for some sixty years, until his death. (It was von Wolzogen who originated the *leitmotif* and its use in the *Ring*.) In the main, the articles that were published in the sixty-one volumes of this periodical were generously supportive of the composer and his works. If many of these writings seem to be more popular than learned, including those of Wagner himself, through the years the contents are surprisingly interesting in that they reveal in several ways the deep idolatry that Wagner enjoyed, both during his life and after his death.

   Between 1878–1883, the journal was sponsored and published by the Bayreuther Patronatverein (Bayreuth Patrons Society), an organization founded by Wagner to encourage and to promote purchase of certificates to assist financially in the production of the premiere of the *Ring*. In 1884 the journal came under the wing of the

Allgemeiner Richard Wagner-Verein (General Richard Wagner Society). Upon the death of Hans von Wolzogen, in 1938, journal matters were assumed by Bayreuther Bühnenfestspiele (Bayreuth Folk Festival), and other organizations.

Indexes of the articles published in *Bayreuther Blätter* will be found in Volumes 50, 55, and 61.

3. *Parsifal: Halbmonatsschrift zum Zweck der Erreichung der Richard Wagner'schen Kunstideale* (*Parsifal: Bimonthly Publication for the Attainment of Richard Wagner's Artistic Ideals*). Vienna, Austria; founded in 1884 and published intermittently since that date.

This journal administration apparently takes much pride in stating that the periodical was founded on the first anniversary of Richard Wagner's death.

4. *Revue Wagnérienne* (*Wagnerian Revue*). Paris, France; Feb. 8, 1885–July 15, 1888.

This journal, published irregularly, was founded by the French author Edouard Emile Dujardin (1861–1949). Although the publication lasted only three years, in that time among its more celebrated contributors were the French composers Camille Saint-Saëns (1835–1921) and Gabriel Fauré (1845–1924), the French poets Stéphane Mallarmé (1842–1898) and Paul Verlaine (1844–1896), and the Hungarian Franz Liszt (1811–1886).

5. *Richard Wagner Jahrbuch* (*Richard Wagner Yearbook*). Stuttgart, Germany; 1886.

This publication, published and distributed by Joseph Kuerschner, ceased publication after the issuance of the first volume.

6. *The Meister* (*The Master*). London, England; 1888–1895.

This journal was founded and edited by William Ashton Ellis (1853–1919). It was Ellis who translated Wagner's prose works into English (eight volumes), and who authored a six-volume biography of the composer, and also translated, again into English, several volumes of Wagner's letters. Ellis was educated as a physician, but he turned from his profession in order to devote himself to things Wagnerian. George Bernard Shaw, himself a writer on Wagner matters, was instrumental in securing a pension from the Civil List for Ellis, "for service rendered."

7. *Richard Wagner Jahrbuch.* (*Richard Wagner Yearbook*). Leipzig/Berlin, Germany; 1906–1913. German language.

This publication was issued annually (1906, 1907, 1908, 1912, 1913) for a total of five volumes, with no publications in the period 1909–1911. The journal was under the editorship of Ludwig Frankenstein.

8. *Richard Wagner*: Vienna, Austria; October 1, 1908–1909.
   This short-lived journal carries beneath its title the following description: *Illustrierte Blätter für Wagner'schen Musik, Kunst, und Literatur* (*Illustrated Journal for Wagner-like Music, Art, and Literature*).

9. *Tribschener Blätter: Zeitschrift der schweizerischen Richard Wagner Gesellschaft* (*Tribschen Journal: Periodical of the Swiss Richard Wagner Society*). Lucerne, Switzerland; Since 1956. Published irregularly.

10. *Die Gesellschaft* (*The Society*). Österreichische Richard Wagner Gesellschaft (Austrian Richard Wagner Society). Graz, Austria; Since 1959.
    The original publication was more a newsletter-type periodical. The society and its publication eventually underwent numerous changes, and beginning in 1984 the publication was titled *Richard Wagner Jahrbuch* (*Richard Wagner Yearbook*), and was published annually through 1988.

11. *Feuilles Wagnériennes: Bulletin d'Information de l'Association Wagnérienne de Belgique* (*Wagnerian Leaves: Information Bulletin of the Wagner Association of Belgium*). Brussels, Belgium. Published irregularly, since 1960.

12. *Monsalvat: Revista Wagneriana* (*Monsalvat: Wagnerian Journal*). Barcelona, Spain; since December, 1973.
    This journal frequently accepts articles on subjects other than Wagnerian matters. (Monsalvat, the location that served as the stage setting for *Parsifal*, is a mountain-like hill that is located some twenty miles north of the city of Barcelona.)

13. *Richard Wagner Blätter.* (*Richard Wagner Journal*). Bayreuth/ Tutzing, Germany. Since 1977.
    During the years 1977–1980, the headquarters for this publication were in Bayreuth, Germany. During that period, there was no fixed schedule of publication of the journal. In 1981, the headquarters were transferred to Tutzing, Germany, and from that date until 1988, the journal was published four times a year. The publication carried the following words: *Aktionkreis für das Werk Richard Wagner* (*Circle of Action for the Works of Richard Wagner*).
    Indexes of the articles published are to be found in Vol. 1 (1977), Vol. X (1986), and a partial index in Vol. XII (1988).

14. *Bulletin du Cercle National Richard Wagner* (*Periodical of the National Richard Wagner Circle*). Paris, France; n.d. Published irregularly.

15. *Wagner.* Publication of The Wagner Society of London. Wickford, Essex, England. Published quarterly since November, 1980.

This journal publishes articles of a scholarly nature on the "music, life, thought, and reception of Richard Wagner." This Society also publishes a second periodical entitled *Wagner News*, which appeared in 1980 and which is devoted to news about coming events, reviews of performances, and articles of a more generalized nature, all, of course, relative to Wagner. Each of these periodicals has a circulation of about 1200.

16. *Leitmotive. The Journal of the Wagner Society of Northern California).* San Francisco, California. Published quarterly, since February, 1985.

This relatively unpretentious journal was first issued as a newsletter-type publication, but its thematic focus was soon modified, and it has now gained an expanding reputation for presentation of substantive articles, interpretative as well as scholarly, on matters Wagnerian.

There also have been numerous newsletter-type publications that have been produced by Wagner societies throughout the world. Some of the current periodicals of this type originate in Brussels, Chicago, Dallas, Denver, Graz, Houston, Leipzig, London, Lyon, Munich, New York, Phoenix, Strasbourg, Sydney, and Vienna.

Index

Index

197

32; his dwelling, 35; *Ring* premiere, 109; in *Die Walküre*, 140, 141; early singers, 158, 162, 167
Hungarian (language), first non-German *Ring*, 116
Hungary, 113, 116
hürnen Seyfrid, Der, 53

Iceland, 60, 62, 63–64, 68
Icelander, 60
incest, 30
instruments, 12, 128–29, 130
Introduction to the Nibelungenlied See, Einleitung in das Nibelungenlied
"Investigation into the History of the German Heroic Saga," *See*, "Untersuchungen zur Geschichte der deutschen Heldensage"
Isolde, Wagner's child, 81
Isolde (role), early singers, 160, 165, 170
Italy, 54, 68, 113, 149, 160

Jachmann-Wagner, Johanna, 109, 159
Jackmann, Hans, 159
Jähns, Friedrich Wilhelm, 133
Jäide, Luise, 109, 157, 159, 162
Jank, Christian, 167, 168, 169
Janowski, Marek, 150
Jesus of Nazareth, *See, Jesus von Nazareth*
Jesus von Nazareth, 59
Jewishness, 163
Jordan, Wilhelm, 54
Judgment Day, 55
Judgment of the Gods, See, Göttergericht
junge Siegfried, Der, 19, 41–42
Jungian (*Ring*), 123

Kapellmeister, 127
Karajan, Herbert von, 149
Karlsruhe (Germany), 70, 165
Kastner, Emmerich, 109, 160
Kaufmann, Anna, 167
Keene, Richard, 104
Keilberth, Joseph, 146
Kharkov (Russia), 162–63
Kinder- und Hausmärchen, 66
Kindermann, August, 162, 167, 168
King Gibich, 31

King Marke, 156, 158
King of the Gibichungs, 25, 28
King of the Gods, 20, 23, 26, 30, 35, 36, 37, 88, 140, 141
King of the Rhine, *See*, Rhine King
Klage, Die, 65
Klingsor, 159
Knappertsbusch, Hans, 147, 151
Königliche Kapelle betreffend, Die, 127, 129, 132–33
Kopisterie, 103, 158n
Kraus, Clemens, 147
Krausse, Robert, 88
Kriemhild, 64, 68
Kritische Gange, 56
Kundry, early singers, 157, 161, 165
Kunst und die Revolution, Die, 4
Kunstwerk der Zukunft, Das, 5, 8, 14
Kurvenal, 156

Lachman, Karl, 61, 70, 71
Lalas, Demetrius, 109, 160
Lammert, Marie, 109, 160
Land of the Giants. *See*, Riesenheim
Land of the Gibichungs, 36
Landgrave of Thuringia, 56
"Last Request," Wagner's, 107
Last Supper, 13
"Lays of the Gods," 61
"Lays of the Heroes," 62
leading motive, *See*, Hauptmotiv
Lebanon, 104
legend, 55, 56, 57, 61–62, 64–65
Lehmann, Lilli, 109, 160–61
Lehmann, Marie, 109, 161
Leipzig (Germany), 3, 44, 70, 80, 89, 112, 115, 129, 158, 163, 164, 165, 168
Leipzig Opera, 112
leitmotif, 133–39
Lemberg (Poland), 116
Leonoff, Karoline, 167
Lettish (language), 116
Levi, Herman, 153, 155
Levine, James, 151
Library, Richard Wagner, *See*, Richard Wagner Library
Library Room (Wahnfried), 98
Liebesverbot, Das, 55, 73, 153
Liechtenstein, Prince, 107
Lied von hürnen Seyfrid, 53

Index

202

Index

Index

Index

sword, 29, 35; pulls sword from tree, 28, 35; names sword, 35; relationships, 31; appearances, 32; in *Die Walküre*, 140, 141, 164; *Ring* premiere, 109; early singers, 161, 165, 167

Siegmund and Sieglinde, the Punishment of the Valkyrie, See, Siegmund und Sieglinde, Der Bestrafung der Walküre

Siegmund und Sieglinde, der Bestrafung der Walküre, original title, 19; a third poem, 42; argument, 42; composed (drama), 42–43; change of title, 43

Siegrune (Valkyrie), 20, 29, 31, 32, 109, 167

Siehr, Gustav, 109, 164

Sigurd, der Schlangentöter, 53

Siguró (Siegfried), 62, 63–64

Sigurds Rasche, 53

Simrock, Karl, 67

singers, interested in *Ring*, 99–101, 101–2; training, 102; acting, 102–3; quarrels, 105–6; *Ring* premiere, 109

"Sketch," 38–39, 42, 45, 52–53, 59, 180

sleep, 30

Slovenian (language), 116

socialism (*Ring*), 123

society (human), *Ring*, 123

Society of Patrons, *See*, Patronatverein

Society, Richard Wagner, *See*, Richard Wagner Society

Solti, Sir Georg, 148

song theorie, *See*, Liedertheorie

"Song of Ecke," *See*, "Eckenlied"

Song of the Horned-Skinned Siegfried, See, Lied von hürnen Seyfrid

Song of the Nibelung, See,Nibelungenlied

sound reflector, *See*, Schalldeckel

sources (Ring), poems, 52–53, primary, 61–65; secondary, 65–71

Sources and Research Relating to the History of German Literature and Language, See, Quellen und Forschungen zur Geschichte der deutsche Literatur und Sprach

southern version (Siegfried tale), 63

Spain, 57, 60, 64

spear, 28, 30, 35, 36, 37, 88, 141, 142, 143

speech, 118, 120

Spring of Wisdom, 37, 88

"Spring Song," 140

Staatsoper (Vienna), 112, 137

Stabreim, 119–20

stage-festival-play, 8, 12, 43

Stehle, Sophie, 167, 170

Stockholm, 115, 116

Stranger, The, See, Der Fremdling

Strasbourg (France), 81

strophe, 119

"structure, is finished, The," *See*, "Vollendet der Bau"

Sturluson, Snorri, 67–68

Style (Bayreuth), 101–3

subjectivity (*Ring*), 121–22

Suddeutsche Philharmonie Orchestra, 149

suicide, Ludwig II, 80

Summary of Dutch Folk Literature of Earlier Times, See, Übersicht der niederländischen Volksliteratur älterer Zeit

Swan-knight, 57

Swarowsky, Hans, 149

Sweden, 60

Swedish (language), 116

Swedish (people), 60

Swiss Family Robinson, The, See, Der Schweizerfamilie

Switzerland, 4, 41, 73, 113

sword, *See*, Notung

Symphony (Beethoven), 15, 85, 129

Tannhäuser and the Songfest on the Wartburg, See, Tannhäuser und der Sängerkrieg auf Wartburg

Tannhäuser (role), Paris, 161; Heinrich Vogl, 165

Tannhäuser und der Sängerkrieg auf Wartburg, 4; source, 55–56; poem, 56; first title, 56; "grand romantic opera," 56; step toward creative goal, 59; Ludwig II, 75, 76; Vienna, 104; Paris, 161; leitmotif, 136; dates, 154; early singers, 159, 161, 165, 169

Tarnhelm, forged by Mime, 22, 26, 33, 35, 36; used by Fafner, 23, 24, 25, 37;

Index

Volk, 5
Volksbuch, 53, 54
"Vollendet das ewige Werk," 104
"Vollendet der Bau," 103–4
Volsa, *See,* Wälse
Volsung, Siegfried, 13, 19, 28, 62;
    Siegmund, 28, 29, 30, 35; Sieglinde,
    30, 35; fathered by Wotan, 36; *Ring,*
    142, 143; *See also,* Wälse
Völsungasaga, 61, 63–64, 181
Vorspiel, 39, 45n
vows, Brünnhilde and Siegfried, 36
vulnerability, Siegfried, 23, 25, 28

Wadsworth (England), 104
Wagner, Albert (brother), 159
Wagner, Cosima, bears Wagner's three
    children, 49, 81; reading Hebel and
    Jordan, 54; wife of Hans von Bülow,
    170; *Diaries,* 54, 64, 70, 94–96, 103–
    4, 157; in Bayreuth, 72; residing with
    Wagner, 80; divorced from von
    Bülow, 81n; Sgraffito, 88; offers inher-
    itance to Festival, 96; inherits
    Bayreuth property, 97; develops Festi-
    val, 97, 156; turns Festival over to
    son, 97; Bayreuth 'style,' 103; 1896
    Ring, 112; favorite *Ring* music, 140;
    on Emerich Kastner, 160; on Ernst
    Ritter von Possart, 169; on Angelo
    Quaglio, 169
Wagner, Friedelind, 150
Wagner Heldentenor, 164
Wagner heroic tenor, *See,* Wagner Hel-
    dentenor
Wagner, Minna, Wagner's first wife, 48,
    81
Wagner, Richard, dates, 3; his art, 3–4,
    5, 46; his life, 3–4, 46; essays, 4–5;
    art theories, 5–8, 9, 10, 73, 136; de-
    tractors, 8–9, 10; influences on, 10–
    11; publications about, 11; studies
    myth, 13, 54–58, 59, 120; Revolution-
    ary, 40–41; self exile, 41; years in
    exile, 41, 46, 73; the conductor, 41,
    85, 86; indecision, 40–41; four
    poems, 43, 73; jailed, 46, 77; creative
    style, 46–47; conducts, 47; Mathilde
    Wesendonck, 48; affair with Cosima,
    49, 80, 81n; to build theater, 50, 73;

finishes *Ring,* 50, 99; works with
    Raupach, 54; living in Paris, 54; Bel-
    lini influence, 55; thematic direction,
    55; attracted to legend, 55–57; letters
    and prose writings, 60; *Ring* sources,
    60–71; state of confusion, 58; first
    view of Bayreuth, 73; resides in
    Bayreuth, 72; working in Magdeburg,
    73; considers singers' needs, 74, 99–
    101; Ludwig II becomes benefactor,
    76–77, 77–80, 87, 89; first wife, 48,
    81; leaves Munich, 81; approves
    Wagner Society, 82; opposition, 83;
    Festival Theater cornerstone, 83–85;
    announces *Ring* premiere, 82, 104;
    cancels *Ring* premiere, 85; searches
    for singers, 85, 86, 99; requests more
    funds, 86; contacts royal families, 87;
    on tour, 89, 103, 104; rehearsing
    Ring, 89, 103, 104, 106; Schalldeckel,
    94; André Grétry, 94–96; to repay
    debts, 96–97; to emigrate, 96; his
    magnetisism, 98; on singers, 99–101;
    on operatic singing, 102–3; meets
    with Ludwig II, 106; the Meister,
    106; "Last Request," 107; London
    concerts, 111–12; desires second festi-
    val, 111; to put *Ring* in three cities,
    112; *Ring* to Newmann, 112–14;
    copyright laws, 112n; publishes *Ring,*
    117; reading *Ring,* 117; on poetry,
    117–18; on poetry and music, 118–
    19; on drama, 120–22; *Ring* meaning,
    124–26; reads Schopenhauer, 125; on
    orchestras, 127–28, 129; in Dresden,
    39, 93, 127, 128; designs tuba, 129;
    orchestral seating, 129–33; von
    Weber's remains, 133; on leitmotifs,
    135–36, 138; conducts premieres of
    his works, 153, 154; brother Albert,
    159; Emerich Kastner, 160; Hector
    Berlioz, 161; opposes dual role for
    singers, 161; coaches singers, 164,
    165; recommends Hallwach to Lud-
    wig II, 168; with Wüllner, 170–71;
Wagner, Siefried, 88, 97
Wagner Society of London, 158
Wagner tuba, 129
Wagner, Wieland, 97, 98
Wagner, Winifred, 97

Index

ment of curse, 30; relationships 31, 125; appearances, 32, 139; embeds sword in tree, 36; Wälse, 35; fathers Volsung race, 36; orders World Ash felled, 37; drinks from Spring of Wisdom, 37; takes branch from World Ash, 37; to Nibelheim, 42, 140; Wagner studies, 58; Sgraffito, 88; George London, 116; wills his own downfall, 125; *Ring* premiere, 109; Wagner on, 126; in *Das Rheingold*, 139, 140; in *Die Walküre*, 140, 141, 162; in *Siegfried*, 142; early singers, 103–4, 162, 164, 167, 168

Wüllner, Franz, 154, 167, 170–71
Württemberg, 168
Württemberg, King of, 107

"Yet Another," 57
Young Siegfried, The, *See, Der junge Siegfried*

zarzuela, 158
Zimmer, Hermann, 109, 165
Zuccalmaglio, Florentin von, 54
"Zukunftmusik," 7
Zumpe, Hermann, 109, 165
Zürich, 41, 46, 73, 85